Is It I, Lord?

Is It I, Lord?

Pastoral Psychology and the Recognition of Guilt

BY ARNOLD ULEYN

Translated by Mary Ilford

HOLT, RINEHART AND WINSTON
New York   Chicago   San Francisco

Acknowledgments

GRATEFUL ACKNOWLEDGMENT is made to the following publishers who have so generously granted permission to reprint from their publications:

Crowell, Collier & Macmillan, Inc., New York, for passages from *Diary of a Country Priest* by Georges Bernanos, copyright © 1937 by Macmillan Company; Darton, Longman & Todd, Ltd. and Doubleday & Company, Inc., New York, for excerpts from *The Jerusalem Bible*, copyright © 1966 by Darton, Longman & Todd, Ltd. and Doubleday & Company, Inc. Used by permission of the publishers; Division of Christian Education of the National Council of the Churches of Christ in the U.S.A., New York, for excerpts from the *Revised Standard Version of the Bible*, Catholic Edition, copyright © 1965 and 1966 by the Division of Christian Education of the National Council of the Churches of Christ in the U.S.A. Used by permission of the publishers; Harper and Row, Publishers, Incorporated, New York, for passages from *Pensées*, by Blaise Pascal, translated by M. Turnell, copyright © 1962 by Harper and Row, Publishers, Incorporated; Paulist and Newman Press, New Jersey, for passages from *St. Gregory the Great, Pastoral Care* (Ancient Christian Writers Series Volume 11), copyright © 1950 by Newman Press; G. P. Putnam's Sons, New York, for passages from *A Very Easy Death*, by Simone de Beauvoir, copyright © 1966 by G. P. Putnam's Sons; Sheed and Ward Inc., New York, for passages from *Vipers' Tangle* by Francois Mauriac (1932), and for passages from *Veil of Veronica* by Gertrud von LeFort (1934); World Publishing Company, Cleveland, Ohio, for passages from *Tartuffe & Other Plays* by Molière, translated by Donald H. Frame, copyright © 1967 by New American Library.

Contents

nisms, "psychisms," or structures?—A typology of defense
mechanisms—The self and the defense mechanisms—Shifting responsibility—The background of exculpation and self-
justification—The parables and the defense mechanisms

Introduction

We should like to begin by explaining the purpose, plan, and method of this study.

Purpose

All pastoral action in the Church, and more specifically that of the priest-pastor, is directed ultimately at helping men to find their proper relationship to God. In the broad sense of the term, "pastoral" or "spiritual" help covers every form of the apostolate: its aim is to give men a deeper faith, a firmer trust, and a more ardent love of God and of their fellow men. In other words, the ministry of salvation means cooperating in God's supreme design of gathering all men in unity; it means building, completing, and, where necessary, rebuilding the ecclesial community of Jesus Christ, a ministry which furthers communion between men and God, and of men with each other.

Of this many-sided pastoral action, the present work examines only one aspect: how men can be helped to become aware of their condition as sinners, and by what means one can arrive at a Christian confession of sin.

Here it is relevant to remark that, compared with the average man of earlier days, our contemporaries do not appear to have achieved a sense of guilt to a normal degree. In particular, they appear immune to the agonizing question which has always troubled a really religious man: how can I, a sinner, find favor and be saved? On the contrary, modern man is embarrassed and humiliated by the doctrine of redemption, of salvation through another. He balks at admitting his guilt, while showing a high degree of sensibility to the sufferings and evils of existence. Instead of personal guilt, he has a sense of absurdity in the presence of the insoluble riddle of life. Everything, it seems, inclines him to reverse roles and to call God to account.

Nevertheless, for every Christian the crucial question remains the same: how can we stand before His gaze? The essential thing for each of us is to recognize that we are guilty and that we have to rely wholly on God's free pardon. Only the man who recognizes that he cannot achieve salvation through his own unaided powers will be saved through Christ Jesus, "unto the praise of the glory of his grace" (Ep 1:6).

Plan

Since the introduction is written after the book is finished, it gives the author a chance to look back at the origins of his study.

The starting point for the present work was an examination of the host of expedients to which we all resort to escape the consciousness and experience of guilt: such defense mechanisms as repression, projection, compensation, rationalization, and minimization. This led necessarily to the question of the source of this tendency to make excuses, and of the whole process of what we call hardening of the heart. Afterward, biblical perspectives gradually opened up on the possibilities of healing the hardened heart, of awakening the somnolent conscience. It was then that we saw clearly that indirect argument, or preaching through parables, was the remedy most commonly used by Jesus and the prophets. Immediately, the pastoral qualities needed to carry on the exercise of this prophetic function of arousing the consciousness of guilt and announcing the offer of divine mercy became apparent. This brought our inquiry full circle, since the confession of our sin presupposes that we put an end to our attempts at exculpation and that we stop resorting to defense mechanisms.

And because the circle was closed, with the starting point meeting the terminal point, a two-way traffic was possible, and we felt that it would be more logical, and therefore preferable, to invert the order of thinking. Which led us to the plan we have adopted here.

In his prophetic capacity, the pastor must awaken men to a sense of their guilt. Without the experience and the confession of our condition as sinners, there is no possibility of salvation. Indeed, in the Christian perspective, salvation consists essentially in being pardoned and rescued by a redeeming God. But sinful man stubbornly refuses to recognize his guilt. To the very degree that he sins, he separates himself from God, makes himself blind to the truth and hardened of heart. He must therefore be flushed out of his imaginary covers and helped to reach the sunlit regions of the earth. And the most effective way of getting him to realize and to acknowledge his error is indirect admonishment. That is the means used by the prophets, who speak in parables in which the sinner faces himself as in a mirror and comes to make a personal value judgment concerning his conduct. Since resistance to self-accusation follows the lines of the defense mechanisms uncovered by depth psychology, we have to identify this apparatus of protective weaponry if our ego structure is to be amended and our numbed hearts brought to life. Through recognition of the systems of exculpation, as through the parables, man can be brought to face his own image, and hence to become aware of his sin and to confess it.

Method

Since pastoral psychology is situated on the borders between theology and psychology, its mode of operation must derive from both these sciences. Since this duality is the source of constant tensions, pastoral psychology, instead of being something clear and well defined, more often resembles a rather dangerous no man's land.

The theologian is a believer who is attentive to the word of God and endeavors to penetrate the mentality of the biblical authors and to exploit the riches of their imagery. He nevertheless remains dissatisfied so long as the revelation transmitted through the Bible and the Church is not reborn in his own thinking, which he keeps attuned to the questions and investigations of his contemporaries.

The psychologist, on the other hand, proceeds from facts which he can observe in human existence. Like the biologist and the sociologist, he attempts to organize and comprehend empirical facts in order to utilize the knowledge acquired in practice. Moral psychology and religious psychology are thus very close to the applied sciences; they tie in with mental hygiene, pedagogy, and psychotherapy.

Theology is based on divine revelation, whence it derives a knowledge of what we ought to be and of the values which we should respect. As a normative science of faith, it judges from above. Psychology, on the contrary, proceeds empirically and observes the given data at ground level. We are thus dealing with two modes of approach which, from a strictly methodological point of view, could and should be distinguished. Too often we let ourselves be carried away into overstepping the boundaries of our particular science and field of competence. This happens, for example, when the psychologist, intoxicated by his discoveries, thinks that nothing exists outside his own observations. He then begins to think in too naturalistic a manner and closes his mind to certain values. Conversely, the theologian may lose contact with empirical reality; caught up in an exaggerated spiritualism, he may become alienated from life, to the point of potential charlatanism.

A caveat against confusing the methods and competence of one discipline with those of another, against a superficial harmonizing which leads only to ambiguity, is therefore wholly in order.

This does not mean, however, that the theologian and the psychologist are not called upon to face each other on the common ground of their investigation, living man, who is not what he should be in the sight of God. To avoid so productive a dialogue and such collaboration in order to preserve methodological integrity is absurd. It means opting for a facile coexistence, since the two roads can never meet. But it is no solution at all to the over-all problems of the phenomenon of man, which fall as much within the purview of theology as within that of psychology.

While the denigrators of pastoral psychology fear, sometimes justifiably, that the sacred ministry will be turned into a mental-hygiene clinic, or into a system of research or initiation into psychological terminology, its champions rightly believe that the apostolate has nothing to lose from substituting for a vague empiricism a more precise knowledge of human nature and of the dynamics of the unconscious.* In pastoral psychology, there can

* A. Léonard, *La Vie Spirituelle, Supplément*, 1955, p. 206.

be no irreconcilable or inevitable conflict between the preaching of faith and psychology.

To use an illustration, a pastor with sound psychological training, but without deep enough conviction of the truth of the Gospel to witness to it, might be compared to an experienced mountain guide summoned to bring aid to a gravely injured man and who, being familiar with the topography, successfully negotiates the dangerous climb only to find, at the top, that he has forgotten the medication. The analogy may also be applied in reverse: the compassionate pastor clasps the precious remedy in his hands, but cannot find the path which would lead him to the person in distress. In other words, a theology which is very rich in content may prove very poor, and even valueless, if the pastor lacks the psychological knowledge needed to reach man's heart.

This is the psycho-pastoral perspective in which we hope to justify the method employed in the present study.

We draw our certainty and take our rule from the word of Scripture. We also lend attentive ear to the spokesmen of ecclesiastical tradition, and especially to the most authoritative among them—St. Augustine and St. Gregory the Great. We thus situate our study from the outset in an ecumenical perspective, and this enables us to carry on a dialogue with the Protestant Churches. For in those Churches, the Christian conscience appears to be more deeply marked by a sense of guilt, and the Christian is urged to cast himself wholly on God's mercy and God's readiness to pardon.*

At the same time, we have endeavored to utilize the recent findings of depth psychology with a view to achieving a more valid pastoral approach to the human person.

This aim, incidentally, explains the somewhat analytical character of the method we have followed. The distaste in our day for analysis, and what is known as hairsplitting, is undoubtedly a healthy reaction to the sterile quibbling and juggling with concepts and formulas in earlier years; we are right to insist on the importance of an over-all view of the mystery of salvation and on the primacy of faith, hope, and charity. But this does not mean

* We may recall, in this connection, the idea of *simul justus et peccator;* the doctrine of *sola fides* and *sola gratia;* the *articulus stantis et cadentis Ecclesiae.*

that we should reject a detailed and even technical analysis of Christian existence in its origins, dynamic development, and expression. Such an attitude would be altogether unjustifiable. It would involve, first of all, a great impoverishment, a foolish jettisoning of the results of centuries of painstaking labor. Indeed, earlier generations, who were not afraid of intellectual calisthenics, achieved some quite remarkable results in this area. Moreover, such a rejection would make it impossible for us to reply satisfactorily to a number of questions raised by our contemporaries; a reflective man today wants more than broad perspectives and vast syntheses. He is particularly responsive to the analysis of his existence and conduct offered by phenomenology, psychology, biology, and sociology.

It is a dangerous illusion to think that the Christian vision of man and his existence can be propagated without taking account of the present contribution of analytical science. Key words such as dynamism, structure, growth processes, mechanism, superego, integration, and so on, have gained increasing currency. As Schopenhauer put it: it may be easy to preach morality, but it is harder to explain it.

However, to prevent any misunderstanding, let me say right away that this book is not for those who are interested in little dodges or formulas. In the apostolate, makeshift devices are quite useless. Only a thorough and balanced understanding of the structure of the moral and religious life can make us wise. Such wisdom will find expression in prudence and pastoral skill if the pastor succeeds in putting his knowledge into practice at the right moment. How to do this will vary, of course, depending on whether he exercises his ministry in the form of preaching, private discussion, or group work.

Finally, if we desire to understand and help others, we have to begin by knowing and accepting ourselves. Only a pastor deeply convinced of his condition as a sinner who needs the grace of divine pardon will be capable of prompting his fellow man to admit his guilt and of receiving that admission.

A. U.

University of Louvain
Louvain, Belgium
June, 1968

You who read this,
where you arrive at the same conviction, walk with me;
where you share my hesitations, seek with me;
where you observe your error, recall my explanations;
where you discover my error, call me to order.
So that together we may follow the road of charity
  and turn our steps toward
Him of whom it is written:
seek always His face.

ST. AUGUSTINE
De Trinitate, I, 3,5

I

The prophetic function in the Church

Kerygma and catechesis

Through the tremendous scriptural revival which has taken place in the Catholic Church in recent decades, we have rediscovered a number of vital elements of the pastoral function which had been virtually forgotten.

For example, we have become more familiar with the New Testament concept of the apostolate and pastoral care as primarily a service of Jesus Christ (St. Paul always liked to refer to himself as the servant, the *doulos* and *diakonos* of the Lord) and as assistance to the community of the Church. This is in direct contrast to the attitude of earlier generations, who tended to place the main emphasis on the authority of the hierarchy.

We have also come to see more clearly that this ministry, even in its liturgical and sacramental form, must be in the first place a preaching of the Word. And we have begun to reflect, in particular, on the two fundamental ways in which this assistance through the Word must be given if we are to carry on, in the same spirit and by the same methods, the preaching begun by Jesus Christ and continued in the early Church.

First comes the proclamation of the good news: the kerygma. The missionary-apostle announces God's offer of salvation; he sketches the fundamentals of the mystery of redemption, the lineaments of the person of Christ and the principal elements in His teaching, as well as the principal duties of man. The object of this universal kerygma is the radical conversion, or *metanoia*, of the listener; it is aimed at bringing the listener to give his unreserved assent to Jesus Christ and make Him the very pivot of his existence. This first stage, which leads to the option of faith and to baptism, is followed by instruction or teaching: the *didache*, *didaskalia*, or catechesis. The fundamentals of the message are more amply set forth and developed in an organic and detailed presentation. The object of this second stage is to stabilize the conversion and consolidate the personal commitment of the new believer.[1]

Prophecy

There is one element, however, which remains in the background and often falls into oblivion—prophecy.

St. Paul's epistles, especially, enable us to give a precise definition of this important pastoral service.[2] In several passages we find listings of ecclesiastical responsibilities, of charismas, or gifts of the Spirit. Without going into the controversial aspects of the subject, we shall recall the principal classifications: apostolate, prophecy, and teaching. In St. Paul's mind, these are the essential functions through which the community of the Church is created, built up, propagated, and strengthened. His first letter to the Corinthians (12:28) makes it clear that while other gifts of the Spirit, such as ruling or healing or speaking diverse languages, may be more spectacular, they are nevertheless merely accessory as compared with the first three, which stand by themselves. And if we consider that the apostle, as the founder and father of the ecclesial community, is in a sense above and outside that community, our attention will focus especially on the teachers and the prophets, who ensure the continuation, here and now, of the work begun by the apostle.

Exegetes warn us against the error—still very widespread—of understanding prophecy as the prediction and revelation of an unknown future. Not that such a concept is altogether erroneous. In the Apocalypse, for example, the word "to prophesy" frequently means "to reveal and make known that which is to come."

Nevertheless, even here the prophetic proclamation is also a call to conversion (11:3), and Chapters 2 and 3 address prophetic exhortations to the Christian communities. And this applies even more in St. Paul's writings, where the term has mainly a moral connotation: the prophet is above all God's mouthpiece, announcing the divine will. His function is related to the Mystery, the gnosis, and the apocalypse (cf. 1 Co 13:14). But the hidden things which he reveals and manifests are related primarily to the religious and moral life of the ecclesial community. His action is one of admonishing, reprimanding, encouraging, consoling, instructing, and exhorting.

Prophetic preaching is distinguished principally by its appositeness to the realities of the existing situation; it is a matter of discerning, putting into words, and proclaiming what God wants, here and now, of Christians. The accent is on the adaptation of divine revelation to the present time (*aggiornamento*), or on the new marching orders implicit therein. Prophecy supplies the word and the light needed for the everyday life of the Church.

Here, incidentally, we come to the real difference between the functions of teacher and prophet—two ministries which complete and perfect one another. Both teacher and prophet are committed to preach the word of God to men. They speak in the name of Jesus Christ and by the action of the Holy Spirit, but in different ways. The teacher must preserve, hand down, and interpret the doctrine of Christ: this is an extension of the kerygma. He is bound to the text of tradition and seeks to deepen Christians' knowledge of doctrine and morals through the didactic method of catechesis. To that end, he interprets the Old Testament in the context of Jesus Christ and of the early Church. The teacher has much in common with the rabbi of the Law who ensures the continuity of tradition by safe-guarding and interpreting the revealed and changeless norms of doctrine and morals. The prophet's function, on the other hand, is to render God's word ever more active and relevant. The gift of prophecy, the greatest of the charismas, is manifested in a preaching full of freshness and freedom, in the interpretation of the existing situation in the light of divine revelation. Prophetic preaching is thus very different from teaching. Its purpose is to jolt and awaken the audience, if necessary. The prophet is dynamic, exacting; he speaks boldly and without beating about the bush. He is not afraid of obloquy or misunderstanding.

As we said before, these are two complementary apostolic functions which mutually influence each other. The teaching of valid doctrine would soon become fossilized without prophecy to infuse it with new life, and prophecy, without constant contact with tradition, would degenerate into a fanaticism tinged with illuminism.[3]

It might be appropriate here to sound a warning against the tendency to see a radical opposition between the terms "function" and "charisma," as though one applied to a purely institutional element and the other to an extraordinary gift of the Spirit. Such a view does not correspond to the realities of the early Christian community. The apostolate, the teaching ministry, and prophecy were regarded not only as responsibilities and functions but also as charismatic gifts, as we see in St. Paul's letter to the Ephesians (4:17–12): "Each one of us . . . has been given his own share of grace, given as Christ allotted it. . . . And to some his gift was that they should be apostles; to some, prophets; to some, evangelists; to some pastors and teachers; so that the saints together make a unity in the work of service, building up the body of Christ."[4]

Reading this passage in its context, we find that St. Paul is attempting to explain the nature of the grace that Jesus Christ grants us and the purpose for which it is given—namely, to build up the single Body of Christ and subject the universe to His lordship.

Paul, in speaking of the specific gifts of grace, had in mind those with particular functions and ministries in the Church. It is in and through these functions that grace becomes incarnate, as it were, and presents itself to us in visible form. The individuals who exercise the apostolate and the prophetic function are thus themselves in the fullest sense of the term charisms or gifts of grace at the service of the ecclesial community. For Jesus Christ raises up apostles and prophets to minister to the faithful and thereby to build up the very body of the Church.

Thus function and charismatic gift are by no means to be regarded as contrary or mutually exclusive realities. St. Peter writes in his first epistle: "Each one of you has received a special grace, so, like good stewards responsible for all these different graces of

God, put yourselves at the service of others. If you are a speaker, speak in words which seem to come from God; if you are a helper, help as though every action was done at God's orders" (1 P 4:10–11).

Recalling the words of the two great apostles, that prophets and teachers embody the grace through which God leads men to Himself and unites them to one another in Jesus Christ, we should be careful not to conceive of the role of grace in the process of conversion as a kind of *deus ex machina*, as something which falls from heaven and directs men from without, or against their wishes and judgment. God's grace uses human means; for example, the pastoral action of our fellow men. It is through their preaching and witness that God acts in the Church and that the Church's sphere of action is expanded. The apostle is an integral element in the economy of salvation, since he makes it effective. The pastor-prophet is not an adjunct to the immanent action of divine grace, but the true instrument of that grace. He is the Holy Spirit's fellow witness to the truth, giving resonance to the Word.

The prophet as the instrument of reconciliation

In the endeavor to define the pastor's prophetic role still more closely, we shall take as a starting point the text in which St. Paul represents the apostolate as the ministry of reconciliation:

"It was God who reconciled us to himself through Christ and gave us [i.e., the Apostles] the work of handing on this reconciliation. In other words, God in Christ was reconciling the world to himself, not holding men's faults against them, and he has entrusted to us the news that they are reconciled. So we are ambassadors for Christ; it is as though God were appealing through us, and the appeal that we make in Christ's name is: be reconciled to God" (2 Co 5:18–20).

Pastoral action, then, consists in reconciling men with God and throwing a new bridge, as it were, across the abyss. But this also means, of course, that the abyss should not be minimized; man's sin should not be taken lightly. As Jeremiah writes: "All are out for dishonest gain; prophet no less than priest, all practise fraud. They dress my people's wound without concern. 'Peace! Peace!' they say, but there is no peace" (Jr 6:13–14). The Hebrew word for peace is *shalom*; it means "all is well; everything is going splendidly." But the first duty of the prophet-evangelist must be to make men conscious of their condition of alienation and enmity with God. By order of Yahweh, Hosea was to call his child "No-People-of-Mine" to symbolize the situation of his fellow citizens.

The ambassadorial function—to revert to the Pauline image— implies a high sense of responsibility and honor. The ambassador must represent his nation or his head of state; he must present their point of view, assert their rights, seek to achieve understanding with the other party. The apostle must be first and foremost the spokesman of Jesus Christ and faithfully transmit his message to men: "be reconciled to God!" That is why he will constantly draw attention to the latent or open conflict separating God and man. He will show the reasons for the conflict. He will introduce the light of revelation into the murky caverns of perdition. Thus he brings the offer of divine love, which takes the initiative and pardons. He points to the cross and says: "That is how much God loves man!" "For our sake God made the sinless one into sin, so that in him we might become the goodness of God" (2 Co 5:21).

It is obviously correct to say that the role of the preacher of the faith and of the Gospel is to bring the Good News. But the big question is this: are those to whom you are speaking really seeking the Good News? Are they awaiting an important message? Is anyone really interested in all this? As a pastor, one cannot but reply that this so-called Good News is in fact rarely "news," and still less "good" news. It would seem, quite simply, that if the news does not strike home, it is because no one wants to be freed from his wretched condition. The offer is there, but there is no demand. Only the man who realizes that he lives under oppression and in slavery can be freed. Only the man who is aware of his need for pardon and grace is capable of accepting the proffered reconciliation with relief and gratitude. "May it not be that many assiduous churchgoers who recite the Lord's Prayer, including the words 'Forgive us our trespasses,' have no desire whatsoever that their sins may be forgiven, for the excellent reason that they absolutely refuse to recognize them?" [5]

In the Beatitudes, Jesus expressly states the *sine qua non* for receiving salvation and entering the kingdom of heaven: blessed are those who are hungry and thirsty; blessed are those who realize their own poverty and indigence . . . St. Paul, too, was very conscious of this correlation. In his apologia before King Agrippa, he narrates the Lord's words to him on the road to Damascus: "I have appeared to you for this reason: to appoint you as my servant and as witness of this vision in which you have seen me, and of others in which I shall appear to you. I shall deliver you from the people and from the pagans, to whom I am sending you to open their eyes, so that they may turn from darkness to light, from the dominion of Satan to God, and receive, through faith in me, forgiveness of their sins and a share in the inheritance of the sanctified" (Ac 26:16–18). In other words, he regards it as his essential task to get men to recognize that they are guilty and have no choice but to throw themselves on God's mercy and generosity. Hence, in his letter to the Romans, Paul logically begins his "gospel" with a ruthless examination of conscience intended to persuade all men, Jews and non-Jews alike, to recognize their guilt and confess their sin, "so that every mouth may be stopped, and the whole world may be held accountable to God" (Rm 3:19). And again: "Therefore you have no excuse, O man, whoever you are, when you judge another" (Rm 2:1). Only after thus clearing the ground does he proceed to proclaim the good news and the offer of reconciliation.

Apostles and pastors are *assistants* of Jesus Christ. Their role is to extend God's saving arm. Their ministry is to succor and support the sinner, so that "you who once were far off" might be "brought near in the blood of Christ" (Ep 2:13).

The "elenchein"

Against this background, St. Paul's use of the word *elenchein* for prophetic preaching is apposite. The word covers a number of concepts. In its broadest sense, it means confronting a man with his guilt and urging him to mend his ways; in other words, appealing to his conscience. More specifically, it means showing up, bringing light to bear on a situation (Ep 5:11–14); revealing a man's dispositions and character (Jn 3:20; 16:8); persuading him of his errors; admonishing, correcting, refuting, unmasking, getting him to exercise self-criticism (Tt 1:9; 1:3; 1 Tm 5:20; Rv 3:19).

The most important text, here, is 1 Corinthians 14:23–25, where St. Paul contrasts prophetic preaching with the gift of tongues: "Unbelievers coming into a meeting of the whole church where everybody was speaking in tongues would say you were all mad; but if you were all prophesying and an unbeliever . . . came in, he would find himsef analysed and judged by everyone speaking; he would find his secret thoughts laid bare, and then fall on his face and worship God, declaring that God is among you indeed." A characteristic of prophetic utterance, therefore, is that it is made in clear and comprehensible language; the prophet instructs, teaches (14:19) and encourages (14:31).

Through the prophet's *elenchein*, hitherto hidden sin and error are brought to light. The discovery produces a crisis in a man's life; he is ashamed; he must confess his fault. It is an anticipation of the last judgment (cf. 2 Tm 4:1). What was hidden and remained secret is unmasked by the preacher of faith. And this, indeed, is the very heart of prophetic preaching: it penetrates to the falsehood that is latent in every man. The prophet co-operates with God by manifesting His light to a world which seeks refuge in the darkness of sin, that is, in falsehood and illusion. Like Jesus (Mt 5:14), Paul compares Christians to light. The role of light is to illumine, to show up the evil deeds of sinful man so that he too may be transformed into light.

But this will be possible only if the language of prophetic preaching is intelligible and intelligent, a language that other men can understand. Only thus will the result be achieved; only thus will the hearer fall flat on his face, adore God and acknowledge: truly God is among you! Falling flat on one's face, according to the Bible, is man's reaction when confronted with God's self-revelation (epiphany); His terrible majesty brings us to our knees.

In the attitude of adoration, man arrives at truth; he is literally in his place, the place of a creature who lives through God and for God. In a sense, every Christian is constantly in the position of the unbeliever who "comes in"; through the prophetic preaching of the Church, he is constantly confronted with the truth which triumphs over him. It would therefore be mistaken to reduce the kerygma to the first message of salvation addressed to non-Christians, as though within the community of the Church there was nothing left but catechetical instruction. The authentic apostolate is always both kerygmatic and prophetic, for the people of God are in constant need of conversion and renewal.[6]

With the concept of *elenchein*, we have rediscovered an essential element in the function of the pastor-prophet. Contemporary pastoral theology can only benefit from the newly placed emphasis on this authentically New Testament aspect of preaching. This kind of prophetic preaching has been exercised through the Law and the prophets, by Jesus Christ, by the Holy Spirit, and by the Church. For proof, we need only glance at a concordance.

The various texts concerning *elenchein* may be arranged as follows:

1. *Elenchein* is attributed:
   to the Holy Spirit as regards the world (Jn 16:8);
   to Christ in glory as regards the Church (Rv 3:19);
   to Christ at His second coming on the day of the parousia (Jude 15);
   to the leaders of the ecclesial community (1 Tm 5:20; 2 Tm 4:2; Tt 1:9; 1:13; 2:15);
   to the faithful among themselves (Mt 18:15; Ep 5:11).
2. In its passive form, the verb expresses the experience of sinful man confronted with:
   the Law (Jm 2:9);
   God (12:5);
   the light of revelation (Jn 3:20; Ep 5:13);
   the prophet (Lk 3:19, 20; 1 Co 14:24);
   personal conscience (Jn 8:9).

The principal texts dealing with *elenchein* through Jesus Christ and through the Holy Spirit are in St. John.

In the discourse with Nicodemus (Jn 3), we learn that the Redeemer's mission is to be the light of the world which saves men. In that capacity, He makes manifest men's evil deeds. But sinners hate the light and flee from it, for fear that their sin will be made known.

In His farewell discourse (Jn 16), Jesus promises to send the Paraclete (the Helper, the Intercessor), who will convince the world of sin, of righteousness, and of judgment. In his magnificent commentary on St. John, St. Augustine gives the following explanation of this text: Jesus sends the Holy Spirit to His disciples so that *through them* He may confound men, show them their sin, and bring them to an awareness of their guilt. "For through the Holy Spirit charity is spread abroad in the hearts of Christians. And charity banishes the fear which might prevent them from reprimanding the world, and gives them the boldness they need. The Holy Spirit confers on them the strength to love, dispels anxiety, and secures for them the freedom they need to reprove sinners." [7]

We therefore ask the same Spirit, in the Pentecostal sequence, to heal the manifold ills of our hearts: to make the rigid heart flexible, the cold heart warm, the sullied heart clean, the sterile heart fertile, the tortuous heart straight.[8]

The prophet's responsibility

The prophetic function and the pastoral duty of admonishing (*elenchein*) constitute a tremendous responsibility. St. Paul dwells on it with insistence in his second pastoral letter to Timothy (4:1–5):

> I charge you in the presence of God and of Christ Jesus who is to judge the living and the dead, and by his appearing and his kingdom: preach the word, be urgent in season and out of season, convince, rebuke and exhort, be unfailing in patience and in teaching. For the time is coming when people will not endure sound teaching, but having itching ears they will accumulate for themselves teachers to suit their own likings, and will turn away from listening to the truth and wander into myths. As for you, always be steady, endure suffering, do the work of an evangelist, fulfil your ministry.[9]

The "in season and out of season" might appear to conflict with the pastor's duty to show tact in his dealings with others. But the injunction might more logically be applied, as St. John Chrysostom applies it, to the preacher himself: preach the word of God at all times, even when you have neither inclination nor leisure for it. That interpretation, moreover, agrees with the exhortation to "endure suffering," for the preaching is often bound to prove unwelcome to those who hear it.[10] But the *elenchein*, or appeal to conscience, must be pursued with unflagging patience. Reproof and exhortation must be based on instruction and doctrine; the preacher must explain the reasons for the conduct he recommends. Offensive aggressiveness is out of place. In 2 Timothy 2:25 and Galatians 6:1 we read that only the pastor who speaks with evangelical gentleness is capable of helping others. He must realize, further, that the value of his preaching depends not on the applause of his audience, nor on whether they like to hear him, but rather on whether his words penetrate to their very consciences.

We can judge how seriously Paul took his responsibility as a prophet from his farewell discourse at Miletus, which may justifiably be called his pastoral testament to those endowed with responsibilities in the Church: [11] "Therefore I testify to you this day that I am innocent of the blood of all of you, for I did not shrink from declaring to you the whole counsel of God. Take heed to yourselves and to all the flock, in which the Holy Spirit has made you guardians, to feed the church of the Lord which he obtained with his own blood" (Ac 20:2–28).

It is an agonizing thing to be sent as a prophet. Ezekiel poignantly compares the prophet's responsibility with the sentry's; failure to sound the alarm means responsibility for catastrophe:

"Son of man, I have appointed you as sentry to the house of Israel. Whenever you hear a word from me, warn them in my name. If I say to a wicked man: You are to die, and you do not warn him; if you do not speak and warn him to renounce his evil ways and so live, then he shall die for his sin, but I will hold you responsible for his death. If, however, you do warn a wicked man and he does not renounce his wickedness and his evil ways, then he shall die for his sin, but you yourself will have saved your life. When the upright man renounces his integrity to do evil and I set a trap for him, he too shall die; since you failed to warn him, he shall die for his sin and the integrity he practised will no longer be remembered; but I will hold you responsible for his death. If, however, you warn the upright man not to sin and he abstains from sinning, he shall live, thanks to your warning, and you too will have saved your life" (Ez 3:17–21).

St. Paul was clearly referring to this Old Testament text; if the prophet fails to fulfill his mission, his hands are stained with blood; he is guilty of homicide through omission and negligence.

In ever-new variations, the pastor is reminded that he must not pander to his hearers' tastes; that he must have the courage to draw their attention to dangers of which they are unaware; that he must use God's standards to determine what is error and sin (cf. Ez 18:21–32; Jr 6:17; Ho 9:7; Ha 2:1). Woe to the shepherds who are too lazy, too careless, or too cowardly to speak out! They are responsible for the eternal death of those who die through their silence (cf. Is 56:9,10).

It is therefore not surprising to find the theme of pastoral responsibility so constantly recurring in the writings of the Fathers. As an example, we might cite this extract from a commentary by St. Augustine on Ezekiel 34:

> We could tell you, "Lead dissolute lives, live as you please! For God allows no one to perish. All that is needed is that you should go on believing. His mercy is infinite. Has He not given His life and His blood for you? How then could He damn you? . . . He has created all things for your enjoyment . . ." If we preached that, we should assuredly have more listeners and disciples. We would displease only a few people and win many to our cause. But in that case we would be proclaiming our own ideas, and not the Word of God or the doctrine of Jesus Christ. Like bad shepherds, we would be feeding ourselves, and not the flock . . .[12]

Boldness and meekness of the prophet

To carry out his prophetic function of helping men to become personally conscious of their sin (*elenchein*), the pastor must have strength of mind and a resolute character. He should be endowed with the apostolic virtue of *parrhesia*—outspokenness and intrepidity. This is made possible for him by the Holy Spirit (cf. Ac 4), the Paraclete who, as St. Augustine says, bestows a strong love and dispels the fear of criticizing the world.[13]

But while this prophetic admonishment contains bitter truths and scathing accusations, the pastor's manner and action must be characterized by meekness, brotherliness, and humility.

It is interesting that Gregory the Great prefaces his remarks on the pastor's duty to confront the sinner with his faults by stressing the equality of the pastor who, as man, is not above others and is sent not to lord it over others but to serve (2 Co 1:23; 4:5). The pastor is neither to take an attitude of superiority to the sinner nor denounce him, but stand at his side. And when St. Gregory speaks of "bringing back those that have strayed" and "bandaging the wounded" (Ez 34:4), he insists on the kindness with which this must be done. It is clear that this great pope was concerned first and foremost to eliminate any thirst for domination, any despotic, aggressive, or triumphalist attitude among his clergy.

> Often . . . the fracture is made worse by an unskillful liga-
> ture, so that the lesion causes even greater pain from being
> bound up too tightly.
> Wherefore it is necessary that, when the wound of sin in the
> subject is repressed by correction, even the restraint be most
> carefully moderated, lest the feeling of kindness be extinguished
> by the manner in which the principles of discipline are exercised
> against the sinner. For care must be taken that loving kindness,
> like that of a mother, be displayed by the [pastor] towards his
> subjects, and correction given as by a father. In all such cases
> treatment must be bestowed with care and circumspection, lest
> discipline be too rigid, or loving kindness too lax.[14]

Jesus himself reminds us that *elenchein* must always be a fraternal remonstrance. St. Matthew inserts the passage in his Chapter
18, which he conceived of as a manual of the Christian life for the
use of the ecclesial community, based on humility, concern for the
disinherited, fraternity, and clemency.[15] Matthew 18:15–17 raises
the problem of sin. The sin is that of one's fellow man in general,
and not a personal offense. "If your brother does something
wrong, go and have it out with him alone, between your two
selves. If he listens to you, you have won back your brother." It
is up to the Christian who sees his fellow sinning to take the first
step; he must go to him and help him to realize what he is doing.
And this must be done with a view to getting the sinner to repent.
One must act as a brother and a neighbor, through genuine concern for the good of his fellow man, who through sin is separating
himself from the communion of life. Matthew places the accent
on the personal and private character of the reproof; there is to be
no hue and cry. The first step must be taken in strictest confidence, so that the offense may remain hidden and the honor of
the person concerned may be safeguarded. If this fraternal remonstrance remains ineffective, then one should try to settle the

matter before a few witnesses, and eventually in the presence of the whole community. In all probability, the reference here is to Leviticus 19:17–18: "You must not bear hatred for your brother in your heart. You must openly tell your neighbor of his offense; this way you will not take a sin upon yourself. You must not exact vengeance, nor must you bear a grudge against the children of your people. You must love your neighbor as yourself."

The first generations of Christians reflected much on the problem of pastoral admonition and fraternal correction. The conclusions which they reached are quite clearly reflected in the following letter of Dorotheus of Gaza (sixth century), which sums up the apostolic wisdom and psychological perspicacity of his predecessors:

If you are put in authority, take care of your brothers with a severe heart and the bowels of mercy, teaching them by deeds and word what they must do . . . When offenses occur, do not become excessively angry, and without getting excited explain the harm that comes from them. If you have to impute blame, do so in a suitable manner and wait for the appropriate moment. Do not be too much on the lookout for little faults, like a strict judge. Do not continually reprimand; that is intolerable, and familiarity with reproof breeds insensibility and contempt. Do not command imperiously, but submit the matter humbly to the brother; this mode of action stimulates, is more persuasive, and instills peace in our fellow man.

If a brother opposes you and you are disturbed at the time, restrain your tongue so that you say nothing to him in anger, and do not let your heart be aroused against him. Remember, rather, that he is a brother, a member in Christ and an image of God threatened by our common enemy. Have pity on him, for fear that the devil might seize him when he is in the grip of anger and put him to death through malice, and that a soul for which Christ died (1 Co 8:11) might perish through our negligence.

Remember that you too are subject to the same judgment of wrath. Let your own weakness make you compassionate toward your brother . . . Do you fear to harm your brother through your patience? But the apostle commands us to conquer evil with good (Rm 12:21), and not evil with evil. And the Fathers, for their part, say: "If you are roused to anger when you reprimand another, then it is your own passion that you are satisfying" (Macarius). And no reasonable man destroys his house in order to build his neighbor's. If your agitation persists, then do violence to your heart and pray in these terms: O God of goodness, lover of souls, in your ineffable goodness you raised us up out of nothingness into being so that we might share in your possessions, and through the blood of your only Son, our Savior, you recalled us, after we had strayed from your commandments; now help my weakness and calm the turmoil in my heart, as once you calmed the stormy waters. Do not, even for a moment, be bereft of your two children, put to death by sin, and do not be obliged to say to us, "What did it serve that I shed my blood, that I descended into the regions of the dead?" (Ps 30:9); or again, "I tell you solemnly, I do not know you" (Mt. 25:12), because your lamps have gone out for lack of oil. Once your heart has been stilled through this prayer, you can then, with prudence and humility, according to the apostle's precept, correct, rebuke, and exhort (2 Tm 4:2), and with compassion tend and restore your brother, like a sick member. Then the brother on his part will receive the correction in all confidence, condemning his own hardness. Through your own peace, you will have pacified his heart.

Let nothing, then, estrange you from the holy teaching of Christ: "Learn from me, for I am gentle and humble in heart" (Mt 11:29).

For it is necessary above all things to take care to remain at peace, so that our hearts are not agitated, even for good reason or in connection with a commandment, in the conviction that we carry out all the commandments for the sake of charity and purity of heart. If you treat your brother in this way, you will hear the divine voice saying to you: "If you utter noble, not despicable thoughts, you shall be as my own mouth" (Jr 15:19).[16]

Nevertheless, it is a fact of experience that the prophet almost inevitably errs in the direction of excessive severity in his reproofs. *Elenchein* is a dangerous weapon. It is extremely difficult to be aroused about the offenses we see and to reprove without being carried away by anger. The pastor is virtually always drawn into using intemperate language; his criticism becomes destructive. In this way, instead of encouraging men, he discourages them. That is why he must constantly recognize his own faults and ask pardon for them. In the tenth chapter of his *Regula pastoralis*, St. Gregory expresses this idea in a striking image. If a man goes into a forest, as we read in Deuteronomy 19:4–5, to cut wood with his friend, and accidentally kills his friend when the axe head slips off the handle, he may save his life by fleeing to a city of refuge. On this, St. Gregory comments that we go into the forest with a companion each time we undertake to reprove our neighbor. We cut wood, without evil intention, when we rebuke another's faults in charity. But the axe flies out of our hand when the rebuke is too severe. And the blade slips out of the handle as soon as excessively severe words arise out of a rebuke. This language strikes and kills our friend, since the proffered insults destroy the spirit of charity in him. The only thing to do, in that case, is to do penance and flee to one of the three cities of refuge: faith, hope, and charity.

In reproving humbly, like a brother, we remember our own frailty and take account of the social aspect of the human condition; and this implies that sin is also a collective phenomenon.

"Brothers, if one of you misbehaves, the more spiritual of you who set him right should do so in a spirit of gentleness, not forgetting that you may be tempted yourselves. You should carry each other's troubles and fulfil the law of Christ. It is the people who are not important who often make the mistake of thinking that they are. Let each of you examine his own conduct; if you find anything to boast about, it will at least be something of your own, not just something better than your neighbor has. Everyone has his own burden to carry" (Ga 6:1–5).

Commenting on this text, St. Gregory writes: "It is as though [St. Paul] meant . . . that when the sight of another's infirmity is displeasing, reflect on what you are, that the spirit may moderate itself in its zeal for reproving, fearing in its own case that which it reproves." [17]

This social aspect of sin appears more relevant than ever today when we live more than ever in close communion and in groups. This is also true of our moral and religious life, not only the individual but also, and especially, the community as a whole is put to the test and tempted by evil.

When we carry out the duty of *elenchein*, therefore, we should not exaggerate the responsibility of individuals. For each of us is caught up in the meshes of the collectivity, which thinks, reasons, and acts. In our day, more than in the individualistic eras of the past, we have to base our examination of conscience on the responsibility and culpability of the group, on the solidarity and latent complicity of all in evil. Every pastor is able to observe that characteristic abuses exist in the different social classes, professions, races, and communities. The ethos of a group, its mores and usages, set the tone and, in the literal acceptation of the term, govern as anonymous great powers, expressing themselves in the general mentality, life-styles, fashions, laws, advertising, etc. These are the collective standards of immorality, hatred of God, idolatry of wordly values. It is extremely difficult, if not impossible, for the individual to escape the influence of these great powers, or even to become aware of them.

A pastorate which is to be just and merciful (John XXIII's inaugural address to the Second Vatican Council is worth rereading in this connection) should, above all, apply itself to persuading men who are enslaved by collective evils to acknowledge and confess those public sins together; only then can a sincere and effective individual *mea culpa* emerge from their midst. We, therefore, have first to acknowledge collectively, in the first person plural, that all of us, together, tolerate or maintain intolerable situations (the accent here is on sins of negligence or omission), after which we can consider our own individual responsibility. Only thus will the way be opened to a general reform, for example, as regards genuine respect for basic human rights, the spirit of tolerance, the equitable distribution of wealth, and so on.

The prophet's starting point: nature and grace

To carry out his prophetic function adequately, the pastor must start with the premise that every human being is a sinner.

That is a fundamental point of faith. God reveals to us the universality of sin and the need for pardon which all men have in common, without exception. As we read the Scriptures, we constantly come up against this disturbing generalization. The words "all" and "no one" recur like a refrain. "If there is one of you who has not sinned . . ." (Jn 8:7); "If you, then, who are evil . . ." (Mt. 7:11); "No one is good but God alone (Mk 10:18); "All have sinned . . ." (Rm 3:23; 2:1; Ep 2:3); "For there is no man who does not sin" (1 K 8:46); "There is no virtuous man on earth who, doing good, is ever free of sin" (Qo 7:20); "No one is virtuous by your standards" (Ps 143:2); "Every one of us does something wrong, over and over again" (Jm 3:2).

Only those who are in good health, the Lord remarks with perhaps a touch of irony, have no need of a physician. And St. Cyprian was expressing a fundamental conviction of the early Church when he said: "Man experiences and learns that he sins daily, since he is enjoined daily to ask pardon for his faults."

If we wish to transmit faithfully the kerygma of the Apostles as summarized by St. Luke (cf. Ac 2:38; 3:19–26; 5:31; 10:43; 13:38), the theme of sin and pardon, offense and grace must occupy a central place. We have to see to it that our prophetic preaching is a veritable *elenchein:* an intelligible language (1 Co 14) that enables the hearer to become personally conscious of his own sin. Evangelization can be existential and effective only if it is accompanied by instruction in the Christian sense of sin. And such instruction presupposes pastoral relations which lead the sinner to repent, through complete conversion and return to God (*metanoia*).

No one with any experience in the matter will dispute that these pastoral relations are a very delicate matter. *Metanoia* is really the existential point of impact between nature and grace.

In his remarkable book on the theological dictum, *gratia supponit naturam,* Stoeckle points to the grave repercussions on moral education which could result from an incorrect interpretation of this axiom.

Supernatural salvation presupposes a natural substratum. Divine grace can develop only on a human substratum which lends itself to it. But everything will depend on what is considered a "natural disposition" to supernatural life. Stoeckle cautions against two by no means imaginary dangers.

The first is minimizing the experience of guilt and the redemptive aspect of grace. It would be very wrong not to help modern man to become really aware of his sin and of his need for pardon. Too often we are misled by our concern to promote mental health and emotional stability and to spare the individual any harmful guilt complexes. It is in the area of education and youth activities especially that this first danger arises. Unfortunately, the self-satisfied man who believes in his own righteousness—and we find him not only in the well-known garb of the pharisee!—may be endowed with rich natural gifts while being incapable of being really seized by grace, at least in the concrete situation of salvation history, which is characterized by sin and divine pardon. This is because he lacks the personal experience of the existential need for liberation which would cause him to acknowledge his own deficiencies and seek a dialogue with the God of salvation.

The second danger is that of maximizing. Some pastors will have to resist the temptation to consider a natural disposition to dejection and depression, or feelings of insecurity or inferiority, as a particularly favorable predisposition for the reception of divine grace.

If melancholic characters and related personality structures are naturally inclined to emphasize human helplessness, that is no reason for thinking that this makes them providentially ready for supernatural grace. Such more or less neurotic dispositions often conceal a tendency to live one's inferiority in a sterile manner, retreating into a shell and confining oneself to a monologue. These are obstacles, not predispositions to God's pardon; far from being accentuated, every effort should be made to remedy them.

A healthy awareness of my own guilt presupposes a value judgment and a personal understanding of my failings and offenses: I could and should have acted otherwise. It presupposes also that I experience my faults as breaking the dialogue with God, and not simply as the violation of an abstract norm or the misunderstanding of an impersonal value. This is the natural disposition on which grace can operate constructively; the *culpa* can be transmuted into a *felix culpa* to the degree that the person who confesses his fault opens himself to the God who brings salvation.[18]

To foster a sense of sin in a genuinely Christian manner is perhaps one of the most difficult and delicate aspects of home education and pastoral action. We are in constant danger of going from one extreme to another. What we have to guard against, in particular, is prompting baseless guilt feelings: anxiety, shame, self-contempt arising out of facts, situations, or actions where there can be little question of personal responsibility—for example, birth, corporeity, sexuality, ability, environmental disadvantages. Each of us has good enough cause to recognize our real faults and offenses without having to impute guilt where there is none. As St.

Augustine so strikingly puts it, we are not asked to seek out a failing which we do not have, but to find one which we do have without realizing it.[19]

The pastor must remember, moreover, that his job is not to sift and weigh the precise dose of culpability of persons or groups. The purpose of prophetic remonstrance is not to inventory all the failings, omissions, and transgressions of which his fellow man is guilty. Christian ethics is not an atomizing casuistry which breaks down each action to its smallest components; it is dynamic and aims at detecting, through the maze of individual motivations and the tangle of superficial modes of action, the fundamental design which governs the individual's total behavior.

Still less should there be any question of precipitately and triumphantly interpreting suffering and trials as the chastisement for some, perhaps hidden, fault. If St. Paul's method (see 1 Co 11:29–32) is adduced in support of such an approach, it would be well to remember the severe judgment which Job's friends drew upon themselves from Yahweh for perceiving a causal link between suffering and personal guilt. And to a similar question by the disciples concerning the man born blind, Jesus replied: "Neither he nor his parents sinned; he was born blind so that the works of God might be displayed in him" (Jn 9:3).

Notes

1. See the principal texts where these two functions of preaching are explicitly mentioned: Mt 4:23; 9:35; 28:19–20; He 6:1–2. Of the abundant literature on this biblical renewal in the pastorate we may cite the following: J. Kahmann, *De Bijbel over de prediking van het Woord*, Roermond-Maaseik, J. J. Romen & Zonen, 1961; A. Seumois, *Apostolat*, Rome, 1961; *L'annonce de l'évangile aujourd'hui* (Parole et Mission), Paris, 1962; I. Hermann, *Kerygma und Kirche* (Festschrift Schmid), Ratisbon, 1963.
2. The principal works consulted are the following: H. Greeven, *Propheten, Lehrer, Vorsteher bei Paulus*, in Z.N.T.W., 1952; Friedrich, *Profètès*, in *Kittels Wörterbuch N.T.*; A. Heschel, *The Prophets*, New York, Harper & Row, 1962.
3. In connection with this relationship between teaching and prophecy we immediately think of the two tendencies—conservative and progressive—manifested at the Second Vatican Council.

4. See H. Schlier, *Der Brief an die Epheser*, Düsseldorf, Patmos-Verlag, 1957.
5. H. Thielicke, *Wie die Welt begann*, Stuttgart, Patmos-Verlag, 1959, p. 207.
6. See H. Schlier, *Le Temps de l'Eglise*, Paris-Tournai, Casterman, 1961.
7. St. Augustine, *In Johannem*, Corpus Christianorum, Series Latina (Steenbrugge), 36, 565. This series will be referred to throughout this work by the letters C.C.L.
8. It would take us too far to inventory all the New Testament texts dealing with the awakening of the sense of guilt. We might, however, cite some passages in which St. Paul describes the pastor's mission as being to turn men away from evil; to warn them; to rebuke them; to persuade them of their error. See 1 Co 4: 14–16; Col 1:28; 3:16; 1 Th 5: 12–14; 2 Th 3:15.
9. See C. Sqicq, *Saint Paul, les épîtres pastorales*, Paris, J. Gabalda, 1947.
10. "For the moment all discipline seems painful rather than pleasant; later it yields the peaceful fruit of righteousness to those who have been trained by it" (He 12:11).
11. J. Dupont, *Le discours de Milet*, Paris, Editions du Cerf, 1962.
12. *Sermo 46 de V.T.*, C.C.L., 41, 534.
13. D. Smolders, *L'audace de l'apôtre selon Saint Paul*, Collectanea Mechliniensis, Louvain, Nova et Vetra, 1927.
14. *Liber Regulae Pastoralis* (see St. Gregory the Great, *Pastoral Care*, Westminster, Md., Newman Press, 1950, p. 66, in the series of Ancient Christian Writers, no. 11). This work has understandably been regarded in the Western Church as an ideal guide for pastors. Gregory the Great is remarkable for his great good sense and balanced judgment. This practical-minded Roman was a subtle psychologist. At the same time, he knew his Scriptures thoroughly, having meditated upon them all his life, like his master Augustine. From his namesake, Gregory of Nazianzen, he borrowed this definition of pastoral action: *est ars artium, regimen animarum*.
15. See W. Trilling, *Die Hausordnung Gottes*, Düsseldorf, Patmos-Verlag, 1960.
16. Dorotheus of Gaza; see *Ouvres spirituelles* (ed. L. Regnault and J. de Preville), Paris, Editions du Cerf, 1963, second letter. Published in Greek and French.
17. *Liber Regulae Pastoralis*, p. 82.
18. B. Stoeckle, *Gratia supponit naturam*, Rome, Herder, 1962.
19. C.C.L., 40, 1649.

2

Importance of the confession of sin

The contemporary approach to sin and guilt

As we reflect on the priest's prophetic function, on the training of conscience and the sense of sin, and on the pastoral theology of the sacrament of penance, we find ourselves confronted by two apparently contradictory facts. On the one hand, there is the loss of the sense of sin which, according to Pius XII's celebrated dictum of October 27, 1946, is undoubtedly the most dangerous phenomenon in the modern world. On the other hand, psychologists and specialists in mental hygiene are constantly voicing concern about exaggerated guilt feelings and anxieties which in many of our contemporaries reach neurotic proportions.

Clearly these observations do not relate to the same individuals. One of Hesnard's grossest errors was to think that a morbid guilt feeling was the product of an individual's recognition that he was a sinner. The truth is just the contrary. Morbid guilt feelings arise rather out of the refusal to admit one's sin and out of the presumptuous attitude of the man who claims that he is blameless.

There is of course a pseudo-guilt; that has been amply proved by psychoanalysis. Many people are genuinely tormented by unmotivated guilt feelings. They are overwhelmed by anxiety and shame or by an inferiority complex, none of which implies the existence of any real sin. They regard any attitude of independence or lawful enjoyment as sinful. They believe they are responsible for circumstances or situations which are normal and healthy or which involve no responsibility: corporeity, success, accidents. Or again, they exaggerate their guilt by applying excessively rigorous standards.

But there also exists a pseudo innocence. This is the case with those who believe in their own righteousness, either because they do not see their real failings and offenses, or because they refuse to see them. Depth psychologists are increasingly aware of this phenomenon.[1]

Only a genuinely Christian guilt experience can resolve this dilemma. The individual who realizes his fault, who accepts responsibility for it and repents, can develop in an atmosphere of confidence and pardon. He will not perish in the asphyxiating grasp of a morbid guilt complex, nor will he succumb to the equally morbid illusion of impeccability. Nietzsche wrote: "An uneasy conscience is a sickness; but it is a sickness akin to pregnancy." [2] In other words, it bears within it the seed of a new life.

Sin, confession of faults, contrition, and penance are themes which many preachers would like to expunge from their programs. The faithful, they feel, do not want them. Or again, they consider that contemporary pastoral theology should put the emphasis on essentials, and the Christian life is essentially that of achieving union with God and men through faith, hope, and love.

It is undoubtedly true that sin and contrition have too often in the past been separated from the theological virtues, and stressed at the expense of essentials. To that extent suspicion and hostility in regard to this theme are legitimate. But an authentically Christian presentation of sin and penance as exemplified in the Scriptures and the liturgy specifically stresses their vital relation to faith, hope, and love. Far from being in conflict or competition with each other, they are dimensions and elements of the Christian existence which are in essential agreement.[3]

If less importance is placed on sin and the sense of guilt in our day, this may be due, in part, to the mentality and existential experience of twentieth-century man. Work, technique, and industry are primary values in the eyes of our contemporaries.

That being the case, it is natural that the sectors in which material influences predominate should hold pride of place for modern man and constitute his main centers of interest. To *homo technicus* it makes little sense to look back over the past—an attitude which must underlie any sense of sin and contrition. The development of material progress and the accelerating pace of new inventions never shift into reverse. At best, obsolete machines and other devices are preserved in museums as curiosities. This is true of the earliest locomotives or airplanes. Technical progress always moves forward from the stage of development already attained, with both present and past left behind forever.

It is logical for the technician to look solely to the future. To regret the past or to contemplate now obsolete achievements is in his view a pure waste of time. And no one senses this more intensely than the young man who sees a whole life stretching out before him, with its unlimited possibilities. An inquiry conducted by *La Vie Spirituelle* in 1946 elicited the following response: "The saints of tomorrow will be not so much penitents as kings of creation."

Such an attitude is healthy enough and undoubtedly very effective from a technological point of view. But the danger is to generalize it and allow it increasingly to dominate our way of thinking, feeling, and acting. It becomes a style of life, a mentality, the spirit of an age. Gabriel Marcel has repeatedly cautioned against this danger. "The modern world, to the degree that it draws support from Promethean values, tends inevitably to the denial of sin, and indeed requires such a denial for its own glorification." [4] In his curiosity about everything, modern man's gaze is trained on the future, on the unending progress of science and technology. One need not be a pessimist or a prophet of doom to see that this man, intoxicated by his achievements, is in danger of forgetting that his discoveries are two-edged. They can be used either to make our world more habitable or to destroy us all: the decision in favor of constructive or destructive use rests with man himself. That decision does not come out of the clear blue sky; it is the product of a fundamental attitude. But such an attitude, or existential orientation, germinates and develops out of man's past. If a man's existential option is defective or morally wrong, he must, above all, recognize that dangerous malady, so that he may be able to remedy it by conversion and contrition. In other words, the realization of sin and the confession of our guilt assume a vital and indeed planetary importance. This applies also, and indeed especially, to the *homo technicus* of our generation.

The truly Christian sense of sin can arise and develop only where the other essential elements of Christianity exist: contact with the living God, the conviction that man is capable of choosing freely, and faith in the supernatural.[5] Contact with God comes first, because when faith withers or vanishes, we no longer realize that to sin is to refuse to recognize God as God and to love Him; it is a breach in the I-Thou relationship caused by our own personal stand. The man who lives a purely secular life regards sin as a moral or social evil, as failure to respect an abstract standard, transgression of an anonymous law, or disregard of the rights of others. To quote Pascal: "Man's knowledge of God without an awareness of his own wretchedness leads to pride. An awareness of his wretchedness without the knowledge of God leads to despair. The knowledge of Jesus Christ represents the middle state because we find in it both God and our wretchedness." [6] The sense of sin presupposes a sense of freedom and responsibility. The man who is not convinced that he has to make his own basic option and personally bring it to fulfilment cannot possibly recognize his culpability.

The sense of sin, finally, develops only in the context of eternity —*sub specie aeternitatis*. The man who takes no account of an endless life beyond death strips his life on earth of its serious and decisive character as a journey and a commitment.

In this threefold perspective, the acceptance of our sin becomes both possible and profitable. The sinner can: become aware of his guilt, recognize his sin and realize that he has committed it; recognize his malady, assume his condition as a sinner and repent; acknowledge his wretchedness and confess his sin; deplore his offense; express regret for it and display his repentance; apologize; attempt to make amends for the offense committed; be prepared to suffer the consequences; expiate and make satisfaction; ask pardon, implore mercy, and accept reconciliation; revise his former style of life; begin a new existence by a radical conversion and a firm purpose.

Like every other process of growth or development, the process of conversion comprises several stages. Our purpose in this study is to make some contribution from the point of view of pastoral psychology to certain stages in Christian *metanoia:* the realization of our culpability and the confession of our sins.

The Bible and confession of sin

In the Old Testament, acknowledgment of sin constitutes the essence of the return to Yahweh. Without such acknowledgment, there can be no healing of the breach with God caused by sin. Only a frank and unqualified *confiteor* can bring about a genuine reconciliation and conversion.

This requirement is explicitly stated in Numbers 5:6–7: "If a man or woman commits any of the sins by which men break faith with Yahweh, that person . . . must confess the sin." Throwing oneself face down on the ground, fasting, and all other penitential practices are of value only to the extent that they symbolize a contrite heart; see Joel 2:12–13: "Come back to me with all your heart, fasting, weeping, mourning. Let your hearts be broken, not your garments torn; turn to Yahweh your God again."

Yahweh desires that the sinner should acknowledge his defeat and recognize his guilt toward the One he has offended. The Hebrew word *kanah* (to humble oneself), used in this context, had originally a secular connotation: the submission of a defeated enemy or of a vassal to his victor (see Jg 8:28; 26:41; 1 K 21:29; 2 K 22:19; 2 Ch 12: 7,12).

That is why confession of sin holds a central place in the principal liturgical texts in which man asks pardon of God (see 1 S 7:6; 12:10; 2 S 12:13; 1 K 8:46–50; Ezr 9:6; Ne 1:6; 9:2; Ps 32:5; 38:18; 41:4; 51:3–4; 106:6; Je 3:25; 14:20; Nb 21:7; Jg 10:10–16). One of the most striking texts occurs in Daniel (9:5–6): "We have sinned, we have done wrong, we have acted wickedly, we have betrayed your commandments and your ordinances and turned away from them. We have not listened to your servants the prophets, who spoke in your name . . ." It is the gesture of one who surrenders unconditionally, humbly submits and, acknowledging his guilt, accepts in advance whatever the injured party decides. "We have sinned. Do with us as you think fit" (Jg 10:15). The admission of one's sin is a repudiation of self and a

throwing of oneself on God's mercy. So long as we are not prepared to make a frank and unequivocal confession of our sin, and
resort to all kinds of expedients to avoid such painful self-
accusation, we only aggravate our position. "He who conceals his
faults will not prosper; he who confesses and renounces them will
find mercy" (Pr 28:13). And Jeremiah puts these words in
Yahweh's mouth concerning Judah, which has sinned gravely:
"You say, 'I am blameless . . .' And here I am passing sentence
on you because you say, 'I have not sinned' " (2:35).

Psalm 32 (1–5) expresses it still more clearly:

> Happy the man whose fault is forgiven,
> whose sin is blotted out;
> happy the man whom Yahweh
> accuses of no guilt,
> whose spirit is incapable of deceit!
> All the time I kept silent, my bones were wasting away
> with groans, day in, day out;
> day and night your hand
> lay heavy on me;
> my heart grew parched as stubble
> in summer drought.
> At last I admitted to you I had sinned;
> no longer concealing my guilt,
> I said, "I will go to Yahweh
> and confess my fault."
> And you, you have forgiven the wrong I did,
> have pardoned my sin.

Any comparative study of religion shows that confession of sin is
a reaction common to all men. Its significance, however, is not
everywhere the same. Among some Eastern peoples, confession
was employed as a form of autotherapy. Alongside many other
remedies, it was used to rid oneself of a variety of ills. The individual names and confesses the sin as in an exorcism he might name
the demon by which he believes himself to be possessed. And to
be quite sure not to leave any out, he accuses himself of every
imaginable sin and misdeed, both known and unknown.[7]

The Bible, on the other hand, attributes no magical or automatic power to the confession of sins. In the Old Testament, the
sinner does not inventory his faults in order to neutralize their

nefarious effect. What he acknowledges is not so much the number and species of sins committed as the fact of having sinned and being a sinner. The important thing is to admit that we have failed in our duty, that we have been rebellious and unfaithful, in order thereby to vindicate God's righteousness. It is significant, in this connection, that the admission "I have sinned" is completed by the statement, "the Lord is in the right" (Ex 9:27). In many instances, indeed, the latter statement in itself constitutes an admission of guilt (see 2 Ch 12:6; Lm 1:18; Ne 9:6–37; Ba 1:15; Dn 3:26–45; 9:4–19).

This tribute to divine righteousness is another way of proclaiming the individual's own responsibility for the ills which have befallen him. To say that God is right is to say that we cannot blame Him for anything, that His justice is not in question. I alone am responsible for the consequences of my sin. In a word, to confess one's sins is a form of praising and glorifying God in the midst of suffering and misfortune. By recognizing his own guilt and the righteousness of God, the sinner ceases to protest against his fate. He gives glory to God and commends himself to the divine mercy.

This typically Semitic association of concepts is crystallized in the term *jadah*, which has that dual connotation. Hence also the Greek *homologein-exomologesis*, the Latin *confiteri-confessio* and the French or English *confession*, which suggest both the idea of glorifying God and that of acknowledging our sins. In Daniel's "great prayer" (9:4–19), the ambivalence of the word *jadah* is particularly apparent: "To you, O Lord, belongs righteousness, but to us confusion of face . . . because we have sinned against you."

To persuade Achan to admit his misdeeds, Joshua says to him: "My son, give glory to the Lord God of Israel, and render praise to him [*jadah*]; and tell me now what you have done; do not hide it from me" (Jos 7:19). Some exegetes believe that this formula literally reproduces the exhortation which the priests of the post-exilic Temple addressed to the Israelites who came to accuse themselves of their transgressions.

We find the same parallelism throughout the New Testament. *Homologein* means to express one's agreement with the announcement. It is a twofold assent: to say yes to God and to confess

Christ, and to say yes to one's own sinful condition and confess
one's misdeed.[8]

The relationship between these two ideas is by no means fortuitous; it is theologically well founded. It becomes very clear when
we recall that sin in fact means saying no to God, refusing
obedience and respect to Him. When I admit my guilt, I recognize what I am and what I have done. Hence, to be contrite and
to confess one's sin is to say yes to God and to ask His pardon. To
confess Jesus Christ is to put the reparation of what has happened
in His hands. In effect, therefore, we are dealing with two facets of
one and the same attitude. It is impossible to confess God's glory
and goodness positively without negatively confessing one's own
sin.

In the New Testament, the following passages deserve particular
attention: Matthew 3:5-7: the people come to John the Baptist
and confess their sins; while St. Paul insists (Rm 10:8-10) that a
man must confess with heart and lips that Jesus Christ is Lord and
Savior. Confession of sin too must be both interior and exterior.

St. John insists (1 Jn 1:8-10) on the absolute necessity of avowal
of sin; to believe that we can live in communion with God without
such avowal is a dangerous illusion. "If we say we have no sin in
us, we are deceiving ourselves and refusing to admit the truth; but
if we acknowledge our sins, then God who is faithful and just will
forgive our sins and purify us from everything that is wrong. To
say that we have never sinned is to call God a liar and to show that
his word is not in us." It may be noted here that the Apostle
requires not only that we confess our sinful condition in general,
but that we should acknowledge our particular sins too. St. James
(5:16) finally lays down a practical rule of conduct: "So confess
your sins to one another, and pray for one another, and this will
cure you."

Confession in the Church's tradition

The Church Fathers, who always remained very close to the
Scriptures, devoted a considerable portion of their preaching to
this theme.

St. Augustine deliberately gave his autobiography the ambiguous
title of *Confessions*. The confession of his weakness, of his sin,

and of his guilt turns into a paean of praise of God and a tribute to the divine mercy.[9] We can learn from the Psalmist, he writes, how to praise God and render Him homage. On the one hand, we do this by enumerating the benefits received from God, by proclaiming His marvelous interventions and His salvific action, as in Psalm 105; on the other hand, by telling the sad tale of our own sins, as in Psalm 106.

"Acknowledge before God that your sin is something *you* have committed, while *He* is responsible for your good action. The sinner, on the other hand, imputes the evil he does to God and attributes the good he does to himself. When he has done something good, he says: I have done it. And if he has done something wrong, then he looks around for someone to accuse of it so that he need not confess God." [10]

We find the same approach throughout the liturgy. This applies in particular to the structure of the eucharistic celebration, which constitutes the center of our prayer life and should serve as the norm in our relations with God, according to the adage: *lex orandi, lex credendi, lex vivendi.*

In the *Didache,* we read the following precepts which go back to apostolic times: "In the assembly [*ecclesia*], confess your sins and do not betake yourself to prayer with a bad conscience" (4:17). "Gather together on the Lord's day, break the Bread and give thanks, after first confessing your sins, so that your sacrifice may be pure" (14:1).

This is clearly an echo of St. Paul's injunction: "Everyone is to recollect himself before eating this bread and drinking this cup" (1 Co 11:28).

The present liturgy of the Mass has faithfully retained this ancient Christian form of eucharistic celebration. We begin with the *Confiteor*: bowing humbly, we confess our sin to God and to one another. At the Offertory, the consciousness of our sin is revived: "Father, receive this spotless host, which I offer you for my numberless sins, offenses, and negligences." And before we take part in the banquet, we remember that we can approach God only in humility: "forgive us our trespasses," and we strike our breasts in true contrition: "Lord, I am not worthy that you should come under my roof." It may therefore legitimately be said that the Eucharist proper, which begins with the thanksgiving prayer of the Preface, constitutes the response to the *evangelium*, the Good News that God offers us His grace.

It should also be noted that our confession of faith, the *Credo*, contains a form of admission of guilt. This is apparent from its structure, which is based on three verbs: *credo* in unum Deum; *confiteor* unum baptisma in remissionem peccatorum; *expecto* resurrectionem. The admission of our guilt, therefore, must not be separated from our confession of faith.[11]

Obviously, the Church does not invite us to say: "I believe in sin." We confess the *forgiveness* of sins. And to confess, in the sense in which it is used in the Creed, implies far more than to acknowledge and publicly admit our misdeeds, more even than to be overwhelmed by the consciousness of our sins or tortured by remorse. Judas, after all, did not deny his sin; his remorse in fact led him to destroy himself. To confess, in the liturgical true sense of the word, means acknowledging God as our merciful Redeemer and asking His pardon. And this presupposes faith and trust on our part. In order to confess our sins in the spirit of the Gospel and the Creed, we must at the same time proclaim our faith in the salvific action of Father, Son, and Holy Spirit.

From the point of view of pastoral activity, this means that any instruction of the faithful concerning confession of sin necessarily implies instruction in faith.[12]

Guilt experience and confession

Only when a man has reached a critical point in his experience of guilt, a point at which he feels his strength failing him, is he capable of uttering his *confiteor*, of asking pardon and obtaining mercy. His dissatisfaction and uneasiness must have become so intolerable as to make a "normal" life difficult if not impossible. The realization that he has reached a frontier and that he is powerless to cross it cause him to look for help, rather as a man suffering unendurable pain goes to the doctor. What he wants, however, is not to be excused or acquitted (neither does the patient want to learn that there is really nothing the matter with him), but rather to implore mercy and pardon of Him toward whom he knows himself to be guilty. The analogy, of course, comes from Jesus Himself: "It is not the healthy who need the doctor, but the sick. I did not come to call the virtuous, but sinners" (Mk 2:17).

The "virtuous," here, must be understood in the sense in which the scribes and Pharisees used the word. They are those who rely on their own merits and believe they have found favor in God's eyes through their scrupulous observance of the Law. Luke's Gospel in particular presents Jesus as showing a marked preference for sinners: the parable of the Pharisee and the publican (Lk 18:9); the three parables of the lost sheep, the lost drachma, and the prodigal son (Lk 15); the story of Zacchaeus, "for the Son of Man has come to seek out and save what was lost" (Lk 19:10).

This does not, of course, mean that the sinner can have access to the Kingdom without changing his way of life, but rather that any man who wants to live in union with God must first recognize his sin and acknowledge that he is a sinner. Only then can there be a real change of heart or conversion (*metanoia*). That is what St. Augustine sums up in the cogent dictum: "prima ergo intelligentia, ut te noveris peccatorem"—the first thing we must understand is that we have to acknowledge that we are sinners.[13]

This basic experience, without which there does not really exist any possibility of salvation, is described with unequalled realism by the author of the book of Job. Because of its profoundly human overtones, this passage is perhaps preferable to the account of the grandiose vision in Isaiah, which is better known and often quoted.[14]

> *Now I have had a secret revelation,*
> *a whisper has come to my ears.*
> *At the hour when dreams master the mind,*
> *and slumber lies heavy on man,*
> *a shiver of honor ran through me,*
> *and my bones quaked with fear.*
> *A breath slid over my face,*
> *the hairs of my body bristled.*
> *Someone stood there—I could not see his face,*
> *but the form remained before me.*
> *Silence—and then I heard a voice,*
> "*Was ever any man found blameless in the presence of God,*
> *or faultless in the presence of his Maker?*"
>
> (Jb 4:12–17)

The speaker here is Eliphaz, one of Job's friends. He is describing what he experienced during a prophetic vision. It was a revelation from on high, without human agency. The emphasis is on perception through hearing rather than through sight. A voice whispers and approaches stealthily like a thief in the night. It is a soft voice, not a roaring. Yet this verbal revelation is somehow frightening. Terror grips the whole person, even his physical being. There is an obscure, unidentified presence here. Its contours are unclear: God, the invisible Being. Confronted with God, man is seized with mortal anguish, or rather, he experiences his own creaturedom, his own guilt. This is the point of existential encounter between the conscience and the Creator-Judge.[15]

He who is righteous is also pure of heart. But no one is pure before God. Each one of us has to admit with heavy heart: I stand before God empty-handed and I cannot meet His demands; I stand before God with sullied hands and I am unable to cleanse them. In the verses that follow (18 *et seq.*) the thought is carried further: even the servants of God and His angels are subject to the same judgment.[16]

According to the teaching of Jesus, the virtuous man is a sinner who has been justified by God. We are purified and saved freely. God grants us what we cannot achieve for ourselves.

St. Paul, who originally shared the Pharisees' conception of sin and righteousness, came after his conversion to a Christian view identical with that of the synoptic gospels.

Before his encounter with Christ on the road to Damascus, he gloried in his descent from a holy people rather than from "pagan sinners" (Ga 2:15). "As far as the law can make you perfect, I was faultless" (Ph 3:6). But then Jesus Christ entered his life, He who "came into the world to save sinners, of whom I myself am the greatest" (1 Tm 1:15). And Paul realized that he could find favor with God only through faith in Jesus Christ. The true peace of the Christian conscience is not the fruit of our merits and works but rather of our faith and trust in the Redeemer. The Christian is not a righteous man in good standing with the Law and his conscience. Nor is he a sinner overwhelmed by an intolerable sense of his guilt. He is a sinner who has been saved and cleansed through God's goodness. Thus the biblical conception of justice (or righteousness, or holiness) is truly paradoxical. The just man is not the blameless man who fulfills his obligations to the letter; he is the sinner who knows and acknowledges his iniquity; who asks pardon and is thereby justified by God, that is, finds favor with Him. We become just to the degree that we confess our iniquity.

"There are only two kinds of men: the good who believe themselves to be sinners; the sinners who believe themselves to be good," observes Pascal.[17] Nietzsche's sarcastic comment, therefore —"The aim of Christianity is not to bring the Christian to a higher morality, but rather to make him increasingly conscious of his guilt" [18]—is only a half-truth.

The basic reason why we can never overemphasize the importance of the confession of our faults is that this is the condition *sine qua non* for obtaining mercy. God gives Himself only to the humble, the famished, the poor, and the little. The sated He leaves to their solitude. "God refuses the proud and will always favor the humble" (1 P 5:5; Jm 4:6). "For everyone who exalts himself will be humbled, and the man who humbles himself will be exalted" (Lk 14:11).

Grace, writes St. Augustine, operates like rain. Only the valleys are filled with the beneficent waters. The heights, on the other hand, remain dry. We do not grasp an outstretched hand unless we realize, like a drowning man, that we are in distress and will perish without help. If we condemn ourselves, we shall not be condemned by God.[19]

"This is how your God speaks to you: 'your sin must in any case be punished, either by yourself, or by me.' Sin, therefore, is punished, either by the man who repents or by God who condemns. And what is repentance if not indignation against oneself?" [20]

The following comment by a Jewish rabbi is pertinent in this connection. We must admit that we are sinners "like a criminal who appears before the magistrate. So long as he denies his guilt, he is beaten. If he confesses, he is condemned. But with God it is altogether different. So long as a man does not confess his offense, he is condemned. But once he confesses it, he is acquitted." [21]

The fruits of confession

The first result of the confession of guilt is that the sinner pauses and stops. He realizes that he has taken the wrong road and he is concerned to reconsider and alter his course. What is done, of course, is done. The past is irreversible and cannot be blotted out. This applies to the objective world around us. To wound or to kill are irreparable actions. But we can to some extent repudiate our own past, that past which has become a part of ourselves. For man is not merely an element of nature. It is given to him to be able to take a personal stand concerning himself, and to modify his basic existential option. Because we are free, we are able to criticize and disapprove of ourselves, particularly when we accept God's laws in a spirit of faith and listen to His word, which, sharper than any sword, penetrates to the very heart and judges our most intimate thoughts and feelings (He 4:12). Naturally, we should not of course suffer the judgment of our conscience passively, as though it was the voice of a stranger telling us "you have acted wrongly." We have to make the judgment of our conscience our own value judgment and take it actively to heart, so that it becomes a judgment in the first person: "I have sinned."

St. John calls this accepting the Word (1:12) and "coming out into the light, so that it may be plainly seen that what a man does is done in God" (3:21). It is a matter of "wanting to have a conscience," as Heidegger puts it. By identifying himself with his best self, man is reborn and accepts the values he had previously denied or has just discovered.

This restructuring is attended by pain and suffering. It implies a detachment from one's own past and a disintegration of the former ego, which had been embodied in a reprehensible style of living.[22] For all restructuring involves some degree of destruction. The grain of wheat must die before it can give birth to new life.

We must be careful, however, not to put exclusive emphasis on this first aspect of confession, which psychologically is the most striking. *Metanoia*—the total alteration in our style of life—is important. But ultimately the principal aspect is the religious one—the pardon we receive from God. If we neglect this aspect, we take a purely moralistic approach; contrition and conversion are thereby reduced to an expiation and rectification achieved through our own powers. Pardon and God's favor are not obtained by amendment, or by reparation for injustice committed and harm done. That is why, from a doctrinal and pastoral point of view, it seems unjustified to represent confession exclusively as the sacrament of penance. It is as much, if not more, the sacrament of God's pardon.

Conversion, repentance, the turning away whereby the sinner breaks with evil and with himself (his past) in order to turn to God, constitute an absolutely necessary condition for acceding to the kingdom of God and obtaining salvation. But reconciliation nonetheless remains a pure gift of God; it cannot be obtained automatically through conversion or the confession of the sin. That is why the convert must implore God's pardon. "Repent therefore of this wickedness of yours, and pray to the Lord that, if possible, the intent of your heart may be forgiven you" (Ac 8:22). That is why we *celebrate* the mystery of pardon. For the main thing is not the sins we have committed but what God does: to pardon and to set free.

We have to be on our guard, however, against a number of misapprehensions. To pardon (absolve, be reconciled) is not the same thing as clearing a person, excusing him, closing one's eyes to what he has done. That would mean disregarding the real guilt, forgetting it, not taking it into account, justifying it. In this way, we diminish or deny responsibility and declare the culprit partially or totally innocent, that is, just. Nor does pardon mean understanding. One who grasps the particular structure of a mode of conduct, who takes account of all kinds of extenuating circumstances, of personality traits, of antecedents and of other factors which confer a relative character on responsibility or eliminate it, will be inclined to "excuse" a great deal. But to the same degree he will no longer have to grant pardon.[23] Nor do measures of clemency and amnesty coincide altogether with authentic pardon. An amnesty can be granted by one who is in a position to remit a fine or a penalty that has been imposed. Finally—and not the least important point—the idea of pardoning should not be confused with that of calming, reassuring, and freeing a person of his guilt feelings, stifling remorse.

Pardon and grace

To grasp the full meaning of Christian pardon, we must listen to the biblical overtones of the word.

The Old Testament language concerning the forgiveness of sins is richly varied, being taken from different areas of living.

Some expressions are of secular origin: blotting out the offense; not taking it into account; forgetting it; letting it pass; freeing the sinner from the meshes in which he has been trapped; unfettering and absolving; closing one's eyes to the offense; casting it behind one's back or into the bottom of the sea; healing a man of the sickness which is sin. Other expressions are taken from the language of law: acquittal; declaration of freedom or redemption from the power of sin. A good number, finally, are taken from the language of religious ritual: washing and purifying, remitting, covering, and reconciling.

Nevertheless, there is always one essential precondition: to confess one's sin and to ask pardon (see Ps 32; 51; Gn 50:17; 1 S 25:28; 2 S 19:20; Jos 7; Jr 14:20; Jb 4; Ezr 9:15; Ne 9; Dn 9:7–19). We find it very clearly stated by Jeremiah (3:12–13):

" 'Return, faithless Israel,' says the Lord.
  'I will not look on you in anger, for I am merciful,' says the Lord;
  'I will not be angry forever.
  Only acknowledge your guilt,
  that you rebelled against the Lord your God . . .
  and that you have not obeyed my voice,' says the Lord."

A careful study of the synoptic Gospels and the Acts leads to the conclusion that the forgiveness of sins is regarded in those texts as the essence of salvation; there is nothing that man needs so much as pardon, and pardon is granted by Jesus at baptism.[24]

In the later New Testament writings, other expressions appear more often: reconciliation, redemption, justification, sanctification, purification.

Jesus Christ takes our faults upon Himself. Through perfect self-abandonment in a spirit of love and obedience to the Father, He is the new Adam who destroys in His person the enmity and the rebellion of man against God (see Ep 2:16). He who carries the cross assumes the real weight of our offense, so that we are effectively delivered from it.

When God pardons, He in fact offers us His grace and readmits the sinner to the ranks of His friends. He restores the covenant which we had broken; He is reconciled and reunited to us (at-one-ment). The act of pardoning is also the act of creating new love. The sinner who had fled far from his native land and from his destination is repatriated.

Strictly speaking, therefore, we remain guilty and at fault. But God, whom we had offended, welcomes us back freely to His love, to which we no longer had claim. He accepts us in spite of our unacceptability. He does not close His eyes to our transgression, neither does He justify it. He does not forget, but He pardons, because He does not bear malice, does not demand a penalty, and does not impute our offense to us subsequently. But we obtain this pardon only if we unconditionally assent to God's judgment.

Thus the difference between the true concept of pardon and its caricatures, mentioned above, lies in that *from* which the sinner is freed and *that which* is given to him.

Without sincere confession of our fault, then, there is neither pardon nor liberation. Hence, a pastoral activity aimed at fostering an existential life of faith must begin with an experience which in some sense is familiar to everyone: that of subjection followed by liberation. For those whose territory was formerly under enemy occupation, the weary wait for liberation comes easily to mind. For victims of natural catastrophes, liberation means rescue from fire, flood, earthquake, landslide. The erstwhile prisoner who hears the heavy prison door close behind him feels relief; he is free. The student who has successfully completed a decisive examination can breathe freely once more. The sick man who has been cured is free from pain and fear of death. A person beset by difficult problems or financial worries heaves a sigh of relief when he extricates himself thanks to expert advice or a windfall . . . The great O Antiphons of the Advent liturgy are particularly rich in content in that respect. Charged with an emotion that is wholly biblical, they reflect the Church's longing for deliverance from the darkness of captivity, from death and solitude, from sin, and from the misery of being cut off and alienated from God.

What about the more perfect?

One might sometimes wonder, however, whether all this applies equally to Christians who are more advanced in the ways of the Lord and more intimately united to God. As the believer sanctifies himself, does confession of sin become less urgent? Or do santification and sense of guilt advance side by side, so that the goal is never in fact reached? The answer to the latter question is affirmative, if we take St. Paul seriously when he says that we must never boast of any personal merit (1 Co 4:7), and that any over-estimation of oneself in this area leads inevitably to pharisaism, pride, and complacency.

Confession of sin is not gradually rendered nugatory, to be replaced by a consciousness of our own worth and holiness. The humility of the true believer never ceases to grow. And this ever-deepening humility relates not only to sins committed in the past, but also to persistent guilt. It was his most faithful disciples that the Lord taught to pray daily: "Forgive us our trespasses." And the liturgy places on the lips of the whole Church the words of the centurion: "Lord, I am not worthy that you should come under my roof." What a contrast with the statement of the elders: "He deserves this of you" (Lk 7: 4–5)!

The closer we get to the Lord and the greater the influence of His Holy Spirit upon us, the more clearly we perceive that we are sinners.[25] It is not without a profound theological reason that the feeling of existential guilt should be of such vital importance.

Man's vocation is to experience gratitude to God and love Him in return. God's joy is to save those who were lost, to grant His pardon and to reconcile men to Himself. His joy is soteriological. But we can be grateful to someone only to the extent that we realize the magnitude of the debt that has been remitted. Only a man who is conscious of his own indigence and dissatisfied with himself can understand the meaning of merciful pardon.

These ideas underlie the parable of the two debtors (Lk 7:41). Jesus has just been speaking of the divine clemency and Simon, the Pharisee, who regards Him as a prophet, invites Him to dinner, though somewhat coldly and with scant ceremony. A woman of ill repute, on the other hand, reacts to the good news with great gratitude, joy, and love. Jesus uses a parable to answer Simon's wordless criticism of the fact that He allows Himself to be touched by so unrespectable a person. What Simon lacks is a sense of gratitude. And why? He is not sufficiently aware of his sin and of his need for pardon. "For this reason I tell you that . . . her many sins must have been forgiven her, or she would not have shown such great love. It is the man who is forgiven little who shows little love" (Lk 7:47).[26]

It is widely recognized today that the sacrament of penance is passing through a crisis. If we want to resolve that crisis, we have among other things to reflect thoroughly on the implications of the points made above. Few sacraments have developed so radically in the course of the centuries as that of penance. Our present liturgical practice differs enormously from that of the primitive ecclesial community. St. Jerome, St. Augustine, St. Gregory of Nazianzen, St. John Chrysostom, for example, never went to confession. It is good that we should be aware of this historical evolution.[27]

Nevertheless, these great figures of the early Church demonstrated a sense of sin far more intense and personal than that of the majority of our contemporaries. It would be gravely illogical to infer from the nonexistence of private and frequent confession that they attached less importance than we do to the confession of their sinful condition, the entreaty for pardon and a constant *metanoia*. It is rather the reverse that is true.[28]

Unceasing confession

Our confession must be a *cogitatio*, says St. Augustine. Just as we must constantly praise and give thanks, so we must ceaselessly recall our sin. The man who forgets what he has been freed from also forgets to thank his liberator. To preserve in my memory both my sin and the mercy that God has shown me is the best means of remembering the Savior. For remembrance and thanksgiving go hand in hand.[29] And St. Gregory the Great cautions us against being misled by the argument that "all that is needed is to sin no more and to live a better life." He points out that when the writer ceases writing and adds nothing to his text, he does not thereby erase what he has previously written. Only the constant recollection and confession of our guilt can heal us of the wound we have inflicted upon ourselves. "I have my sin constantly in mind" (Ps 51:5).[30] To cite a modern authority: "Remorse is linked to the exercise of a practical remembrance, not intellectual but living and direct . . . An amnesic—the point is highly significant—will not really repent of an act he has forgotten, not for lack of moral sense but for lack of memory. The principle of remorse resides not in the reality of the action committed but in the permanent significance of that experience, in its incorporation in the totality of one's life. There is no remorse for an act which is not directly remembered." [31]

We can never sufficiently acknowledge our distress since we shall never sufficiently know the grace we receive. To quote Jean Guitton: "The act of adhering to the Giver is an incessant act. It might perhaps be summed up in that word of assent, that 'yes' which Lavelle called the deepest of all words. To be converted is to say 'yes' to God. But we shall never have done with saying it." [32]

Admission and remission

There is another, rather subtle and dangerous, misunderstanding concerning pardon to which we should draw attention.

While the Bible, the tradition of the Church, and the liturgy insist without respite on the necessity for humble confession of our sinfulness if we are to be saved, that does not mean that confession of sin is itself the cause of pardon and salvation. Such a concept would negate the gratuitousness of God's generous love. Strictly speaking, contrition has of itself no expiatory power and can neither bring about reconciliation nor enforce it. Confession places us in the dispositions required for the reception of God's pardon and the experience of His grace.[33] The only thing we have to offer Him is our broken and contrite hearts, our self-condemnation. We cannot expect forgiveness and salvation unless we throw ourselves entirely on His clemency. There can be no question whatsoever of merits or good works capable of influencing God's will to pardon. "May we be accepted by you, Lord, in a humble spirit and a contrite heart," is our prayer at the eucharistic celebration, echoing Daniel (3:39; see also Ps 51:16–17). Thus the famous expression, *sola gratia,* is undoubtedly theologically sound in this context.

We can go even further. Not only the favor we find with God but even the confession of our sin and the conversion themselves are gifts of God. For it is God who invites us and grants us the possibility of returning to Him. When we acknowledge and confess our sinful condition, we do so under the influence of the Holy Spirit. He it is who, through His coming, confounds the world in the matter of sin and unbelief, to lead it to the fullness of truth (see Jn 16:8–13). "Therefore I want you to understand that no one speaking by the Spirit of God . . . can say 'Jesus is Lord' except by the Holy Spirit" (1 Co 12:3).

St. Augustine writes on this point:

> The Holy Spirit is present in the man who confesses his sin. For it is already a gift of the Holy Spirit when an offense you have committed displeases you. To the impure spirit sins are pleasing; they displease the Holy Spirit. Although you are still engaged in asking pardon, you are nevertheless already united to God, since you hate the evil you have committed. You both reprove it. There are therefore two of you combatting your fever (sin)—you and the Doctor. Consequently, since the confession and punishment of sin in man cannot come from himself, it is impossible for anyone to condemn himself without the gift of the Holy Spirit.[34]

Confession and catharsis

So far, we have been emphasizing the primary importance of confession of guilt if we are to find favor with God. But insistence on this strictly religious aspect does not rule out the consideration of what might be called the intrahuman result of confession. In all ages, men have known that the fact of expressing oneself and pouring out one's heart produces a cathartic effect. The legend of King Midas is an example.

A repressed guilt feeling poisons the whole system. It grows and gains ground like some anonymous power, causing an ever increasing distress in a man's affective life and ultimately disrupting his inner balance. In an allegorical interpretation of Acts 10:13, St. Augustine writes that just as the Jews were not permitted to leave the blood in slaughtered cattle, so we cannot try to stifle the actions of which our conscience accuses us. We have to try to find some outlet through the acknowledgment of the fault. Sin is a concentration of pus; by confessing, man is unburdened and purified.[35] "Satan is never so happy as about those who do not express their most intimate thoughts," observed the Desert Fathers, who possessed a very thorough knowledge of the human heart in this respect.[36]

It is therefore clearly one of the pastor's most important duties to create a pastoral climate favorable to this cathartic outpouring of the heart. For the genuine admission of sin is not achieved in isolation and solitude, on the basis of introspection. Confession bears fruit only if it grows on the fertile soil of interpersonal relations. And such relations must fulfill several conditions if they are to eliminate the attitude of self-defense which blocks the admission of sin. A man will open his heart in an atmosphere of confidence, security, and acceptance, when there is a prospect of understanding, respect, and pardon.[37]

On this point, the sayings of the Desert Fathers, some of which we cite below, contain suggestions worth consideration in pastoral activity.

A deep awareness of his personal guilt will prevent any hard and pitiless judgment on the pastor's part. "He who bears his own sins does not notice those of others." "So long as a man finds something to complain about in himself, he respects his brother. But as soon as he is satisfied with his own righteousness, he has a tendency to find his brother worse than himself." The man who places himself in the right relationship with God—that is, who kneels down humbly—also places himself in the right relationship with his neighbor: beside him, not above him. He goes down into the muddy water to help him and does not remain on the high bank whence he can only cause the drowning man to sink deeper down and finally perish. The following anecdote is quite striking in this connection. At an assembly of monks, there was criticism of a brother who had committed some fault. Then one of those present rose, went out and returned with a heavy bag of sand on his back, and carrying a small basket of sand in his hands. That, he said, is how we dismiss from our field of vision the host of our own sins, while judging the petty sins of our neighbor.[38]

Nevertheless, the quest for catharsis can in its turn give rise to all kinds of erroneous ideas and motivations concerning confession. And experience teaches us that this is very often the case in connection with the sacrament of penance.

Thus it can happen that a person seeks through sacramental confession to rid himself of the distressing feeling of having offended God and living at enmity with Him. Yet the peace and reconciliation which are given us in absolution do not wipe out the fact that we have broken our covenant with Him. Even after finding mercy, we remain conscious that we are sinners. Contrition is definitely an evangelical virtue which must develop constantly and which is never superfluous, not even after our sins have been forgiven. The notion of sacramental absolution as a kind of vacuum cleaner which removes the superficial grime from our hearts, so that we find ourselves completely blameless after all, as though there had never been anything wrong in the first place, is an unworthy caricature. Quite the contrary: Confession is intended to deepen the consciousness of our sinful condition, not to lessen or eliminate it.

Pascal writes on this point: "One day a man told me that he was filled with joy and trust when he left the confessional. Another told me that he remained a prey to fear. This made me think that the two of them together would have made one good man, and that each lacked something insofar as he did not possess the feeling of the other." [39]

It is equally out of place to look primarily for reassurance in confession.[40] To think that we shall be at peace as soon as we have verbalized a transgression or a failure is a very dangerous thing. For it easily degenerates into an attitude compounded of magic and scrupulosity: We confess in the greatest possible detail in order to be able to say, "There, now I'm rid of it all!" Christian peace grows out of a humble confession to God that we remain sinners and that we put our trust unreservedly in His Son, Jesus Christ, who bestows His grace upon us. "The holier a person becomes, the further he knows himself to be from his goal, and yet he is more and more confident, more and more balanced." [41]

Authentic evangelical joy is given to those who recognize their sinfulness and who learn the Good News. The consciousness of sin and its admission banish anxiety and renew confidence in the divine mercy. The man who confesses his sinful condition knows that this humility frees him from sin, because it is accompanied by the grace of God (cf. Ps 130: *De profundis*). As one of the Desert Fathers put it, "Better a man who has sinned, but who knows that he has sinned and who does penance, than one who has not sinned and thinks he has acted rightly." [42]

Notes

1. As is shown in this final statement by H. Haefner (*Schulderleben und Gewissen*, Stuttgart, Klett, 1956, p. 180), in which he sums up the results of his inquiry: "We are led to conclude that there is no psychological and spiritual health without continual anxiety and guilt, without doubts and permanent self-challenge."
2. *Zur Genealogie der Moral*, II, no. 19.
3. See B. Haering, *Pastorale du péché*, Paris, Desclée, 1962; J. Pohier, "La pénitence, vertu de la culpabilité chrétienne," in *La Vie Spirituelle, Supplément*, 1962, p. 331.
4. *Monde moderne et sens du péché*, Paris, P. Horay, 1956, p. 29.
5. See M. Blanchet, in *Monde moderne et sens du péché*, Paris, P. Horay, 1956, p. 46.
6. Blaise Pascal, *Pensées*, translated by Martin Turnell, New York, Harper, 1962, p. 212.
7. See A. Falkenstein, *Sumerische und Akkadische Hymnen*, Zurich–Stuttgart, Artemis Verlag, 1953, p. 272.
8. The term *confessio* in the Latin Church did not acquire the sense of sacramental confession to a priest until the eighth century. Previously the term had had the much more general meaning of confession to God. This semantic contraction corresponds to the greater frequency of sacramental confession at the time, as the practice of public penance gradually gave way to that of private penance. An extreme of devalorization was reached when *confessio* became synonymous with "confession penny." See C. Vogel, *Pastorale du péché,* Paris, Desclée, 1962.
9. See M. Verheyen, *Eloquentia pedisequa*, Nijmegen, Dekker & van de Vegt, 1949; J. Ratzinger, "Originalität und Uberlieferung in Augustinus' Begriff der Confessio," in *Revue des Etudes Augustiniennes*, Paris, 1957, p. 375.
10. *Enarr. Ps.* 91, C.C.L., 39, 1280.
11. From the fourth century onward, the article of faith concerning forgiveness of sins, which had originally been considered as the fruit of baptism, was related to sacramental absolution. See J. N. D. Kelly, *Early Christian Creeds*, New York, McKay, 1960.
12. "The faith of the Christian believer does not bear primarily on an interpretation of evil, its nature, origin, and end. The Christian does not say: I believe in sin, but: I believe in the forgiveness of sins. Sin receives its full significance only retrospectively, from the present instant of 'justification.'" P. Ricoeur, *Finitude et culpabilité*, Paris, Aubier, 1960, p. 286.
13. *Enarr. Ps.*, C.C.L., 38, 231. Cf.: "Initium operum bonorum, con-

fessio est operum malorum" (*Tract. in Joh.*, C.C.L., 36, 128); "Initium justitiae nostrae, confessio est peccatorum" (*In I Ep. Joh.*, IV, 3).

The Council of Trent expressly defined that consciousness of sin constitutes an essential element of the act of faith (DZ No. 798). We might recall, in that connection, Pope John XXIII's appeal for the confession of our sins (*Poenitentiam agere*) in preparation for the Second Vatican Council. The invitations of the Netherlands and German hierarchies are also instructive; see *Kath. Arch.*, 1962, p. 953.

14. We can distinguish three phases in Isaiah's religious experience which we may call, according to the dialectical mode, thesis, antithesis, and synthesis. 1. God is holy and absolutely pure. 2. I, a man, am a sinner (consciousness of distance). 3. In His mercy, God pardons me (experience of proximity).

15. Hebrew has no equivalent for "conscience." The term generally used is "heart," the source of thought, sentiment, and will. A text such as this one proves once again that psychic phenomena can be known and masterfully described even without the use of technical terms. Whence the danger of confining research, in the present case for example, to passages where the words *suneidesis-conscientia* occur.

16. "What man can say, 'I have cleansed my heart, I am purified of my sin'?" (Pr 20:9). (Cf. Jb 14:4; 15:14–16; 1 K 8:46; Qo 7:20.) Incidentally, the prophetic experience which Eliphaz describes here is of an altogether different kind from the formalist theology, learned by rote, which he proposes to Job in other passages, where he appears as a rather clumsy pastor. See F. Horst, *Hiob*, Neukirchen, Neukirchener Verlag, 1962.

17. *Op. cit.*, p. 324.

18. *Menschlich, allzu menschlich*, no. 141.

19. "We deserve to be pardoned only if we do not pardon ourselves." P. Guérin, *Vérité et religion*, Paris, Presses universitaires de France, 1962, p. 185.

20. *Sermo 19 de V.T.*, C.C.L., 41, 252. See similar passages: *Enarr. Ps. 66*, C.C.L., 39, 864. "Qui confessus fuerit homini, punitur; Deo qui confessus fuerit, liberatur" (C.C.L., 41, 379); "Fac confitendo propitium, quem negando non facis nescium" (C.C.L., 39, 1026).

21. H. L. Strack and P. Billerbeck, *Kommentar zum Neuen Testament aus Talmud und Midrasch*, Munich, C. H. Beck, 1956, vol. I.

22. "We repent of an act which we recognize as our own, yet in which we do not recognize ourselves. Remorse manifests a discordance between us and ourselves, an inner conflict between two elements, one of which in our eyes is more valuable than the other." G. Gusdorf, *Mémoire et Personne*, Paris, Presses universitaires de France, 1951, vol. II, p. 358. There are some very interesting data on con-

trition in a recent work by A. Esser, *Das Phänomen Reue*, Cologne, Hegner, 1963.

23. Kindly acceptance, the tolerant and permissive attitude of the psychoanalyst and the counsellor, is probably a secularized form of the Christian *justificatio impii*. Religious pardon has been, as it were, leveled down and reduced to a psychological and empathic understanding. If the tolerance of certain therapists sometimes verges on indifferentism or is imperceptibly transformed into acquittal and absolution (to understand is to forgive), that is a misuse of the method of acceptance which in fact does not help the patient at all. The permissive approach, properly applied, avoids both condemnation and approval. And it is today a solidly established fact that excellent results may be obtained by that method, even from a pastoral point of view. See A. Uleyn, *Empathische therapie en empathische omgang met schuldgevoelens*, Gawein, 1961, and R. Hostie, *Pastoral Counseling*, New York, Sheed & Ward, 1966.

24. Cf. the principal passages where the technical term *aphesis* occurs: Mt 1:21; 26:28; Mk 1:5; Lk 1:77; Ac 3:20; 7:60; 22:16.

25. There is a magnificent text on this theme in Dorotheus of Gaza, *op. cit.* (see note 16 to chapter I), p. 197.

26. The Semitic languages have no specific term for "gratitude." That is why the evangelical text speaks of "love" and "return of love." See J. Jérémias, *Les paraboles de Jésus*, Le Puy, X. Mappus, 1964. With St. Paul, too, the attitude of thanksgiving so predominates that it may be regarded as basic to his spirituality. L. Beirnaert writes in *Psyche*, no. 18–19, 1948: "Thanksgiving presupposes a deep sense of having been delivered from danger, of being reconciled with every being in a friendly universe. It bursts out like a song of freedom and salvation: we were lost and now we are saved, we were abandoned and now we are loved! Its explosive character comes precisely from the felt contrast between the former situation, which remains alive in the living memory, and the new situation. We should note, further, that thanksgiving is always addressed to someone; we give thanks to . . . It is therefore somehow accompanied by the sense of an outside initiative, which has broken the barriers and knocked down the walls of the prison in which we had been enclosed hitherto. It bursts out when the agonizing drama has been resolved in a freedom received as a gift."

27. See B. Poschmann, *Busse und letzte Oelung*, Fribourg, Herder, 1951; P. Anciaux, *Le sacrement de la pénitence*, Louvain, Nauwelaerts, 1960, and "Sacrement de pénitence" in *Lumière et Vie*, Saint-André-les-Bruges, 1964.

28. In support of this statement, we might cite the following appeal of St. John Chrysostom: "That is why I ask, beg and entreat you ceaselessly to confess your sins to God. I do not want to induce you to do it as on a stage, in full view of your companions in wretchedness, and I would by no means oblige you to reveal your faults to

other men. Lay bare your conscience in the presence of God, show him your wounds and implore Him to heal them; turn to Him not as to a censor, but as to a doctor. In any case it would serve you nothing to be silent, since He knows everything. Speak, therefore, for it is to your advantage. Speak so that, having set out all your sins, you may then withdraw clean and freed from your sins, and so that you may thus be exempted from the intolerable ordeal of a public confession." (Translated from the French text: *Sur l'incompréhensibilité de Dieu*, Sources chrétiennes, no. 28, Paris, 1951, p. 301.)

29. *Enarr. Ps.*, C.C.L., 39, 1046.
30. *Liber Regulae Pastoralis* (see note 14 to chapter I). In the Greek Church, too, there is emphasis on continual confession.
31. G. Gusdorf, *Mémoire et Personne*, Paris, Presses universitaires de France, 1951, vol. 2, p. 358.
32. J. Guitton in *Monde moderne et sens du péché*, Paris, P. Horay, 1956, p. 243.
33. For more details on the theology of contrition, confession, and absolution, see C. Vogel, *op. cit.*
34. *Enarr. Ps.*, C.C.L., 38, 611. See also the remarks on *elenchein* as a prophetic charisma in the previous chapter.
35. *Enarr. Ps. 86*, C.C.L., 39, 980.
36. See H. Doerris, "Die Beichte im alten Mönchtum," in *Festschrift Jeremias*, Berlin, Tüpelmann, 1960, p. 239.
37. See R. Hostie, *Pastoral Counseling*, New York, Sheed & Ward, 1966. The fine distinction made by C. Le Chevalier (*La confidence et la personne humaine*, Paris, Aubier, 1960, pp. 199–202) is also instructive.
38. See H. Doerris, *op. cit.*, who seems to be unaware, however, that this is a very ancient fable told by Aesop (ed. A. Hausrath and H. Hunger, *Corpus fabularum Aesopicarum*, Leipzig, no. 229): "Jupiter gave us two sacks. He placed the one containing our own failings on our backs and the other, weighted with the failings of other people, on our breasts. Thus we cannot see the evil in ourselves. But when others do anything wrong, we see it right away."
39. Pascal, *op. cit.*, p. 343.
40. See A. Henry, *La contrition et les autres actes de la réligieuse pénitente*, Paris, Editions du Cerf, 1963, p. 81.
41. L. Beirnaert, *op. cit.*, p. 501.
42. See H. Doerris, *op. cit.*

3

Parables: an indirect method of bringing man to confess his sin

The parable as an analogy

In the first Chapter we considered the prophetic responsibility of the priest: the priest's office is to warn and to arouse the consciousness of sin (*elenchein*).

To clarify the scope of this pastoral function, there followed some considerations on the importance of the confession of sin. We believe, as St. Ambrose puts it, that no one can be saved without confessing.[1] Turning again to the prophetic function, we shall now examine the method to be followed to sensitize the sinner's conscience.

The Old Testament prophet acts as the envoy and spokesman of Yahweh, announcing salvation. But again and again we read in the Bible of false prophets; apparently the chief characteristic of the "genuine" prophet is that he is honestly prepared to voice unpalatable truths and, where necessary, to caution against dangers.[2]

It has recently been shown that the prophecies of doom should not be regarded as being mainly compounded of threat and invective. The true function of the prophet of woe is to establish a fact, as in a court of law. His hearers are in the position of the accused in the dock. The offense imputed to them is clearly substantiated and the penalty announced.[3] We may call this whole mode of action *elenchein*.

Some of the prophets do not mince their words in rebuking an evildoer in God's name. Elijah is the prototype of these, taking King Ahab to task with a boldness matched only by the acerbity of his tone (see 1 K 20). But in general the prophets proceed in a more "psychologically" appropriate manner: carefully, and with a view to convincing the offender. They clothe the accusation and the basis for it in a parable or in a symbolic action.[4]

The use of parables is instructive. Our preaching can only gain from a study of the methods of the great masters of the Word of God, and of Jesus Christ Himself, who used analogy in preference to any other method.

The primary purpose of a parable is to illustrate an invisible or a supernatural reality. We might call it a type of visual education based on the analogy existing between certain situations in everyday life and realities which escape the perception of our senses. In our own day, there has been a fortunate rediscovery of the charm and value of myths, legends, and stories. In fact, allegory and symbol possess a universal and timeless relevance, not only because they are so vivid and appeal to the imagination, but also because they awaken an emotional resonance and a dynamic response. They correspond to the archetypes of our being, to the deepest strata of our affectivity, where thought, feeling, and will are not yet differentiated. That is why we delight in the repetition of myths and parables of the most distant times—just as one never wearies of contemplating a work of art or a landscape, of listening to a symphony or tasting a familiar dish.

Philosophers and psychologists warn us that excessive rationalization and conceptualization destroy mystery. This warning is particularly applicable to theology and preaching. An abstract and purely notional approach dries up the wellsprings of esthetic and religious experience; in such an arid desert the affective life remains undernourished.[5]

We should therefore say that the purpose of the parable is to arouse us to an experience of culpability rather than to give us an idea or an awareness of guilt. To conceive of and to become aware of something are operations of the intelligence, which gives its assent on the basis of an argument or logical demonstration. To experience, on the other hand, is an operation involving the entire human being with all his faculties—his thought, his heart, and emotional life, his will and his aspiration. That is why the experience will lead to the commitment of the entire personality, of one's whole life. Logical demonstrations and awareness, by contrast, are derivatives of dynamic experience. Experience, ultimately, is an intimate conviction in which everything that the person concerned thinks and feels is integrated. That is why it is impossible either to achieve or to eliminate genuine experience by purely rational means. An argument is addressed solely to the intelligence and directed to the building up of conceptual knowledge. Being purely rational, it elicits only cold assent and a wholly abstract grasp of truth. It does not necessarily speak to the whole man and cannot, therefore, produce existential conviction.

Obviously experience and rational knowledge are not mutually exclusive. A skeleton is not a whole man; yet without a bone structure there can be no man. In the same way, while the theoretical proof of guilt and a rational awareness of guilt are not yet an existential experience of guilt, a genuine, personal experience of guilt is not achieved without the support of the intellect. The two go hand in hand. Understanding must be grafted on experience; separated, it will wither away and remain sterile. Experience needs to be reflected upon and rationally explored. Life precedes thought, but its development is climaxed in understanding.[6] In a word, we mean by experience the personal knowledge of a reality, a situation, an idea, or a sentiment—a knowledge procured through life. That is why human experience is both sensory and spiritual.

The parable as an argument and a mirror

But the parables contain far more than matter for comparison. In the Bible it is never their sole purpose to illustrate supernatural realities. In His parables of the sower, the ten virgins, the prodigal son, and so on, Christ is not simply saying that things happen in the kingdom of God as they do in nature or in everyday life. The parable always contains a *call to conversion*. It reveals to the hearer, or the reader, what he is and who he is, how he in fact behaves and how he ought to behave. Through his parables, the prophet seeks to expose, to accuse, and to exhort to amendment. He announces God's will and to that end describes some striking scene. By means of a clear and realistic picture he impels the hearer to reflect, take a stand, and give his assent. The prophet's aim is less to impart new knowledge or more extensive learning than to induce us to understand and revise our basic approach.

However, through the use of parables, God's spokesman avoids making a frontal attack. He helps us to help ourselves, to see ourselves objectively, to become aware of our guilt, and to work out a new orientation for our lives. Comparisons or analogies are linguistic devices which serve to direct our attention away from one object and on to another. The important thing is that, through the analogy, we are enabled to see ourselves in better perspective and thus to make a more accurate judgment. The purpose is not to enlarge our field of vision or to procure fresh information, but to clarify an experience which is in progress; in other words, to induce the listener to judge himself.

Let us take as an example the conversation between Tekoa's widow and King David, described in the second book of Samuel. Amnon, one of the king's sons, has raped his half-sister Tamar. Absalom, their brother, avenges Tamar and kills Amnon. But then he must flee in his turn, for the law of the vendetta is without mercy (2 S 13). In the following chapter, a woman describes a fictitious case in the form of a parable, in order to arouse David's interest and pity. To have no heirs to perpetuate the family name was to lose the sole claim to immortality known to an ancient Israelite. Nothing worse could happen to a man. Subtly, the story further suggests that, in their ruthless zeal for reprisal, the members of the clan are really trying to get rid of the heir in order to seize the inheritance for themselves. The argument proceeds as follows: by upholding the prohibition against Absalom's return, David is depriving the people of God of an heir and of a successor to the throne. Nothing can bring Amnon back to life. In the meanwhile, God has no servant, since Absalom is outside the country. In other words, David is acting just as the imaginary relatives of the widow, who, for the sake of an abstract justice and the law of the vendetta, want to deprive her of her only son (2 S 14:1–7).

Through his parables, the prophet confronts us with ourselves. He holds a mirror before our eyes. If you place a small child before a mirror, he does not recognize himself at first. He is interested, of course, and enjoys the nice child who gazes back at him. But his expression soon changes. What has happened? The simultaneous and parallel movements of his double have made the child discover: why, it's I! The parable has much the same effect. First, we listen to it as to an interesting story, but which does not directly involve us. The characters may or may not be likable—the housewife who has lost a coin, the elder brother who sulks because his father welcomes the prodigal, the dishonest steward . . . until suddenly our expression changes too: "But that man is I!" That is the point at which we, in our turn, have identified the reflection. And we can then reread the story in the first person, as a slice of autobiography. Our own portrait looks out at us from the mirror of the parable—with the sometimes sensational consequences which that discovery entails. We are thus enabled to see ourselves in perspective and in a new light. Without realizing it, we pronounce a judgment upon ourselves.

When we judge our own cause without knowing that it is our cause, we do so with greater objectivity. For it is easier for a mere spectator to render an impartial verdict than for the person involved. So long as we are not prejudiced in the matter, we shall be less inclined to prefer the agreeable, the useful, or the easy to what is true, just, or proper.

Through the parable, the prophet enlightens sinful man concerning himself by revealing his hidden being, his true meaning which had escaped him because of opaqueness and which cannot be made manifest save in the light of God. The parable is to our sinful existence what a lamp is to a diapositive photograph. So long as the lamp remains out, the photograph is invisible; but once the lamp is lit, the design, the color, the relief stand out. In the light of the parable, the significance of my conduct stands revealed; it was present already, but hidden.

A parable is thus an argument or a proof, a didactic or pedagogical method, part of a chain of reasoning intended to convince the audience so that they may judge the situation objectively (that is, otherwise than they are presently doing). The parable is intended to involve the person to whom it is presented. It is really a challenge; it puts a question to him, and at the same time calls him in question.

This point is of capital importance. To forget it is to reduce parables to purely figurative language, to comparisons appealing solely to the imagination or to symbolic relationships.

The prophet who narrates a parable starts off from a divergence of opinion between himself and his audience. The center of gravity of the parable is the point in dispute. The parable is couched, as it were, in a kind of cipher, but the crux of the comparison is at the same time the key to the code. At first the narrator plays along with his audience. He identifies himself with their point of view and their value judgments. The object is to establish a common approach on which they all agree. Unwittingly, the hearer thus becomes the ally of the narrator. There follows a story dealing with an apparently objective case. The obvious reaction is: "A decent or intelligent man really doesn't do this sort of thing!" or "Naturally that's the way he should behave!" But in so doing the hearer has fallen into the trap; it subsequently appears that he has judged his own cause.

By the skillful choice of his story, the prophet has the situation speak for itself. The implications of a man's deeds, of which he himself is not yet aware, become clear through the medium of a comparison. By showing certain similitudes or parallels, the narrator indicates that "this" situation corresponds to "that" one. And he has thereby achieved the aim of his reasoning: to bring the audience, which had originally judged otherwise of the situation, to his own point of view. Once that has happened, it is no longer possible to backtrack: the hearer has become transparent to himself and is sentenced out of his own mouth.

St. Paul uses this method in masterly fashion in his epistle to the Romans. He begins by drawing up a ruthless indictment of the pagan style of life (1:18–32). This must clearly delight the Pharisees to whom he is writing. But just as they applaud him, Paul turns the weapon against them: "Therefore you have no excuse, O man, whoever you are, when you judge another; for in passing judgment upon him you condemn yourself, because you, the judge, are doing the very same thing" (2:1).

The more unexpected the verdict which the prophet seeks to elicit from his audience, the more concessions he must make to them at the start; otherwise the foundations of his argument would be too insubstantial.

Thus, in a successful parable, there is a certain ambivalence. The subject, the comparison, and the development of the story are chosen by the narrator. But at the same time the initial attitude of the audience is taken for granted. The narrator takes it as his starting point and thereby appears to be in connivance with his audience. By skillful maneuvering, however, he achieves victory for his own point of view and obliges the hearer to agree that he must adopt the same point of view.

We should add, further, that the parable really constitutes an *event* and a phase in salvation history. The story changes the hearer's position, since it obliges him to consider matters in another light and to pronounce a verdict on himself. He is given the opportunity to change his attitude. The clarification of his position forces him to take a stand and to choose for or against: for conversion or for a harder line.

Nathan's parable: a prototype

The best illustration of these theoretical considerations may be found in the careful study and analysis of the account of David's sin and Nathan's intervention in the second book of Samuel.

David, Yahweh's annointed, is in a truly lamentable plight after his crime. His conduct has been unbelievably crude, and he has resorted to a revoltingly brutal ruse to safeguard his royal dignity. In his blatant contempt for the word of the Lord (2 S 12:9), he appears as an unscrupulous tribal chieftain. Had the problem at least been a complex one, of imposing dimensions and difficult of execution, in which one could not be too choosy about the means. . . . But this is no more than an amorous adventure, in which he has become involved almost fortuitously, yet certainly deliberately. And he has thereby flouted the religious and ethical rule which has hitherto governed his life. It has been a leap into the void. In what is virtually a vicious circle, David has committed ever graver crimes. But his greatness of soul triumphs in his frank confession of his sin. He does not attempt to deny his responsibility. He acknowledges the nauseating egotism which caused him to take such unscrupulous advantage of his dictatorial power.

Thus the author's intention is not so much to emphasize David's great guilt as his humble confession. The story is a masterpiece; the author manages in a few deft strokes to sketch complex and dramatic situations. While the army of Israel is campaigning under the command of Joab, David strolls out on the terrace of his palace just after the hour of the siesta. As he stands there, he sees Bathsheba, the wife of his faithful officer, Uriah, bathing. He is overwhelmed by concupiscence and immediately sends for the fascinating lady. As the all-powerful king, he has only to give the order. But in so doing, he violates the law of his Lord: "You shall not commit adultery. . . . You shall not covet your neighbor's wife" (Ex 20:14,17).

The affair has awkward consequences: Bathsheba finds she is pregnant. David foresees a number of complications. What will the cuckolded husband and the people of Jerusalem think of him? Panic grips him. He is a prisoner of his own passion. But he soon finds a clever solution. He sends for Uriah, ostensibly to ask for a report on military operations, but really so that the officer can see his wife again. But now further and unforeseen complications arise. Uriah refuses to have marital relations with Bathsheba! He knows what is licit and what is not; even when David gets him to drink, he still acts according to his conscience. His respect for the prohibition against sexual relations in wartime is such that he resists David's attempts to weaken his resolve. Possibly, too, he has caught wind of the affair and his protests are tinged with irony.

David's plan may not have been altogether selfish; perhaps he was trying to protect Uriah and his wife from the miserable consequences of his illicit desire. In any case, at this time David was not intending to marry Bathsheba; otherwise he could have got rid of Uriah immediately. But he is tortured by remorse now that he foresees the consequences of his sin.

The first round is lost. David considers more radical means. If the Gordian knot cannot be undone, it must be cut. But sin is like shifting sands; the more you try to extricate yourself by yet other sins, the deeper you are sucked in.

Uriah must die. The adulterous relationship must not be discovered. "You shall not kill," says the Lord (Ex 20:13). No matter! A king and commander-in-chief possesses great powers. David sends Uriah back to the army with a message for Joab: "Set Uriah in the forefront of the hardest fighting, and then draw back from him, that he may be struck down, and die" (2 S 11:15). Joab is the kind of underling who carries out whatever order he is given without asking awkward questions.

This time the plan succeeds. Messengers return with the news that Uriah has fallen gloriously in battle. But every honorable Israelite knows that David should censure the suicide raid. Joab had realized that the king needed an excuse on this score and sent him the kind of explanation to which David could send a reassuring reply: the fortunes of war are uncertain; do not take the affair to heart; carry on the fight bravely!

David is stilling his conscience. How human, all too human, to make circumstances (chance, "God's will") responsible for lamentable events for which we ourselves are to blame! Rather like the drunken driver who proclaims modern technology responsible for the death of the child whom he has run over through his own fault. David is at ease again. And as soon as the war widow has ceased mourning her husband, he sends for her and marries her. The child can be born without scandal. All is safe and secure.

But God is not duped, and Nathan the prophet arises. David had arranged everything so nicely, but his conduct displeases Yahweh: his selfish adultery, his deceit, his abuse of power, and his murder of Uriah.

Nathan's parable is a masterly and incisive argument intended to jolt the king's conscience and rouse him to a sense of guilt:

> "There were two men in a certain city, the one rich and the other poor. The rich man had very many flocks and herds; but the poor man had nothing but one little ewe lamb, which he had bought. And he brought it up, and it grew up with him and with his children; it used to eat of his morsel, and drink from his cup, and lie in his bosom, and it was like a daughter to him. Now there came a traveler to the rich man, and he was unwilling to take one of his own flock or herd to prepare for the

wayfarer who had come to him, but he took the poor man's lamb, and prepared it for the man who had come to him." Then David's anger was greatly kindled against the man; and he said to Nathan, "As the Lord lives, the man who has done this deserves to die; and he shall restore the lamb fourfold, because he did this thing, and because he had no pity." Nathan said to David, "You are the man. Thus says the Lord, the God of Israel, 'I anointed you king over Israel, and I delivered you out of the hand of Saul; and I gave you your master's house, and your master's wives into your bosom, and gave you the house of Israel and Judah . . .'" David said to Nathan, "I have sinned against the Lord" (2 S 12: 1–13).

It is sometimes suggested—mistakenly—that David could not have been so ingenuous as not to see through Nathan's transparent tale. But it should be remembered that as king he was also supreme judge, and it was therefore quite natural that he should be consulted on a legal case.

Our indignation is easily aroused in the presence of some injustice which does not involve our own security, comfort, status, or pride. The poor man with his only ewe lamb is still among us, and in more ways than one—for instance, in the person of the victims of every kind of exploitation, and of minorities who do not enjoy equal economic, social, or political opportunities. And while we easily condemn other people's faults, we nevertheless passively accept all kinds of institutional injustice and structural violence for which our family, social class, people, or race are in fact responsible.

An anonymous poet, living at a later period, put in David's mouth the penitential psalm, the *Miserere*: "For I know my transgressions, and my sin is ever before me" (51:5).

Before Nathan aroused him to a sense of his sin, David had kept his transgression behind his back; as St. Augustine comments, he avoided looking at himself. That is why he was able to pass such severe and just judgment on the rich plunderer. But the prophet removed his fault from his back and placed it before his eyes, so that he might see that he had passed this severe judgment upon himself. David had sought to remove the speck from his neighbor's eye, not realizing that he had a log in his own (Mt 5:3).[7]

The parable of Jonah

Instead of running through the many parables of the Old Testament, it would seem preferable to analyze another one in order to familiarize the reader with the prophets' methods. We must remember that they were trying to help purblind man to realize his culpability by bringing him to a new value judgment.

The picturesque and sometimes comic details of the slim little book of Jonah conceal astonishing theological depths which place it among the finest of the Old Testament writings. It is therefore most unfortunate that, both in the past and even now, its value has often been disregarded on account of the famous story of the whale. Many people have been unable to swallow that one. And the humorous comment of an exegete that the problem was not really a great one, since the fish had to swallow only a minor prophet, does not suffice to dispel the uneasiness of most readers of the tale.

It is nevertheless only too obvious that the author is not trying to present a historical account or a biography in his small book. Anyone reading it in that spirit does him an injustice. The author has an important prophetic message for his contemporaries, namely, that the goodness and salvific will of God are on an incomparably larger scale than man's pettiness would have it. He establishes a vivid contrast between the intolerant narrow-mindedness of his people and Yahweh's universal love.

To substantiate his view, he uses the technique of the parable in the form of a piece of didactic fiction. Instead of writing "there was once a prophet," he introduces a historical personage, a certain Jonah (cf. the man Job of the region of Hus), counselor and prophet in the time of King Jeroboam II (see 2 K 14:25). In all probability, this man had proposed a program of national expansion and was subsequently revered for it. In a word, he was the embodiment of fanatical patriotism, harboring an implacable hatred for all non-Israelites. The author deliberately sends this Jonah with a message of pardon and a warning to the capital of the odious Assyrian empire.

In the years following the captivity, a bitter resentment and a smoldering longing for vengeance developed in Israel against the

other nations. The people of Israel had suffered so much from
their enemies that they no longer had the slightest wish to serve
Yahweh by bearing witness to His magnanimity and His universal
salvific will (Is 42). On the contrary, the Jewish community lived
closed in on itself, harboring revenge and plagued by xenophobia.
May divine justice descend upon those detested pagans and
destroy them once and for all! Those were times in which God's
emissaries, the prophets, sought to revive the missionary spirit of
their community, as well as concern for the salvation of the surrounding nations.

Our author proposes to awaken the slumbering or repressed
conscience of his audience. To that end, he invents a story concerning which his hearers can render an objective verdict—and in
so doing unwittingly condemn themselves.

There was once, he tells them, a prophet named Jonah. Though
identified with a historical figure—Jonah, son of Amitai—the
name probably also had a symbolic significance. It means "dove,"
a symbol familiar to Israel; perhaps, too, there was added significance in the fact that the dove is a home-loving bird. This prophet
is ordered to preach to the people of Nineveh. Instead, he boards a
boat going in the opposite direction, to Tarshish, to the ends of
the earth. He runs away. Not that he fears the formidable job of
preaching penance or the potential threats of the hostile Ninevites. Jonah is no coward. He proves it by his sacrifice when the
boat is in danger. He runs away from God because he disagrees
with the message which he has to proclaim. It is a message radically opposed to his own ideas about the pagans. His most ardent
desire is to see Nineveh destroyed. He fears that Yahweh may
spare the city if, through his preaching, the inhabitants turn from
their evil ways. Suppose God were to give a second chance to these
odious enemies, just as the potter does not throw away a clay
vessel which has come out wrong, but puts it back on the wheel?
(See Jr 18:1–10.)

Jonah is a man eaten up with resentment, a man who wants to
thwart the divine enterprise of salvation; he desires not the salvation but the destruction of sinners. The listener is at once interested and in sympathy with the narrator. The prophet has acted
just as he would have done.

When, later on in the story, Jonah nobly offers his own life for that of the sailors, the audience fails to note the inconsistency of sacrificing oneself for some pagan sailors and at the same time refusing to believe that Yahweh can save the impious Ninevites. Even the most vengeful Israelite would applaud Jonah's generosity, since the Law commands love of neighbor. Jonah was entitled to have compassion on pagans in this particular case, just as individual Israelites could help individual pagans. But it was inadmissible that Yahweh should take pity on them as a whole! No, vengeance and punishment—these alone were what Yahweh was preparing for them!

The author is using Jonah to show the absurdity of the Israelites' attitude. In the end, our prophet does what Yahweh commanded him to do and goes to warn the Ninevites of the imminence of judgment. But his earlier experience has not made him wiser. He remains as fanatical as ever. When the whole population, with the king and his ministers at their head, are converted and do penance, Jonah does not react as one would expect a prophet to react when he sees that his preaching has produced results. He behaves like a wayward and sulky child. He is so disappointed at God's generosity to Nineveh that he gives way to utter depression, even to the point of wishing he were dead. It is just too much for him to see these detestable pagans escape vengeance and destruction.

It is important to note the reason for Jonah's rebellion and depression as given in Chapter 4, verse 2. He does not want God to be merciful and compassionate, gracious and slow to anger. In other words, he refuses to accept God as the God who revealed Himself to Abraham, Isaac, and Jacob—the generous God of salvation and of the covenant. Here the parable becomes transparent, and there can remain no doubt as to the author's intention. The people of Israel, to the degree that they refuse to serve as the light of the nations, are identified with Jonah. In parable form, there is here a grave warning that, through their resentment and intolerance, the Jews are rejecting the living God and breaking faith with the religion of their ancestors.

The final episode shows Jonah in a still more unflattering light. He has gone to lie down somewhere outside the city to await whatever is to happen. In his bitterness and weariness with life, he is strengthened and consoled by the welcome shade of an ivy-plant which has grown with astonishing rapidity to protect him from the sun's heat. But when on the following day the leaves wither as quickly as they had grown, Jonah is no less disgusted at the destruction of the shrub than he had been at Yahweh's mercy on Nineveh. Here Jonah's attitude, which is that of the Israelites returned from captivity, reaches the peak of absurdity. He laments over the fate of a plant which grows and withers in a day, but objects to Yahweh's compassion for the thousands of inhabitants of a pagan city. Thus the narrator has put the finishing stroke on his story: the internal contradiction in Jonah's behavior is revealed.

The parable puts an urgent question to us too. What is *your* attitude toward Nineveh? Toward Tarshish? Toward Jonah?

The great city of Nineveh personifies those about whom "there's really nothing to be done." The reference is to those categories of people concerning whom we say: You just can't change them! You can expect nothing good of them! Each one of us is to some extent affected by "Ninevitis," or particularism. It is not very hard to identify the reprobate. For some of us they are the teenagers. For others, the older generation, the dodderers. In some circles, the enemy is the bosses, the capitalists, the "haves"; in others, the unions, the leftists. Now it is the Whites, now the Negroes; now the conservatives, now the progressives. Ours is still a time of particularism, of prejudice, and of hatred; of chauvinism, nationalism, and racism.

God's universal clemency, on the other hand, extends far beyond the frontiers of *our* chosen people. He awaits only a sign of contrition to pardon. He is naive enough to believe that even "those" people can still change, and that something *can* be done about them. Meanwhile, we continue to grumble: Why does He make me waste my precious time on something foredoomed to failure?

Do we realize clearly enough that particularism and intolerance are senseless? Have we finally understood that, if we want to have access to the grace of God, we must be prepared to allow others to have a share in its riches too? In other words, that our sentiments must really be catholic and universal? Or are we trying to flee to Tarshish, far from Yahweh, to escape our mission and our responsibility? (Tarshish is where we live in peace and safety. It is synonymous with the time-honored excuses: The importance of my work, my comfort, my delicate health, my spiritual life.) [8]

This paraphrase of the book of Jonah allows us to draw attention, in passing, to yet another characteristic of parables: irony. The prophet who proposes a parable conceals, at least momentarily, what he intends to stress. He plays hide-and-seek, as it were, with his audience. Sometimes a wit untinged by bitterness pierces through the narrative. Then we divine a mischievous gleam in the eyes of the narrator, who clearly takes some satisfaction in his argument. At other times, however, the irony borders on sarcasm.[9]

The parables in the Gospels

With regard to the parables of Jesus Christ, we refer to the many excellent works which have appeared in the past few years on these Gospel texts.[10] Among the principal parables by means of which Jesus sought to elicit from his audience a verdict against themselves, so that they might confess their sins and be converted, we may cite: the vinedressers who are plotting murder (Mt 21:33); the prodigal's elder brother (Lk 15); the wayward children (Lk 7:31); the merciless creditor (Mt 18:23); the two creditors (Lk 7:41); the rich man and Lazarus (Lk 16:19); the marriage feast (Mt 22); the two sons (Mt 10:28); the workers sent to the vineyard (Mt 20); the good Samaritan (Lk 10); the foolish virgins (Mt 25); the Pharisee and the publican (Lk 18:9); the talents (Mt 25:14). Some of these will be discussed in later chapters.[11]

All these parables tell a story in a more or less circumstantial manner, but they provide no simple solution for the problem raised. The answer is not a formula that we can carry away with us for future use, like a recipe. Thus the questions: who is my neighbor? who is entitled to my love and assistance? are answered by the story of the good Samaritan—not by a general, theoretical definition but by an event which takes place somewhere. In this story we discover that our neighbor is the first comer, the person I happen to meet and who needs my help, the person who sees me as his neighbor, his closest companion. In other words, the parable provides matter for reflection. The parables open our eyes on a possible attitude; they do not define it by detailed prescriptions.[12] A reversal of perspective is produced, permitting the emergence of a radically new point of view and the discovery of a hitherto unsuspected dimension of reality.

The parables are constantly paired with the theme of obduracy in the three synoptic Gospels. Mark (4:12), Matthew (13:13) and Luke (8:10) quote—although with notable variations—the harsh words which Isaiah hears from Yahweh when he receives his mission: "Go and say to this people, 'Hear and hear again, but do not understand; see and see again, but do not perceive.' Make the heart of this people gross, its ears dull; shut its eyes, so that it will not see with its eyes, hear with its ears, understand with its heart, and be converted and healed. Then I said, 'Until when, Lord?' He answered: 'Until towns have been laid waste and deserted, houses left untenanted, countryside made desolate, and Yahweh drives the people out . . .'" (Is 6:9–12).

Is this not cruelty verging on sadism? No, indeed, if we recall that Jesus endorsed the words. His message was one of good news. He Himself was God's goodness incarnate. And yet He was rejected and put to death.

In this perspective some light is shed on Isaiah's obscure text. Isaiah could not have intended to imply that God desires evil. God could not desire men's hearts to be hardened. He wants to save them, and to this end He sends His prophet. He sets out to look for His people. But His people live in the intoxication of well-being and do not respond to the divine advances. Whereupon God communicates to Isaiah a doom which he foresees: your preaching will make souls only more stubborn. You will come up against their deafness and blindness. Whence the prophet's anxious question: "Until when, Lord?" And Yahweh explains: Until the good times are over; until men are in need and in the wretchedness of exile. Once they are in darkness, they will aspire to the light.

While the exegesis of this disturbing passage has not yet been altogether clarified, it seems clear that Jesus accepts Israel's obduracy as a phenomenon analogous to that experienced by Isaiah. But He hopes to achieve something in a small group. If He preaches in parables, it is not in order to harden hearts. His parables are aimed at communicating the good news of the kingdom to men who are prejudiced against Him and who harbor hopes compounded of illusions; to men who on this account must make a complete about-face. The parables provide an opportunity for reflection and eventually understanding. But only a part of his audience follows them up and asks for further explanations. Those, on the other hand, who remain outside, exclude themselves.[13] As Pascal puts it, the parables contain enough light for those who want to see, and enough darkness for those who do not.

Notes

1. *Expositio evangelii secundum Lucam, liber VIII*, C.C.L., 14, 330.
2. See E. Osswald, *Falsche Prophetie im Alten Testament*, Tübingen, Mohr, 1962. Thus, for example, Jr 14:13–14: "Then I said: 'Ah, Lord God, behold, the prophets say to them, 'You shall not see the sword, nor shall you have famine, but I will give you assured peace in this place.' And the Lord said to me: 'The prophets are prophesying lies in my name; I did not send them, nor did I command them or speak to them. They are prophesying to you a lying vision, worthless divination, and the deceit of their own minds.'"
3. See C. Westermann, *Grundformen prophetischer Rede*, Munich, Chr. Kaiser, 1960, p. 46.
4. Some parables: Is 5:1–7: the vine; Jr 12:12–14: the wine jars; Ez 16 and 23: the homeless child who is sheltered by a benefactor and subsequently turns his back on that benefactor; 2 S 12: the unjust rich man.
   Some symbolic scenes: Jeremiah (19:1–11) breaks a clay vessel to symbolize the destruction of Jerusalem; he lives alone, in celibacy, just as Israel has been abandoned by God for breaking the covenant (16); Isaiah walks naked through the streets of the capital to announce the future captivity of his fellow citizens (20); he gives his child symbolic names (8:1–4); Ezekiel prepares soiled food as the people will be obliged to do during the occupation; he shaves his beard and scatters the hairs to the four winds, as the Jewish community will be scattered (4:1–5); he disguises himself as an emigrant to symbolize exile (12); Hosea's unsuccessful marriage (1–3) is a replica of Yahweh's grievous disillusionment concerning Israel, his faithless spouse, who scorns his love . . . Cf. G. Fohrer, *Die symbolischen Handlungen der Propheten*, Zurich, Zwingli Verlag, 1953.
5. Cf. L. Ramlot, *L'au-delà du mythe*, Homo symbolicus, Editions de Maredsous, 1964, p. 55; J. Daniélou, *Symbolisme et théologie*, Festgabe Guardini (Interpretation der Welt), Würzburg, 1964, p. 663.

6. J. Lotz, *Metaphysische und religiöse Erfahrung*, in *Archivio di Filosofia*, Padua, Cedam, 1956.

7. *Enarr. Ps.*, C.C.L., 38, 604.

8. The novel by S. Andres, *Der Mann im Fisch*, Munich, Piper, 1963, contains a successful presentation of the Jonah parable.

9. C. Voeltzel, *Le rire du Seigneur*, Strasbourg, 1955; H. Clavier, *L'ironie dans l'enseignement de Jésus*, *Novum Testamentum*, Leiden, Brill, 1956, p. 3.

10. The best introduction to date appears to be H. Kahlefeld, *Gleichnisse und Lehrstücke im Evangelium*, Frankfurt, 1963.

11. Jesus, following the symbolic actions of the prophets of the Old Testament, in His turn performs "expressive" actions. Thus He places a little child in the midst of His adult disciples in order to illustrate their littleness in the kingdom (Mk 9:36); He looks for figs on the fig tree long before the season for the fruit (Mk 11:13; Mt 21:19). The latter procedure appears completely inept in the prosaic order of everyday life. It is a strange and irrational gesture, like that of Jeremiah breaking a good jar or that of Ezekiel shaving in so bizarre a fashion. That is why the prophet gives his audience an explanation of his symbolic act. Actually Jesus is not seeking fruits from the fig tree, but rather a symbolic opportunity for cursing the tree. Not that the tree is guilty, but it symbolizes a reality which does deserve malediction. The people reap no spiritual fruit from Jesus' preaching and are therefore rejected.

12. The tales of the Buddhist sect of Mahayana are based on an analogous existential method: simultaneous revealing and concealing. See W. Gundert, ed., Bi-Yän-Lu, *Meister Yuan Wu's Niederschrift von der Smaragdenen Felswand verfasst auf dem Djia*, Munich, Hanser, 1960.

13. See J. Gnilka, *Die Verstockung Israëls*, Munich, Kösel Verlag, 1961. In the context of blindness and obduracy, it is interesting to compare the evangelical parables with the Greek oracles. Croesus, for example, receives this reply from the oracle: "If you undertake your expedition against the Persians, you will destroy a great kingdom." This statement by the oracle seems ambiguous and enigmatic, just as the replies given to Polycrates and Xerxes are also susceptible of more than one interpretation. The method used by the oracle is intended to challenge man to reflect and think better of his plan. It seeks to cure him of his blindness. But it avoids any outright condemnation; it neither commands nor clearly prohibits. Croesus' mistake is to take account only of the interpretation of the oracle which suits him. His reasoning is egocentric; he allows himself to be carried away by his passion and does not so much as trouble to reconsider the decision he has already made. He refuses to look at the situation in the new perspective suggested to him—a vague enough perspective, doubtless, but one which gives him a chance to emerge from his blindness. Thus the oracle, rather like the par-

able, contains a warning which manifests something while at the same time concealing it. It endeavors to free man from his captivity to himself by making him conscious of the dangerous or evil aspects of his existential option.

See R. Schaerer, *L'Homme antique*, Paris, Presses universitaires de France, 1958, pp. 213–238.

4

The difficulty
of conversion

The hardened heart

Pastoral and psychotherapeutic experience shows that immense forces of inner resistance make self-knowledge very hard. Every man instinctively feels reluctant to see himself, if only for a brief moment, as he really is.

Psychoanalytical treatment is therefore legitimately described as a struggle against the stubborn resistance of the person analyzed. His ego senses the possibility of being unmasked and cured as a threat to his neurotic existential option. The energy of repression is concentrated in a supreme effort to resist the interpretation of his personality structure—at least so long as the subject is not yet mature enough and ready to receive the interpretation which the psychotherapist offers him. The psychoanalytic interpretation can be regarded as successful when the patient gradually begins to understand something of his unconscious attitude to life and discovers himself in the revealing mirror which is held before his eyes.

But psychological self-knowledge is still only an attenuated form of self-criticism as compared with the realization of guilt and the confession of sin of the man who abandons himself to the judgment and the mercy of the living God.

Authentic and existential self-accusation is an extraordinarily painful thing. To acknowledge that I am a sinner is to depreciate myself, to feel and to admit that I am worthless, at least from a certain point of view and in relation to a specific person. And this entails a head-on collison with our spontaneous tendency to make the most of ourselves and our natural desire for appreciation.

Confession of sin has something agonizing about it, for it implies a death to ourselves. It is a disintegration and a destructuring, whereas every living being seeks to preserve and develop his personality. *Metanoia* requires that we let ourselves be made over completely and that we should about-face in order to become a "new man." We have to detach ourselves from the impurity to which our old hearts were attached by so many fibers. The offer of pardon, the prospect of reconciliation, the hope of being reborn and rising again, are not capable of assuaging the excruciating pain involved. "I have never experienced a terror and an agony to equal those which I felt on the day of my first confession," Paul Claudel wrote to Jacques Rivière in 1907. And we may well ask whether on this point there is not a terrible deficiency in many of us. Obviously we cannot always achieve such depths in the experience of pain; at the same time we really should experience something of this agony at each confession. The habit of regularly "going to confession" may be one of the reasons why we lack the dispositions in which alone we can receive pardon and be reborn.

Confession of sin, repentance for one's previous behavior, and the working out of a new existential option—all this is hard for us because we are ill disposed. And this sinful condition itself implies the lack of a quality which is absolutely necessary to conversion and reconciliation with God. The sinner is caught in a kind of infernal mechanism from which he cannot extricate himself. This condition might be compared to that of a psychosomatic disease.

The man suffering from Parkinson's disease lacks precisely that character trait which would enable him to stand the pain resulting from muscular movement. The obese man is prepared to give up anything save an abundance of food. The man with high blood pressure struggles and gets agitated about avoiding excitement, which is the cause of high blood pressure . . .

In each case, our faculty of decision is weak precisely where it is most needed to prevent sickness or sin. For this faculty is itself affected, and it is this powerlessness that should really be cured.

This analogy of disease recurs constantly in the Scriptures and in the liturgy. The sinner, we are told, suffers from all kinds of spiritual maladies. His heart has become hardened and stony; it has withered; it has become impure and sullied; it has become cold and frozen; it has become tortuous and deceitful; it has become darkened. Our sick ego, sensing the cure as a new danger, obstructs the unmasking of the truth about itself.

If we manage to become aware of our guilt and to confess our sin, that is the work of the Paraclete—the *elenchein*. But He exercises His saving influence through the prophets, whose intelligible and revealing words are a grace and a charisma for others (cf. Chapter 1).

We experience our heart as the essence and expression of our personality. It palpitates with joy or expectation; it contracts with pain; it beats violently with fear and anxiety. Sometimes we feel it as it were overflowing; sometimes it seems more like a total void. We open it generously or we close it resolutely. We lock it up or we share it. Our human existence unfolds to its rhythm: in turn slowing down and accelerating, dilating, and shrinking.

"Heart" is one of the typical words of man's spontaneous thought which, even if it does not proceed in a formally scientific manner, nevertheless reaches to the crux of a question. The heart is the symbol of our deepest and inmost center, embracing the totality of our being and embodying its unity. Thus in love we give someone our heart; or we define prayer as a raising of the heart to God; or again, the heart is identified with our instinct for self-preservation, our desire for communion, the direction of our will, our affective life, and the memory of our past experience.[1]

It is doubtful whether such terms as existential option, basic design, propulsive ego, prospective ego, or other technical expressions of modern psychology are more adequate than the word "heart." The fact remains that men have always employed this symbol. And the Bible, in which God speaks to us, is no exception to this rule. It is one of the primitive words, as Karl Rahner calls them, such as time, space, love, being, knowledge. Strictly speaking, it is impossible to define it satisfactorily, because these words are more fundamental than the terms and concepts which we subsequently use to define and explain the reality.

It is therefore erroneous to assert that the Bible and the liturgy are satisfied to use poetic figures or that they use as a symbol what is *really* only a hollow muscle and a biological organ. Man really *is* heart in his thought, in his affective life, and in his will. Through his heart, he borders on the mystery of God. For it is from the bottom of his heart, the source of his actions, that he is good or bad. The heart, says Pascal, is the place of decisions and commitments.

Recalling the biblical expressions concerning sin and guilt, we find: the heart turns away from God (Dt 17:17; Ps 44:18; Is 29:13); the heart becomes gross and insensitive (Is 6:10; Ps 119:70; Ho 13:6); the heart hardens and becomes stony (Ex 4:21; 7:13; Ez 11:19; Za 7:12); it is uncircumcised—that is, closed (Dt 10:16; Jr 9:25); it is darkened (Rm 1:21).

St. Paul compares Christians to a letter written with the Spirit of the living God. Their hearts are not tablets of stone but tablets of flesh, whose sensitiveness and plasticity make them easy to write on (2 Co 3:3). In this image different references to Old Testament texts are interwoven: the stone tablets of the Law on Sinai (Ex 24:12); the law which is engraved in men's hearts (Jr 17:1; 31:33; Pr 3:3); God's promise that, after the Israelites have returned to the promised land, He will replace their hearts of stone by hearts of flesh and a new spirit (Ez 11:19; 36:26).

As a prototype of the man with a hardened heart, the Bible cites Pharaoh (see Rm 9:19). Pharaoh seeks to keep the Hebrews at hard labor and refuses to recognize their right to independence and the free exercise of their religion. Yahweh provides Moses with the means of clearly manifesting His power through a series of plagues. Pharaoh's tendency to capitulate whenever he feels threatened alternates with stubborn resistance and refusal as soon as the danger has passed once more. After unbending temporarily, his heart hardens again and his neck stiffens. Finally the day comes when the Israelites undertake their liberating exodus by force and the Egyptian army perishes in the Red Sea.

Certain expressions in this famous Exodus story suggest, it is true, that Yahweh had hardened Pharaoh's heart. The Bible nevertheless imputes to the Egyptian the responsibility for his inflexibility and regards it as culpable.

It is worthwhile considering the episode of the flight from Egypt from the point of view of the Egyptians. For in their conception, too, the heart plays an important part.[2]

The exodus of the Hebrews (Habiru: a group of Bedouins) should probably be placed in the time of Ramses II (A.D. 1301–1234). It is established that Semitic workers were often employed in the gigantic Egyptian building enterprises: this is evident from many bas-reliefs. Texts have been preserved showing that the immigration and emigration of nomads, who in time of famine often sought the fleshpots of Egypt (Joseph's brothers, for instance), were legally regulated.

As the supreme authority of Egyptian society, which was organized according to static and theocratic norms, Pharaoh had the responsibility for maintaining order firmly and courageously. The Egyptians, like every other people, regarded the heart as the source of human life. That is why the defunct Pharaoh was provided with a spare heart at the time of the embalming of the body. For the body was regarded as indispensable for survival in the next life, and at first the technique of preserving the heart in any durable fashion was unknown. When such a technique was subsequently discovered, the custom was retained of placing a stone scarab in the mummy as a spare heart for the journey into eternity. This sacred coleopteron, like the phoenix, symbolized the future, the resurrection, and the sun god. With their keenness of observation, the Egyptians had noticed that the scarab dug itself in a pellet of cow dung to lay its egg before dying in the autumn. The larva greatly resembles a miniature mummy, and the following spring the insect reappears, as though risen from the dead.[3]

The heart-shaped scarab amulet was supposed to bestow on man a solid heart of stone, with which to confront the obligations which would be laid upon him in the next life and which the ordinary human heart, with its inconstancy, would be incapable of fulfilling.

To die is to undertake the voyage to the nether regions and to answer for one's actions to Osiris. Fine reproductions and descriptions of the scene have been preserved in the Egyptian books of the dead. There we see the deceased's heart weighed in the scales against the symbol of truth, justice, and order. The god of wisdom records the result. A monster, part crocodile, part lion, and part hippopotamus, stands ready to devour the sinner. If the test is successful, the deceased must appear before Osiris.

In a stereotyped formula, the deceased adjures his own heart not to accuse him before the infernal tribunal. "Oh my heart, do not rise up as a witness against me . . . do not accuse me before the ministers of the scales . . ." Through a negative confession, in which every fault is denied, the statements of the man himself and those of his heart should be made to concord and balance each other out.[4]

The appearance before Osiris is a trial in reverse. The deceased enumerates the long series of offenses which he has *not* committed. There is no question of acknowledging his wrongdoing. Yet the deceased has not in fact been an ideal embodiment of all the virtues; this is indirectly shown by the fact that the heart of stone must serve to compensate for the inadequacies of the heart of flesh. Firmness of heart, or force of character, artificially achieved, is thus to make up, magically, for moral deficiencies.

This custom is probably the Egyptian background for the biblical expression *turning one's heart to stone,* but with rather different overtones. What the Egyptians called a "strong and solid heart," as opposed to flabbiness of character, was rejected by the Israelites as stony-hearted, as stubbornness and insensitiveness to the salvation which Yahweh proposed was contrasted with the flexible and tender heart. "They made their hearts like adamant lest they should hear the law and the words which the Lord of hosts had sent by his Spirit through the former prophets" (Ze 6:12). That is probably why character traits which we describe as insensitiveness, stubbornness, stony-heartedness, surliness, inflexibility have acquired a perjorative connotation, whereas in connection with positive qualities we speak of a stout heart, a strong character, firmness, tenacity, vigor, and courage. Thus when St. Augustine, for example, speaks of firmness of character, he avoids the image of the heart and prefers that of the bone: a strong backbone, which enables a man to stand firm under trial and persecution.

However, the Oriental symbolism of the inflexible stony heart and the supple and conciliatory heart seems to appeal less to the inhabitants of the northern regions. As a result of climatic conditions, perhaps, we prefer to speak of freezing, stiffening, congealing; of a rigid attitude; of melting, of softening; of a fixed habit, a prejudice, a behavior pattern which thaws or melts. But these expressions are also clearly of biblical origin. St. Augustine, commenting on Psalm 124, says that our sins do not relax their grip on us, just as ice prevents water from flowing. We are caught, he says, in the ice of our sins, but the Holy Spirit breathes like a warm south wind; then our sins are pardoned and we escape the icy grasp of iniquity.

It is thus not without significance that St. John notes: "it was winter" (10:22) when certain of Jesus' hearers refused to believe in Him and took up stones to stone Him.

In an allegorical exegesis of Psalm 147, in which he allows himself to be carried away by his poetic temperament, St. Augustine succeeds in harmonizing the dual symbolism. Before his conversion, St. Paul was a hard and refractory crystal. He stubbornly opposed the truth. He resisted the Gospel as an ice block resists the sun. Although he listened to Moses and the Scriptures, he refused to believe in Jesus Christ whom they foretold. Compared with Paul, the pagans were but snow—cold, indeed, but malleable. As a Pharisee and a scrupulous adherent of the Law, Paul had the brilliant whiteness of crystal. But at the same time he was hard and icy like a crystal, and he persecuted the Church. Paul felt the cold, of course; he felt abandoned by God. He compared himself to a corpse (Rm 7:23-25). He was not capable of liberating himself. Then came the grace of God, like a spring breeze, melting his hardness and pride. He became like a nourishing loaf of bread, or life-giving, thirst-quenching water. God wished to melt this hard crystal so that we, the men of snow, should not despair . . .[5]

Blinded man

Ophthalmologists speak of scotoma: a yellow spot in the visual field. Psychoanalysis, largely influenced by W. Stekel, has adopted the expression "psychic scotoma" to indicate the repression of emotional contents from consciousness.

A man of considerable literary culture may be endowed with unerring taste and judgment concerning the work of another, yet be incapable of judging his own. The fact that his esthetic standards fail him in this point does not penetrate his consciousness at all. This means that certain conscious criteria slip into the area of the unconscious or are repressed at the moment of contact or conflict with our unconscious infatuation or pride. These are the famous yellow spots in our self-criticism. They "explain" almost any stupidity on the part of intelligent persons and virtually any injustice on the part of upright persons.[6] Man is blinded by passion and by love, so the saying goes. Or again, whom the gods wish to destroy, they first make mad.

A person in the grip of a passion sees everything in the light of that passion. He appreciates things and events only to the extent that they give him the opportunity of satisfying his passion. When such a person claims to see only qualities in the object of his adoration (a woman, a political party, gambling) he is not lying, but expressing what he really sees. Contrary perceptions are neutralized; they cannot cross the threshold of consciousness or, if they do, only as meaningless and indistinct data. In the same way, the clearest warnings remain without effect. All the data which contradict the passion or prejudice are automatically interpreted or rejected, while the favorable indications are eagerly accepted. All this takes place without clear consciousness and deliberation, in a sphere where ideas, impressions, and emotions arise and disappear without articulation.[7]

The idea of psychic scotoma revives an old and universal principle already recognized in the Bible. Hardness of heart and blindness make sinful man his own accomplice; the admission of guilt is so hard for him because, through his sinful attitude, he becomes as it were impermeable to grace and closes himself to the voice of his conscience. "For everyone who does evil hates the light, and does not come to the light, lest his deeds should be exposed" (Jn 3:20). There is a close correlation between hardening or obstinacy and blindness or darkening. Grossness and denseness go hand in hand. Our moral life has repercussions on our moral approach. Sin dulls the soul to the values it betrays. That is the appalling tragedy of the guilty man. His condition and his orientation blind him and mislead him concerning his own sin. His conscience is gradually blunted, his heart rendered insensitive. He becomes less and less aware of his culpability and ends by denying it, either consciously or unconsciously.

It is in the very nature of sin to render the knowledge and admission of the offense difficult, if not impossible. "The more real the guilt, and the closer to the wellsprings of the personality, the more it is dissimulated." [8] That is why to confess means, ultimately, to stop sinning; just as sinning means ceasing to confess. In the context of the Bible, the contrary of being free is not to be determined by another, but to be hardened of heart as a result of sin. Freedom presupposes the opening of the soul, of the spirit, of the eyes and of the ears. Sin is essentially destructive of the self, and in that sense guilt and punishment become a single reality (cf. Rm 1:18–32). The man whose heart is besotted and his sensitivity dulled is not aware of the fact. By sinning, he has rendered himself inaccessible (blind and deaf) to the call of goodness. And because he is unaware of it, it is impossible for him to repent of his offense. He neither seeks nor desires to become sensitive, healed, or converted. And that is why an intervention by God through the agency of prophets or of painful trials is absolutely needed to awaken him from his lethargy.

The cause of this jamming of the understanding must be sought in the fact that sin comes to us in seductive and deceitful appearance. "The devil is your father, and you prefer to do what your father wants . . . When he lies he is drawing on his own store, because he is a liar, and the father of lies" (Jn 8:44). Satan disguises himself as an angel of light (2 Co 11:14). His tactic is to camouflage himself, as do his servants, the false prophets (11:13). He assumes another form to hide his true nature. He tempts man by presenting evil as something beautiful and attractive. Through this disguise, he seeks to seduce Adam—Mr. Everyman—and drag him down into sin, at the same time closing the road to the knowledge and confession of his sin.

In 2 Tm 2:26, St. Paul describes the sinner as a man caught in the devil's snares so that he may do the devil's will. Here Satan is represented as a hunter who captures his prey (men) in nets and traps. The same passage suggests that the sinner is in a state of bewilderment and intoxication. His spirit is clouded. This comparison with the effects of alcohol is also familiar from the Old Testament (see Is 22:12–14; 28:1–4; 7–8; 29:9–10; cf. 1 Tm 3:6).

The context of the passage cited from the second epistle to Timothy also deserves attention. In 2 Timothy 2:22–26, the task of the pastor is defined on the lines of prophetic remonstrance (*elenchein*). He is the Lord's servant, sent to arouse sinners and bring them out of their torpor. He must unseal their eyes and deliver them from their state of captivity, co-operate with God to persuade them to be converted and recognize the truth, so that they may repent and be freed from their bonds. Accepting the Gospel and being converted means recovering health and lucidity of spirit (cf. 2 Tm 3:8).

The manner in which God's spokesman is to fulfill his mission is explained in a few pregnant words. He should not be quarrelsome but act with quiet tact and disarming gentleness; he must be a person with whom one can talk and who is persuasive. He must, further, be a good teacher, able to explain things clearly. In other words, his gentleness must not be simply a matter of being agreeable and understanding. He also has to help others to understand, and he has to bring light. Thus his intervention will have a genuinely educative value.[9]

To sin, then, is to deceive oneself, to blind oneself. It is a consequence of the refusal to obey God, in which the sinner assumes for himself the power to establish, by his own authority, what is good and what is evil. Sin involves such blindness that it becomes impossible for man to see himself as he is, or to recognize his own nature and his true relationship with God. Concealment and dissimulation are of the essence of sin. It is true that the Scriptures often speak, in this connection, of "ignorance." But this is not to be understood as an extenuating circumstance or a lack of knowledge which would excuse the person concerned. On the contrary. It is an ignorance and an alienation of one's being through which man fails to know himself or to recognize himself in his sin. And it is precisely this refusal to see clearly that is his sin.

"So they are without excuse; for although they knew God they did not honor him as God or gives thanks to him, but they became futile in their thinking and their senseless minds were darkened" (Rm 1:20–22). To sin is to refuse to recognize God as God. And this implies a rejection of the truth, of what is. Sinful man denies his condition as a creature; he thereby alienates himself from God as well as from himself. Whence the fatal consequence of darkening, blindness, inability to know God.

Thus sin contains its own punishment: separation, isolation, alienation from God, deliberate solitude. "They are darkened in their understanding, alienated from the life of God because of the ignorance that is in them, due to their hardness of heart; they have become callous and have given themselves up to licentiousness" (Ep 4:18–19).[10] "The god of this world has blinded the minds of the unbelievers, to keep them from seeing the light of the gospel of the glory of Christ, who is the likeness of God" (2 Co 4:4). "But who can detect his own failings? Wash out my hidden faults, and from pride preserve your servant; never let it dominate me" (Ps 19:13–14).

St. Augustine, who could speak from experience, never wearied of meditating on this point. "If one could see the darkness, one could also know one's misdeeds as such. When a man becomes entangled in sin, his eyes are closed and covered, so that he no longer sees his misdeed. For if your physical eye is covered, it is impossible for you to see anything else, and certainly not what is held before your eyes." [11]

It is thus, too, that sinful man perceives the speck in another's eye but not the beam in his own (Mt 7:4). Jesus, incidentally, is not denying the existence of the speck which we see, but warning us against the deceitful practice of hiding our own sins behind our backs.

Man is the being who deceives himself. This theme of illusion has been developed by European thought in a number of variations since the nineteenth century. Thus, according to Schopenhauer, human reason is not the faculty for discovering the objective truth but rather an organ in the service of life, the accomplice of the will, the instrument through which we dangle the necessary illusions before our own eyes. Marx, for his part, describes the ruling classes as deliberately or unconsciously taking refuge in ideologies which are superstructures designed to justify their interests. According to Kant, only the human structure and congenital weakness of our faculty of knowledge prevent us from attaining to truth, just as, according to Plato, the instincts and affects of our physical being hinder us in our knowledge of truth. At the same time, these philosophers emphasize that, if we live in error and are constantly deceiving ourselves, it is not through helplessness or through defective reasoning resulting from some incapacity, but because this is what we want, motivated as we are by our own self-interest. We neither seek nor desire the truth; we disguise ourselves in our mendacious lives and hide behind ideological façades.

According to Nietzsche, we refuse to admit that we are prompted by the will to power. We wrap ourselves in the chaste mantle of morality; we put on a mask and disregard reality. Freud taught that our unaccepted and repressed libido refuses to be stifled. From the subliminal regions, this vital energy continues to exert an influence and to make man neurotic. In its turn, existentialism affirms that man constantly lets himself be involved in an inauthentic existence: he lacks the courage to meet the exacting requirements of authenticity.[12]

"I was blind: now I see" (Jn 9:25)

The indirect method of awakening the conscience (prophetic challenge and parables) is based on a fundamental principle which can be formulated as follows:

Man is capable of recognizing certain value judgments and certain exigencies as of universal validity and of proclaiming them to be mandatory for everyone. At the same time, he can deny their mandatory character and their importance when they impinge on his personal interests. We can call this paradoxical phenomenon, with von Hildebrand, the inability to subsume.[13] Normally we have a general sense of values: thus we realize that adultery, treason, and deceit are abhorrent. And our indignation is spontaneously aroused when we come across others acting in such a fashion. But to discern the relevance of this general principle to our particular case is quite another matter; our personal advantage may stand in the way. Egotism and self-interest may more or less consciously obscure our conscience and prevent an accurate value judgment on our own conduct. And thus we sometimes fail to realize that our conduct partakes, for instance, of the quality of treason. We suffer from partial blindness and scotoma.

It is quite possible to combine ardent philanthropy with utter disregard for the distress of one's neighbor. Dickens, for instance, in one of his novels, describes certain worthy ladies filled with indefatigable zeal on behalf of the morally abandoned young of far-off lands, but quite unmoved by the plight of the destitute children in their own immediate surroundings. Here we have an inability to see, practically and existentially, the presence of a value which we nevertheless recognize—if only theoretically. We do not see a value or an obligation because we do not want to see it. And we do not want to see it because it is in our interest not to see it.

But where it is a matter of judging others, the roadblocks of egotism which make it so hard to apply obvious and objective criteria to ourselves suddenly vanish. Knowledge of others is far from identical with knowledge of self.

It would seem so simple to reduce both to a single denominator: to elaborate an image of man, to decide how human beings in general, including myself, should behave. But a closer look shows that a person may sometimes penetrate very deeply into the psychology of others, yet be unable to achieve genuine self-criticism. A man who has scrutinized human nature scientifically and can discern and analyze the delicate and hidden mechanisms of the human heart nevertheless has no assurance of really knowing his own person. Our representation of self is all too often distorted and blurred by illusions. This illusory image, formed according to our desires, does not correspond to reality as others see it, especially God. And every man who lifts himself up and idealizes himself will be humbled by God (Lk 18:9). As St. Paul puts it: "Therefore you have no excuse, O man, whoever you are, when you judge another; for in passing judgment upon him you condemn yourself, because you, the judge, are doing the very same things" (Rm 2:1).

Our criticism of another may be penetrating and accurate, yet miss the mark. We deceive ourselves because we dissociate our knowledge of others from our knowledge of ourselves. As soon as we isolate our unfavorable judgment of another from a lucid judgment of ourselves we stray from the path of truth and reality. For it is accompanied by an abstraction. We make an exception for ourselves by placing our own case in parentheses, because we entertain an idealized and erroneous view of our own personality. This applies as much to our conscience before the event—we do not hear the invitation to do good and avoid evil—as after it; who has not met people who see no difficulty in acknowledging themselves to be sinners and yet protest furiously when a specific misdeed is imputed to them?

Nietzsche writes movingly: "Lightening and thunder need time, the light of the stars needs time, deeds need time, even after they are done, to be seen and heard. This deed [the killing of God in men's hearts] is as yet further from them than the furthest star— and yet they have done it!" [14]

Aristotle noted that in order to be able to observe a high standard of morality, a man must know his obligations and be conscious of the priority of values; that, in turn, was possible only if he was already leading a healthy moral life. The solution to the difficulty would seem to lie in the awakening of the personal conscience which lies dormant within each one of us, and in its application to our own lives. And so we come back to the prophetic *elenchein,* which seeks to produce the confession of sin through strengthening the sinner's understanding and power of reaction. In the Scriptures we find the prophets trying to confront the guilty individual with his own conscience, really present but forgotten or repressed. The individual thus comes to pronounce his own condemnation. He is judged, as Jesus puts it in the parable of the talents, by his own words and out of his own mouth (Lk 19:22). The value judgment which he utters after hearing the parable bommerangs on himself. An innocent story turns out to be dangerous and challenging.

Camus calls this self-accusation by ricochet. "Should I climb up to the pulpit, like many of my illustrious contemporaries, and curse humanity? Very dangerous, that is! One day, or one night, laughter bursts out without a warning. The judgment you are passing on others eventually snaps back in your face, causing some damage." [15]

Basically, this method of forming the conscience is bound up with the deepest moral evidence present in every man by virtue of his synderesis. It is the first principle or the first intuition which imposes itself irresistibly, and which has been called the golden rule: do not do to others what you do not want others to do to you.[16]

To unmask amounts indirectly to inviting a person to impose on himself what he is spontaneously inclined to demand of another. Use on yourself the same yardstick that you use on others, and do not be more indulgent toward yourself than toward your neighbor. "Do not do yourself what you decry in another," according to the dictum of Pittacus, one of the Seven Sages. This, of course, is a negative formulation of the golden rule. Instead of being urged to extend to all the spontaneous care and love which we show to ourselves, we are exhorted to apply in our own personal case the severity which we show in regard to others.[17]

In this manner our "science," that is, knowledge, becomes "conscience." A transition is made from universal objective validity to practical subjective validity. Through the value judgment he has made concerning the rich man in the parable, David has committed himself. He is a prisoner of his own principles and cannot evade the obligation this entails. Thus we have to judge ourselves by the same standard as we use to judge others in virtue of the self-evident authority which we have ourselves conceded to that standard.

When no one sees or hears us, we can perhaps evade the obligation of fidelity to our own principles. But this becomes much more difficult in relations with other persons. By taking a public stand in the presence of the prophet who proposes the parable, we feel constrained to abide by our declaration of principle. Thus a person who desires the imprisonment of A for committing felony X, but who sincerely refuses to be jailed himself should he commit the same crime or a similar one, may be charged with an incorrect use of ethical language or a lack of logic.[18] In this sense we may speak of training in veracity and impartiality. The guilty man is helped to make a discovery and to acquire a new understanding of reality.

Needless to say, it is a painful experience to be unmasked and condemned by one's own words. Faced with the reflection of my features in the mirror of the parable, I am obliged to experience my behavior or my situation as a loss of personal ethical value. This conclusion, more or less clearly apprehended, is expressed by a guilty conscience and a sense of culpability. I realize that I have played fast and loose with my moral and human dignity, and this wounds my natural self-esteem. My imposture, my insincerity, my lack of authenticity, and my pose become clearly apparent to me. I am a person who sets high standards for others. I support noble general principles. But I do not respect them myself. I lack logic and consistency. I am a hypocrite. My alleged conviction lacks foundation and my moral integrity is a sham. The dignity on which I prided myself and which I flaunted before others is illusory. I am revealed as dishonest: as a man who goes back on his word and on publicly stated principles. I am deflated; my weakness of character and especially my injustice to others now appear in broad daylight.

The repressed contents of consciousness cannot be accepted,

reflected upon, and thoroughly examined save through confrontation with analogous cases. When a man identifies himself with a person who, in other circumstances, has behaved in similar fashion, an unconscious transference takes place. This is so even if he does not make the application in so many words and if he is not yet able consciously to draw the inevitable conclusion: "That man is I! I behave in just the same way!" By the very fact that he has identified himself for a moment with the other case, an integration has taken place: the beginnings of a restructuring of the self, a softening, a thaw. However briefly, he has been able to see himself in perspective.

This triggering of the mechanism of identification and transference accounts for the efficacy of the parabolical technique. That is why in the chapters that follow we shall propose a confrontation with instinctive attempts at self-exoneration as a method of challenging the individual. Systematic group discussion may also produce very useful results in this area, for all the participants in some way identify themselves with what is said in the course of such discussion.

The mirror

Let us take a look back over the ground covered in this chapter.

It is particularly difficult to establish the facts because recognizing them constitutes a threat to our personal security. It means the collapse of the little world we have built up for ourselves. Self-knowledge and self-criticism are so hard for sinful man because of the obduracy and blindness inherent in sin. He can nevertheless be helped to revise his line of conduct by applying to his own person the value judgment which he professes in connection with another. This transition to self-accusation and conversion appears possible to the extent that his potential in the area of knowledge and reaction is activated. By this we mean not so much the sum of his knowledge but rather his existential good will to act effectively; in other words, a combination of qualities which trigger off the new stand.[19]

All this presupposes in the man concerned a consciousness of religious and moral standards and principles, but especially an existential experience. A proof which has been experienced outclasses all demonstrative argument. The most effective approach would seem to be the parabolical method of the prophets: examples taken from life which find an echo in the soul, so that the individual personally acquires a new intuition of the situation and thus gradually comes alive.

In this whole process of *metanoia,* the action of the Holy Spirit plays an essential part. The challenge—*elenchein*—comes ultimately from Him. But divine grace should not be represented as something altogether ethereal, without the slightest perceptible influence. God operates in man through his reason, his affective life, and his will. And to that end He uses ministers. The Christian, and particularly the pastor, insofar as he evangelizes, teaches, and prophesies, *is* a grace and a charisma for his neighbor (see Ep 4:7–13). His mission is to communicate Christ so that the new man may be born. That is why he prefers to speak in parables and indirectly. For it is thus that sinful man will best be able to assimilate the truth. The truth which he discovers himself emerges from his inmost depths, where it was already, although hidden and unrecognized. Significantly, the Greek term for truth (*aletheia*) means to emerge from its covering. But it is also a gift of the God who reveals: something from above, which in the last analysis cannot come solely from within man.

As a subjective entity, our self is in a way inaccessible to us, transcendent of itself. Only by indirect means can the individual come to confront himself through the progressive deciphering of the symbolic behavior patterns submitted to him.

The traditional comparison with a mirror is the most satisfactory, insofar as this mysterious phenomenon can be formulated and understood at all.

The mirror provides man with the means of learning to know himself in his reflection and his image. It enables us to move on to that other reality, which previously had been unrecognized and unreal to us, but nevertheless determined our true being. Through the mirror, reality can be made capable of discovering itself in its reflection.

The parable proposed to man as a mirror produces an analogous effect: it reveals to him his hidden self, it interprets his inner life and shows him the truth. "As in water face answers to face, so the mind of man reflects the man" (Pr 27:19). When we see the attitude and the behavior of another, we recognize our own—provided we want to see. "To listen to the word and not obey is like looking at your own features in a mirror and then, after a quick look, going off and immediately forgetting what you looked like" (Jm 1:23).

So long as a man is young and good-looking, he likes to look in the mirror and remains on good terms with it. The mirror is well disposed toward him. He preens himself before it, and his reflection smiles back at him. But after he has reached a certain age, he generally begins to be annoyed with the mirror. It shows him his wrinkles and his sour face. And that, he feels, is the fault of the mirror. So he thinks that everything will be fine, provided the mirror disappears. We have all heard the saying, of course, that when a monkey looks in a mirror the reflection he sees is not that of a wise man; but we do not apply it to ourselves. So we must get rid of the mirror. And having taken that decision, we must find a good reason to justify it. The mirror, we say, is defective or cracked and reflects a distorted image of reality. Let it be smashed to bits . . .

In his very thorough examination of the problem of culpability, Ricoeur draws attention to the fact that man as it were instinctively uses images and comparisons to express his experience of culpability. "The language of confession is remarkable in that it is symbolical through and through." [20] Thus we speak of stain, of baseness, of captivity, of exile, of a fall. One feels that humanity has been able to penetrate the abyss in which it is plunged only along the royal road of analogy. Everything seems to show that we can express ourselves only through images. Hence Ricoeur begins his study with a description and an interpretation of the symbolic confessions of Jewish and Greek mythology: *the symbolism of evil.* It is a mirror in which we can all recognize ourselves.

Necessity and danger of the unmasking process

How often have we not heard the wry comment that whenever a psychoanalyst examines a patient, he sends even the most normal and the most healthy person away with all sorts of complexes! If a man claims that he does not have an inferiority complex, that is proof that he suffers from a superiority complex . . . And *vice versa*. And a person who believed he had no complexes at all would provide the most serious grounds for alarm . . .

Theologians and preachers should be more careful than anyone else to be very clear-sighted in handling this cheap and commonplace type of argument. The barb might one day be directed back at them. As prophets and sentries, have they, too, not the duty to make men conscious of their malady, their sin, their wretchedness, and their need for divine redemption? And does not the Gospel tell us that it is those who consider themselves to be in perfect health who are the most sick?

Then again, we are told that constant introspection and self-analysis are unhealthy and unproductive. They are symptomatic of a decadent culture, a phenomenon of old age, leading to psychologism, egocentrism, and narcissism. Introspection, it is argued, leads to paralyzing discouragement. We must learn to look away from ourselves, losing ourselves in objective reality, love God and our neighbor . . .

It is, of course, quite possible to misuse the parabolical and analytical methods, which can degenerate into a destructive rage to unmask everything. To arrive at a balanced position, we have to take a number of factors into account. The tendency of a good number of our contemporaries to tear down time-honored values and to reduce alleged values to "it's nothing but . . ." is a phenomenon peculiar to the mentality of recent centuries. Modern man has realized the relative nature of many opinions and attitudes peculiar to certain times and certain environments. History, sociology, and the comparative study of civilizations are primarily responsible for this development.[21]

Nietzsche maintained that all men's aspirations are in fact disguises for his will to power and his spirit of domination. Psychoanalysis, on the other hand, has drawn attention to the role of the unconscious in our affective life; to the libido, the desire to make the most of oneself, the inferiority complex, repressed emotions, childhood experiences, and archetypes which have not been integrated. Whereupon we have the simplistic conclusions: "Show me your subconscious and I'll tell you what's true for you! or rather, what appears true!"

The argument snowballs. Religious and ethical convictions,

philosophical truths and systems—all are merely ideologies, the disguised expression of desires, interests, and repressions. What appears on the well-lit scene of conscious thought, draped in the brilliant mantle of justice, generosity, and truth, has been concocted and brewed in the dark caverns of the unconscious. With eagle eye, the psychoanalyst penetrates all these absurd disguises. He shows up reality for what it is, in all its poverty and nakedness. Ruthlessly he tears off man's masks and, sneering, forces him to look into the disorderly witch's kitchen where his fine ideologies and superstructures are brewed. It is a relentless process. Hardly has one practitioner torn off a protective covering than another comes along and tears off the one below, until nothing is left. There is no authentic face under the layers of masks. Man is simply a series of masks, fitting into each other like the layers of an onion, but without a center . . .

Removing other people's masks is a fascinating occupation, a virtually unending parlor game. It gives the person who indulges in it an agreeable sensation of relief, releasing him from whatever imposes limitations or obligations on him, or demands sacrifices. For he has become too shrewd to go on being taken in by such sublimations. And then there is that delicious sense of superiority —you can look so condescendingly at those simpletons who do not know the truth about themselves . . .

Until one day there appears yet another tearer-off of masks, who in his turn unmasks the very man who was so busy exposing others. For why should not the historian of cultures or the environmental sociologist themselves be influenced by their environment, which imposes a particular mode of thought and a particular approach? Is not the Marxist, too, a member of a class which disguises its will to power under the fine ideology of a classless society and universal liberty—until all are enslaved? Why should the psychologist escape from the illusions and influence of his subconscious, of his unknown desires and repressed appetites? His verdict, therefore, which tears off the masks of others, is suspect; he had better keep quiet . . .

And so the parlor game concludes in general hilarity. Each thought he could fool his neighbor, but in the end he must concede that he was simply fooling himself. He is himself wearing the masks which he thought he could strip from other people's faces.

Or rather, that emptiness and nothingness of his, which according to him is the core of human nature, is wearing the mask. And thus he refutes himself, like the skeptic who, through his doubting, undermines his own system.

The great mistake in this kind of mirror game is to look no further than the desolate scene left after a mask has been stripped off. On the face beneath the mask we see the traits of cupidity, vanity, envy, lust, aggressiveness, passion, obsequiousness, boastfulness, sadism, masochism, etc. And we are content to find nothing more, or nothing else, beneath this grimace. Such heartlessness and nihilism betray the unmasker. Had he pursued his investigation, he would also have discovered authentic values. He would have deepened and clarified his understanding of man and would have realized that other factors too were at work in his victims. He would have concluded that the first mask was not altogether a mask; that that superficial appearance also reflected certain genuine personality traits. Embittered and carping moralists like La Rochefoucauld see selfishness and immoral designs behind all noble conduct. Freud removed the mask of hypocrisy, and the derisive laughter of a brutal sexuality concealed behind it was to pursue him for the rest of his life. Nietzsche experienced cowardice and the suppressed rage and resentment of the physically weak, and he never managed to discover anything more. Adler, to the end of his days, was pursued by the specter of the spirit of domination, of ambition, and the secret will to power.

What we must never forget is that, if no one is as good as he seems, neither is he as bad as he appears. Just as our sentiments are generally mixed and interwoven, and indeed contradictory, because the situation is a complex one, so our conduct is also generally ambivalent and indeed polyvalent. That is why we speak of the superego. A single action may be the result both of instinctive and selfish desires and of more or less generous intentions, superimposed on one another. There is often a convergence of stratified aspirations, arising out of different registers of our personality.

While idealists incline toward moral optimism and have eyes only for what is noble in man, it is understandable that others, by reaction, should draw attention to less glittering features and establish a pessimistic diagnosis. Some conclude that even the guilty are innocent; others counter with the assertion that even the innocent are guilty. It is hard to maintain a balance between overaccusing and overexcusing. Here truth alone can help us; we have to examine, without any bias whatsoever, the complete dynamic substratum of man, and honestly endeavor to sort out the valid intentions from the immoral ingredients. Pharisaism occurs only if we refuse to make this lucid distinction.

The mask-stripper's essential motivation is a loathing of inauthenticity, a refusal to be taken in by a jingle of fine words and high-sounding ideals. But his action, like that of any critic, can be constructive or destructive in form. It can be motivated by respect for man and human values, by a real concern to distinguish the authentic from the inauthentic, by the desire to be humble and truthful. That, indeed, is healthy criticism. It is in that sense that the prophet holds up the mirror before men's eyes. But to snatch off masks becomes a morbid process when negative motivations prevail: perfectionism, an inhuman puritanism, ruthless severity, cynicism, nihilism, and above all the resentment of those who are disillusioned and embittered because they have been unable to fulfill their youthful dreams and therefore take a snarling revenge. In this connection, the following lines from Molière's *Tartuffe* are wonderfully apt:

> *It's true that now her life is most austere;*
> *her years have brought her purity; but still*
> *she's only virtuous against her will.*
> *Uneasy in her dreary solitude,*
> *she finds her one vocation as a prude,*
> *and people feel this worthy woman's sting.*
> *Forgiving nothing, blaming everything,*
> *she rants against the morals of the age,*
> *not out of charity, but jealous rage,*
> *determined for all others to destroy*
> *the pleasures she no longer can enjoy."* [22]

An illustration: the proud and cynical mask-stripper

In his book *The Fall*, Albert Camus describes a former Parisian lawyer in comfortable circumstances who has turned up in a bar in Amsterdam. He is pursued by a mysterious mocking laughter (his uneasy conscience) which taxes him with his selfishness, his pleasure-seeking, his vanity, and his hypocritical philanthropy. After various unsuccessful attempts to escape the shame and remorse he feels, he seems finally to have found the right solution. He becomes a "judge-penitent," a new St. John the Baptist (whence his name, "Jean-Baptiste Clamence") in this desert of stone and water which is Amsterdam. Skillfully but ruthlessly he makes his neighbors feel that their way of life is sickeningly immoral. And at the same time, he fulfills his old life's dream: to maintain his own uncontested superiority. "I'm actually no better than you, but at least I know it and have no illusions about my vulgarity." Through his cynicism and lucidity, he feels vastly superior to everyone else and his vanity and will to power remain unimpaired.[23]

To unmask or to admonish?

The man, be he prophet or psychoanalyst, who tears off other men's masks is in the awkward position of apparently always harboring suspicions and casting doubt on honest intentions. Thus he will suspect the man who conforms to orthodoxy of infantilism and defeatism; the conservative of self-indulgence and cowardice; the revolutionary and the progressive of a spirit of rebellion resulting from an unresolved crisis of puberty. He will detect an unintegrated sexuality and homosexual tendencies in the voluntary celibate, latent aggressiveness behind polemically stated convictions, paternalistic captiousness in certain forms of the apostolate and spiritual direction, lack of balance and adaptability in evangelical radicalism and its seeking for perfection . . .

Basically, however, the problem is not whether we are entitled to cast doubt on a person's idea or to undermine it on the pretext that it is founded on some infantile or neurotic tendency, but rather whether he is entitled to disguise his immaturity or his egotism behind a pseudo-virtue.[24]

We should not forget, moreover, that when we strip away masks, we have a powerful ally in the person of the man who is deluding himself, whether culpably or unconsciously. Man feels a natural horror of being deceived, as well as of all error and illusion, writes St. Augustine. We are oriented to the truth through the very structure of our conscience: memory, intelligence, and will. That is why integrity and veracity are so highly regarded. Honesty, indeed, is a quality which modern man appreciates, expects, and demands. Merciless criticism is directed, preferably of course, against others, especially the highly placed and those in authority. But there are many indications that man does not want to make any exceptions, not even for himself. The conscious concern with authenticity and the austerity which characterize modern art are very revealing in this connection.[25]

There would be little difficulty in adducing abundant proof that mask-stripping is altogether in the spirit of the Bible and tradition. God reveals Himself to man and at the same time reveals—and exposes—man to himself. He wants our radical commitment. He hates half-measures and whatever is merely superficial. He vomits the lukewarm. He demands that good should be done in its totality and evil totally rejected. Our self-abandonment must be complete. Only the pure in heart, those whose eyes are not dulled, will see God. The Sermon on the Mount is particularly significant in this connection. The Lord is jealous and will brook no rival. Therefore "let us examine our path, let us ponder it and return to Yahweh" (Lm 3:40; cf. 1 Co 2:10).

As a spokesman of tradition, we may cite St. Gregory the Great. One of the pastor's principle tasks, he writes, is to expose vices which hide under the cover of virtues. The pastor "should also understand that vices commonly masquerade as virtues. Often, for instance, a niggard passes himself off as frugal, while one who is prodigal conceals his character when he calls himself open-handed. Often inordinate laxity is believed to be kindness, and unbridled anger passes as the virtue of spiritual zeal. Precipitancy is frequently taken as efficient promptitude, and dilatoriness as grave deliberation. Wherefore it is necessary that the [pastor] discern with care and vigilance virtues from vices." [26]

Certain secret faults must therefore be delicately probed. Commenting on Ezekiel 8:8–10, in which the prophet breaks down a wall at the Lord's bidding and sees "filthy things" within, St. Gregory says that Ezekiel represents the pastor, the wall the hardness of heart of the flock. And what does breaking down the wall mean if not getting past the barrier of that hardness of heart by penetrating and careful probing? "By examining certain external symptoms," the pastor "sees into the hearts of his [flock], so that all the evil thoughts therein are disclosed to him." [27]

All things considered, however, it might appear less indicated to use the word "unmasking" to designate the pastoral approach to the sinner. The term has a pejorative connotation for many, evoking images and emotions that are very little "pastoral." Which is why we have used the Biblical term *elenchein*, or admonishment. It is preferable, and more accurate to speak of revealing, opening men's eyes, confronting man with himself; helping men to see and to understand the evidence of something; detecting a disregarded or forgotten offense, exposing sin and furnishing irrefutable proof of guilt. And indeed, the prophet's admonishment through parables consists not in imputing, accusing, or triumphantly pillorying, but in getting the man concerned to discover his sin for himself and realize his guilt.

Accusation or unmasking suggests the intervention of a stranger prompted by animosity and acting to protect himself or to triumph over another. Admonishment and revealing, by contrast, shift the emphasis to man, hardened or blinded, who must be not vanquished but rather persuaded and cured.

The touchstone, ultimately, of a constructive pastoral cultivation of a sense of sin, as distinguished from a destructive tearing off of masks, is the patience and longanimity which the pastor shows in his contact with his neighbor. He knows very well that confession of sin and *metanoia* are the culmination of a long growth process and of a gradually deepening experience of one's sinful condition. We should not demand either of ourselves or of others a startling and complete awareness of our latent, unsuspected, or forgotten guilt. Self-discovery is a long and tortuous voyage of exploration. All man is asked is to move ever closer to the truth, to bring light into his own existence. Instead of hardening his heart and denying all guilt through illusion and blindness, he is asked to become increasingly aware of his sin, to accept his need for pardon, and to live that need, even if he is still beset by certain illusions by reason of the grossness and denseness of his human heart.

It would be Utopian to hope to rid ourselves of all illusions at once. At the same time, it is both possible and necessary to set aside illusions. God does not require of *homo viator* that he should have reached the term of his evolution, but that he should begin and pursue this exploration. And the sign by which he can be sure that this purification has begun is his readiness to look the truth in the face and acknowledge it—to "make truth in himself," as St. Augustine puts it.

When Jesus had cured the blind man at Bethsaida, He asked him, "Do you see anything?" The man, who was beginning to see, said, "I see men; but they look like trees, walking." Then Jesus laid His hands upon the man's eyes, and the man was cured and could see everything plainly (Mk 8:23–25).

Notes

1. Karl Rahner, *Eléments de théologie spirituelle*, Paris–Bruges, Desclée de Brouwer, 1964.
   St. Augustine's incomparably productive teaching on the human heart has been clearly systematized by A. Maxsein in, "Cor im leib-seelischen Gefüge," in *Jahrbuch für Psychologie*, Freiburg–Munich, K. Alber, 1962, vol. IX, p. 55, and in "Das Cor aegrotum," *ibid.*, 1963, vol. X, p. 269.
2. See A. Herrmann, "Das steinharte Herz," in *Jahrbuch für Antike und Christentum*, Münster, Westf. Aschendorff, 1961, vol. IV, p. 77.
3. See H. Jelgersma, *Ex oriente Lux*, 1942, p. 610.
4. See A. de Buck, *Ex oriente Lux*, 1944, p. 23.
5. *Enarr. Ps.*, C.C.L, 40, 2161. We may refer, also, to the thirtieth canto of the *Purgatory* of the *Divine Comedy*, in which Dante describes the heart, frozen by fear of divine punishment, beginning to thaw out in tears.
6. I. Caruso, *Bios, Psyche, Person*, Freiburg, Alber, 1957, p. 129.
7. J. de Finance, *Essai sur l'agir humain*, Rome, Gregorian University Press, 1962, p. 101.
8. P. Ricoeur, *Esprit*, Paris, 1956, p. 308.
9. See C. Spicq, *Saint Paul: les Épîtres pastorales*, Paris, J. Gabalda, 1947.
10. See H. Schlier, *Der Brief an die Epheser*, Düsseldorf, Patmos-Verlag, 1957, p. 212.
11. *Enarr. Ps.*, C.C.L., 38, 111.
12. See M. Landmann, *De Homine*, Munich, K. Alber, 1962.
13. Dietrich von Hildebrand, *Christian Ethics*, New York, McKay, 1953, p. 230.

14. F. Nietzsche, *Joyful Wisdom* (tr. T. Common), New York, Frederick Ungar, 1964, no. 125, p. 169.
15. Albert Camus, *The Fall* (tr. Justin O'Brien), New York, Alfred A. Knopf, p. 137.
16. H. Reiner, *Pflicht und Neigung*, Meisenheim Glan, Westkultur-Verlag A. Hain, 1951, p. 206.
17. Other sayings along the same lines reflect a very ancient wisdom. For example: people in glass houses shouldn't throw stones; the pot shouldn't call the kettle black; physician, heal thyself, etc.
18. Cf. R. Hare, *Freedom and Reason*, Oxford, Clarendon Press, 1963.
19. H. Thomae, *Der Mensch in der Entscheidung*, Munich, Barth, 1960, p. 128.
20. P. Ricoeur, *Finitude et culpabilité*, Paris, Aubier, 1960.
21. See A. Brunner, "Entlarvte Entlarvung," in *St. d. Z.*, 150, 1952, p. 91, from which we have borrowed the ideas that follow.
22. Molière, *Tartuffe and Other Plays* (tr. Donald Frame), New York, New American Library, 1967, pp. 245–246.
23. Albert Camus, *op. cit.*, pp. 139–143 and 147.
24. In the *Cahiers Laennec*, Paris, 1963, vol. I, p. 73, M. Eck describes the unfortunate case of a young idealist who had been in the Resistance, became active in the labor movement and wanted to become a worker-priest. Then he discovered that his revolutionary nonconformism was inspired by an Oedipean rivalry with his father, a capitalist. He eventually settled down to a middle-class style of life himself.
25. See H. Sedlmayr, *Die Revolution der Modernen Kunst*, Hamburg, Rohwolt, 1956, and *id. Verlust der Mitte*, Salzburg, Otto Müller, 1953.
26. *Liber Regulae Pastoralis* (see note 14 to chapter 1), p. 78.
27. *Ibid.*, pp. 80–81. We may also refer to St. John of the Cross, who frequently cautions against illusions as one of the greatest obstacles to man's ascent to God. St. Ignatius of Loyola's rules on the discernment of spirits endorse that view, as do the very thorough analyses of F. Guildore (1615–1684), *Les secrets de la vie spirituelle.* Cf. J. von Hirscher, *Selbsttäuschungen*, 1860 (reissued: Heidelberg, 1947).

Mounier writes: "You cannot, with impunity, dislodge the guilty conscience from the specific point at which it requires of man that he assume his responsibilities. Any attempt to elude the pressure—a temporary pressure if we are prepared to face our offense frankly—only turns pressure into oppression, unpleasantness into an illusory peace achieved at the price of spiritual death" (*Traité du caractère*, Paris, Editions du Seuil, 1947, p. 730).

5

The defense mechanisms
in the service
of exculpation

The exculpatory tendency

As we have shown, sin produces blindness, and even the prospect of pardon fails to mitigate the torment involved in acknowledging our guilt.

On the other hand, the consciousness of guilt is just as agonizing an experience and may eventually become intolerable. The individual who wishes to be relieved of this torment without acknowledging his guilt is obliged to seek some other solution, and resorts to all kinds of excuses. He would like to be cured, but refuses to undergo the painful operation required.

St. Augustine uses a striking analogy to describe the guilt-ridden soul. My heart, or conscience, is my dwelling, in which I live and feel at home. A serene conscience, which does not accuse me, is a spacious dwelling in which I can move at will and where it is pleasant to live. But remorse and the experience of guilt turn it into a stifling chamber, in which I am unable to breathe. A house which for one reason or another becomes uninhabitable puts its occupants to flight.

The guilty man whose heart is assailed by violent remorse is in the position of one whose house threatens to collapse, or whose dwelling is filled with asphyxiating smoke, or who lives under a leaking roof. Men who live under such conditions flee their homes to seek rest and shelter elsewhere—away from their own hearts, in material pleasures. When I am uncomfortable in the intimacy of my own conscience, when my heart gives me no rest, then I try to live comfortably away from home.[1]

The ancient Greeks compared the guilty conscience to a swarm of wasps circling furiously around the guilty man's head; to Furies relentlessly pursuing him; to an abscess causing intolerable pain; to a fever against which one is powerless, unlike the external heat or cold against which one can seek protection. The Congolese use the colorful simile of a jackal with red ants on its tail. In our own day we would tend to use analogies from mechanical devices that jar on the nerves: vacuum cleaners with their monotonous hum, deafening motorcycles, rasping saws, etc.

It is no accident that the pangs of conscience are compared to an accusing voice. These metaphors borrowed from the realm of acoustics emphasize our powerlessness to escape from conscience, since it is far harder to shut ourselves off from importunate sounds than to eliminate undesirable visual impressions. To make matters worse, the source of the sound, in the case of remorse, is deep within ourselves. My conscience is like a power plant, producing feelings of guilt and anguish which cannot be escaped. We carry our torment around with us like a shadow. We are—literally— guilt-ridden, as in a horror story in which the werewolf or the witch pounces on the victim's back and will not be shaken off. Or again, a guilty conscience might be compared to a pilot's earphones: as soon as he strays from his route, the device emits a shrill, whistling sound which continues until he corrects his direction.

The question then arises: what can a man do, and what methods should he use, to rid himself of a guilt feeling that has become intolerable, but without admitting his sin and revising his style of life? This, clearly, is a problem of great importance for moral and pastoral psychology.

It is also a very ancient problem. Aristotle, for instance, pointed to the strategems of concupiscence, which manages to achieve its end through specious argument. The passion by which we are enslaved suborns our logical reasoning processes, disguising itself behind all kinds of sophistries and obfuscations. It is like a band of clever smugglers who elude the customs officers appointed to check on anyone entering the country; or like undesirables who provide themselves with false identity papers, even passing themselves off as government employees.[2]

This is an area where depth psychology, with its very thorough probing of the protective or defense mechanisms, can be particularly instructive.

Biological defense mechanisms

If a captive chimpanzee is served a mushroom in a dish of bananas and other titbits, it will react with physical revulsion. Either it will break the offending fungus into tiny pieces and scatter them as far out of the range of sight and smell as possible, or it will turn away from the food in disgust and go off, disturbed and fearful.

Biology teaches us that every organism protects itself against foreign bodies. The tissues and the blood of living creatures have a faculty of immunization. From its conception, the organism learns to distinguish between friendly and hostile substances. It is thus that certain molecular structures are recognized and rejected (xenophobia). If a particular hostile substance finds its way into the body, special proteins, or antibodies, are produced to neutralize it. This type of reaction seems to be the basic defense mechanism against microbes and viruses.

Thus we have, even on the physiological level, the central phenomenon which is under study here: some realities are incompatible with my structure; they are not suited to my being or my life.

Here, then, we may speak of unconditioned reflexes, a term used mainly in neurology. The literal meaning of *reflectere* is to bend back or to reflect. The perception or representation of certain stimuli provokes an instinctive reaction. The perceptive faculty is reflected in the motor system as in a mirror. This is true, for example, of the patellar reflex. A tap under the kneecap produces a sudden extension of the leg. This spontaneous reaction takes place because the nerve ends have been stimulated by the elongation of the muscular fibers. The nerve ends conduct the stimulus through the sensory nerve to the spinal cord. There the perception is transmitted to the motor nerve of the muscle concerned, as a result of which a sudden muscular contraction takes place.

Among the characteristics of unconditioned reflexes are the following: they are fairly stereotyped; they occur spontaneously and cannot be restrained; they can be easily isolated from other vital phenomena.

Three types of reflexes are generally distinguished.

First, there are the reflexes of appropriation and assimilation: breathing, the sucking of the infant, salivation, and gastric secretions upon contact with food.

Secondly, there are the reflexes of accommodation: with a change in temperature, the blood vessels dilate or contract and the degree of perspiration changes; according to the intensity of the light, the pupils are more or less enlarged.

Thirdly, there are the defense reflexes: the eyelids twitch in a strong wind, in a bright light, or at the sound of a harsh voice; foreign bodies which stimulate the mucus of the throat and nose are expelled by a cough or a sneeze; some animals remain motionless at the least sign of danger: the snail returns into its shell, the mouse is fascinated and paralyzed by a snake or a cat, the hedgehog rolls itself into a ball and sticks out its quills (stiffening, inertia, playing dead); other animals exhibit a frantic agitation: a panic-stricken cat, for example, or an insect circling around a light.

These different reflexes sometimes interpenetrate and it is not always possible to distinguish clearly between adaptation and defense.

To understand the origin and dynamic background of the mechanisms of accommodation and defense, it is best to proceed from what von Bertalanffy has called the law of dynamic equilibrium. The stimuli which provoke tensions are perceived and neutralized by the living creature according to a four-part pattern: the equilibrium is disturbed, and this causes frustration; the organism is in an unpleasant state of tension; a reaction takes place to restore the shattered equilibrium by appropriate action; this results in a normalization and a satisfactory relaxation of tension.

In this context we may consider the mechanisms as a kind of automatic regulatory system spontaneously coming into play to maintain the structure of the organism and eliminate the threat.

Psychic defense mechanisms

For man, too, accommodation, defense, and protection are vitally necessary. Quite spontaneously, we constantly tend not only to maintain our biological equilibrium but also to harmonize our affectivity and spiritual personality. Our ego strives to maintain order in the interior structuring of its affective life, to integrate new impressions and factors as well as new desires, and to achieve and develop a psychic synthesis.

We have to establish a satisfactory balance among the many constituent elements of our lives. Among these are: the energy which comes from below—our needs, drives, and desires; the many and often chaotic impressions which we receive from outside: signals, opportunities, danger; the demands of reality, of society, of authority: our concept of certain standards and our conscience.

Man has sometimes been compared—understandably—to a driver who drives himself instead of an automobile. The motor provides him with energy and speed; he moves toward a goal to carry out a plan; he has to pay attention to dangerous turns and oncoming cars; he has to obey traffic regulations.

Through our perceptive faculties (the senses and the intelligence) we record our observations and experiences: the world outside us, within us, and above us. We attempt to understand reality and we instinctively tend to distinguish between two categories of impressions: on the one hand, what is agreeable, useful, advantageous, and good; on the other hand, what is painful, disagreeable, harmful, and bad.

We react both positively and negatively to these perceptions, maintaining the dynamic stability of our person, accommodating it, protecting it, and possibly restructuring it. To resolve this vital problem, we are equipped with a system of adaptation and protection.

By protection or defense, therefore, we mean an instinctive and almost automatic reaction in the face of a threat, aimed at safeguarding the present structure of our personality. The individual concerned will carry out this reaction by rejecting from his consciousness the perceptions and experiences which clearly conflict with the organizational balance he has already achieved. Faced with an unpleasant fact of observation or with a distressing and humiliating conflict, innate habits, reflexes, and behavior patterns come into play. These are protective mechanisms, defensive reflexes by means of which the individual seeks to dodge a problem, eliminate it, or neutralize it.

For instance, he can deny the existence of the unpleasant experience: this is not allowed, therefore it is impossible and does not exist (repression, negation). Or he can distort the unpleasant experience and rearrange it so that the situation becomes acceptable. For example, I live in the conviction that I am an intelligent and gifted person (image of the ego-ideal). Yet I have to concede that I failed an examination. This contradiction between my representation of myself and the unfortunate fact is eliminated by the argument: "I was unlucky; it was an unfortunate accident" (rationalization); or by the assertion: "The teacher concerned is prejudiced against me and unfair; it's not my fault" (projection); or again, by restoring the threatened equilibrium through substitution or compensation: "I did flunk that exam, but I'm nevertheless blessed with a host of other abilities which more than make up for this quite unimportant diploma" (minimization).

In other words, if our feeling of personal worth, our flattering representation of ourselves, our situation, condition, or ambitions are threatened, and if the tension between what we are and what we should like to be becomes too painful, we resort to all kinds of stratagems and defensive maneuvers. We protect our ego against negative feelings of helplessness and inferiority for fear of suffering a defeat. We believe that these existential experiences will become intolerable and that life with a diminished personality will be impossible if we admit and face up to reality.

Ultimately, therefore, the defense mechanisms serve to maintain the equilibrium we have achieved and to preserve or restore our peace of mind.

In many cases there is absolutely nothing abnormal or morbid in employing certain protective mechanisms. As long as the adaptation to reality takes place smoothly, and the defense mechanisms are used constructively to promote our personal integration, the activity is a healthy one. Every man is constantly assailed and submerged by such a torrent of chaotic impressions that he has to rid himself of at least some of the enormous pressure. It is a form of self-defense which is necessary if we are not to be overwhelmed. We are constantly obliged to test and to establish our defense systems if we are to succeed in ensuring our preservation, our development, and our capacity for action.

This self-protective activity becomes pathological, however, when the mechanisms are used constantly and indiscriminately with a view to escaping reality. This proliferation and degeneration lead to an unalterably static and irreversible style of living, which in fact operates against the best interests of the individual concerned. The individual obstructs objectively accurate perceptions and develops an unhealthy course of conduct which conflicts with reality. He wastes his precious vital energy on unproductive undertakings. He deteriorates and weakens his ego and comes finally to exhibit neurotic, or even psychotic, symptoms.

The progressive discovery and cataloging of the defense mechanisms by clinical psychology is a fascinating story in itself, but any detailed account of it here would take us too far. We shall confine ourselves, therefore, to pointing to the key aspects of the problem.

The study of the protective mechanisms is based on the premise that there exists in man a form of unconscious life. This depth dimension of our personality presents characteristic forms of life, assimilation, and action: stereotyped unconscious modes of functioning or innate behavior patterns.

Sigmund Freud, in his pioneering work, concentrated mainly on the mechanism of repression. The ego unconsciously defends itself against emerging drives and effects (the id). The ego identifies itself with the demands of the external world (reality principle) and with those of society, authority, and conscience (the superego) by totally or partially repressing its limitless longing for pleasure (pleasure principle).

With Adler, on the other hand, the main emphasis is on the search for compensation, and with Jung, on projective activity.

In recent years, the defense mechanisms have come to be considered in a broader perspective. Man defends himself, as it were, on three fronts. In the first place, he defends himself against the sexual and aggressive drives which arise from below, through fear of authority and of accepted standards of conduct; this results particularly in emotional disturbances and neuroses, as psychoanalysis has been able to demonstrate. But he also feels threatened by hostile forces from other directions. He defends himself against the pressure of his superego or of his archaic conscience, so that he may be able to give free rein to his instinctual drives. This may ultimately lead to immoral and psychopathic forms of conduct. And finally, man defends himself also against the external world which he experiences as dangerous and disturbing; in extreme cases, this produces psychoses or mental disturbances.

It has recently been pointed out, moreover, that the defense mechanisms in which the unconscious activity of the ego takes form are not purely intrapsychic phenomena. It would be a mistake to conceive of them as autistic modes of conduct adopted by the ego to avoid anxiety, unpleasantness, and danger. In reality, these mechanisms are methods for regulating the traffic between man and his environment. Repression, projection, sublimation, compensation, transference, and identification are forms in which we achieve our interhuman relationships. They are communication mechanisms which fulfill the social function of initiating contact and maintaining it.[3] They are effective to the degree that they relate to the prevailing concepts and expectations of the environment. Self-protection presupposes a socially acceptable substitution for the original form in which the need or desire was manifested.

Recent research has *experimentally* established the operation of the defense mechanisms. It has been demonstrated, *inter alia*, that a kind of defense system is set up in the individual who has just made a choice. For example, an individual is asked to choose between two household appliances valued at between $15.00 and $30.00. The defense system which is established after he has made his choice consists principally in a tendency to refute any data which might place that choice in an unfavorable light. Any arguments in its favor, on the other hand, are overemphasized.[4] The option which has been made is thus protected and rendered firmer and more durable. It is an extension of what took place at the time of the initial decision: some aspects of the situation are highlighted and others are pushed into the background or attenuated. The more radical and existential a decision is, the more actively the defense mechanisms come into play. We oppose the possible rescinding of the decision made, even before the action that has been decided upon is carried out. We dispute the obviously detrimental consequences of the choice we have made.

Should we speak of mechanisms, "psychisms," or structures?

Objections are sometimes voiced, particularly among those who take a spiritualistic view of man, to the term "mechanism." Does it not imply that we are machines, impotent victims of independent automatisms?

It is a fact that psychoanalysis has borrowed its categories from physics and mechanics, in which the governing factor is conflicts of quantitative energy. This approach could, of course, give rise to a mechanistic and materialistic view of man, but we have to think analogically and remember that the term "mechanism" is a type of image. Through this analogy or symbol we are trying to indicate that relatively independent dynamisms exist and operate in man. They are modes of functioning of the energetic process, not only in the physiological and biological spheres, but also in man's affective and social life. That is why we do not think it necessary scrupulously to avoid a mechanistic terminology and to speak instead, for example, of "psychisms."

This whole problem belongs to the area of philosophical anthropology. As we know, a good many data of psychology still await a satisfactory formulation and integration. The following comments may perhaps throw some light on the matter.[5]

It would be a mistake to regard the defense mechanisms as *things*, substances, or devices. This would be a concession to the tendency to think statically and to *reify* all beings. The defense mechanisms might better be conceived of as faculties or dynamisms of the soul. But at the same time it must not be forgotten that these mechanisms relate to a group of events, phenomena, and activities and that they belong to the sphere of *operation*.

The best solution, we feel, is to use concepts such as structure, configuration, or form. For we are dealing with situations and with constants in human existence, which are formed and established by a reiterated activity based on operational patterns and preestablished modes of functioning. A structure is very analogous to a faculty, but the term implies, further, a constant interaction between being and activity. Man possesses possibilities of action in the form of propensities and innate dynamisms. But the activity determines the faculty itself by giving it a concrete form. What we are dealing with here is the dynamic and historic actualization of a potentiality. With Merleau-Ponty, we may associate the conclusions of behavioral psychology with those of structural psychology (the Gestalt theory).

A Gestalt (form or structure) may be defined as an indivisible entity which we apprehend in its totality, and immediately, as being what it signifies. It appears to us as a phenomenal unity and a configuration implying a precise arrangement of the parts.

By behavior we mean the over-all movement, the totality of the actions and modes of conduct which make up the existence of a human being. Or again: the human personality itself as existing in its totality and reacting to its environment. Combining these two ideas, we conceive of behavior as an over-all configuration, an irresolvable course or melody of action.

We can attempt to understand a structure by discovering the motive of the behavior in question. We then perceive a link between the signifying element and the element signified in a structured entity. Thus we *understand* the experience of fear and anxiety if we know the danger which in fact threatens, or if we know that the person who takes fright is of an asthenic nature and liable to worry at the slightest threat.

Next, we can *explain* psychic phenomena in terms of automatisms or mechanisms which, though observable, are not therefore *understandable*. An intense, inhibited desire (for example, repressed aggressivity) can create anxiety feelings. It is difficult to discover the significance of the permanent relationship between these two phenomena. The person concerned perceives no motive for his anxiety. We therefore conclude from the observations of events proceeding in regular succession that a constant psychic structure is involved: a type of *mechanism* which is responsible for this relationship.

Using this theory, we more easily discover a relationship between phenomena which, taken separately, remain inexplicable. That, basically, is what we expect of a sound hypothesis. But what is most important is that such an hypothesis facilitates diagnosis and helps to free the person concerned of his fear or anxiety. If he regards certain stereotyped actions as produced by a mechanism, he immediately becomes capable of standing back from them and seeing them in better perspective. He objectifies himself to some extent and is therefore better able to detach himself from the action. Take, for example, the mechanism of regression. Innumerable observations have led to the hypothesis that there exists in man a tendency, in difficult circumstances, to seek a solution and some form of consolation in the revival of infantile behavior patterns. One and the same basic attitude and style of life are apparent in the most varied circumstances, so that we can speak of a transposable configuration or structuring, rather as a single melody or leitmotiv may be recognized in a number of compositions which have nothing else in common.

A typology of defense mechanisms

In order to elaborate some kind of typology of certain psychic phenomena, it is customary to use two criteria, form and content.

Let us take the very varied phenomenon of *tendency*. We can ask, first, in what manner and in what form (rhythm, intensity, frequency, tactics) is a tendency displayed? Immediately a host of terms come to mind, permitting a certain classification: tendency, drive, instinct, desire, need, appetite, aspiration, passion, interest, hunger, wish, orientation, purpose, will. Next, we can ask the question: what goal are we striving for under these varied headings? We speak, for instance, of the tendency to make the most of ourselves, the will to power, ambition, self-esteem, etc., according to the nature of the object.

The first classification is based on differences of form; the second is thematic. According to *form* or mode, we distinguish repression, rationalization, projection, compensation, sublimation, minimization, regression, etc. Here we might also subdivide activities into transitive and intransitive ones. We can protect ourselves —like the chimpanzee—either by removing the disturbing object or by turning away and seeking safety: by fight or by flight. In the first category we place repression, rationalization, projection, sublimation, minimization. In the second, we place regression, conversion or somatization, flight and capitulation, compensation.

According to the *content* or object against which we are protecting ourselves, we obtain the following ternary scheme based on the various areas of existence: man protects himself against his drives and needs (the id); against the external world and surrounding reality; against the demands of the superego, conscious standards, his conscience, and God.

The self and the defense mechanisms

But there is another question which appears to us to be far more important than the satisfactory and exhaustive cataloging of the defense mechanisms. It is this: who, actually, is defending himself? What is the agency responsible for the activity which we call self-defensive? The answer is obvious: man's ego. But what do we really mean by that? Who and what is this ego?

The first and most obvious answer is that the ego is the epitome of everything that we represent to ourselves concerning ourselves: the image we form of our own being. It is the image of the self built up from a series of affirmations concerning our possibilities, our past, our present, our plans and future designs. It is enough to consider for a moment the kind of things so many people say about themselves, implying some over-all concept of self: "I've never really had a chance, so far, to be myself." "I feel that I'm not really myself; behind this façade there is concealed my real and better self; I should so much like to be myself, if only for an instant." "I would have been a good musician had my parents given me the means of following my inclinations and getting the proper training." "Fundamentally, I'm a loyal friend, and can be counted on; but when others misunderstand me and make fun of me, I become impossible and savage."

It is clear that this view of the person concerning himself (auto-perception) does not necessarily coincide with the objective configuration of the ego. At best, we can speak of a part of the total personality structure.

The second and much simpler answer is that the ego is the grammatical subject of verbs which we conjugate in the first person singular. "I, Smith, and not Jones, am the starting point and the initiator of a certain action. I am the subject of a number of lived experiences and activities. Thus, for example, I feel a longing for movement and for relaxation."

The personal pronoun "I" here designates a very definite person who has certain sensations, feels emotions welling up, reflects, works out plans, or carries out actions. A characteristic of this "I" is to be *inner-directed*. A two- or three-year-old will still speak of himself as others do about him: "John wants this," "Mary is good." The very young child is satisfied with the third person. The following experiment can help us to grasp the meaning of the experience of the self: if in a group conversation we deliberately avoid the use of "I" or "you" and speak both of others and of ourselves in the third person, we get the impression of approaching all those present, including ourselves, from the outside. A bizarre atmosphere of distance and objectivity is created. We put ourselves outside and above ourselves and others. We regard ourselves as spectators. A third party would express himself in like manner about the members of the group who participate in the conversation. To be able to say "I" or "me," an inner perception is required, and an inner direction.

Thirdly, however, we have to distinguish two elements in this grammatical "I." On the one hand, there is the *center of the ego*, or the nucleus of the personality, which carries out and controls certain actions. On the other hand, there is a wider periphery: the marginal "I" which surrounds the central ego and is at the same time the ground whence this nucleus emerges.[6] Many easily established facts point to the existence of such a structure of the personality.

For example, we are sometimes disgusted about certain things and unable to shake off our bad mood. Often a tune rings stubbornly in our ears when we would like to be able to concentrate on something else. Dreams snatch us far away from our real surroundings, but we cannot drive them away. Often, too, the voice of conscience sounds importunately and aggressively, in opposition to our inclinations and present directions. We passively perceive demands and standards which seem to come from outside and from above.

These are so many phenomena of my psychic and affective life which take place, of course, *within* me, in my self, but without being, as it were, *of* me.

The fringe and the enveloping ground of the self are situated where my lived experiences take place without my personal intervention, although they nevertheless become *my* experiences since I am personally involved in them. They are situated wherever I can say that something is happening *in me:* actions and experiences which I look upon as to some extent alien, as *something* or as *that.* The peripheral self is a reality which actively intervenes in the space delimited by my skin. There is where it can be perceived; yet I cannot be made directly responsible for it, since *that* takes place without the intervention of my personal will. The same is true of ideas which go through my head like lightning shafts, or of feelings of aversion, desire, anger, and fear which in turn grip my heart.

As "I" proper, I am essentially active. The central ego is the element in my personality which regulates its activity and decides how I should behave: "The only reality in the world whose essence is to make itself." [7] In the wider periphery of experience there is also a certain spontaneity but, compared with the nucleus of the self, of a more passive nature. It is not in my power to produce in myself whatever experiences, sentiments, or value judgments I happen to want, nor is it in my power to eliminate them completely once they are in me. I can, of course, refuse the assent of my self, properly so-called, to a thought or a sentiment that arises spontaneously. In that sense, the central self is its own master and possesses freedom of choice. Thus joy can well up in me even before I come to reflect whether or not I shall endorse it. But as soon as I recollect myself, my essential self can, for one reason or another, refuse to assent to it; for example, if I come to realize that it is a malicious joy. At once the feeling is driven from the central self and relegated to the marginal self.

This does not mean that the central self is totally autonomous and independent as regards the content of the peripheral self. The two elements constantly interact. For its activity, the essential self must draw its energy and its material from the enveloping ground of the self. This region of the peripheral self is as it were the womb which surrounds and feeds the nucleus of the personality and whence that nucleus draws its sustenance. It originally consists as much of drives and instinctive desires (the id) as of principles and value judgments (superego and conscience).

The central self is the faculty whereby the individual can integrate his experiences and interior situations in a coherent whole, whether by assimilating or by rejecting them, rather as a biological organism assimilates what is good for it, but rejects what is harmful. "My self is not my being; it is the affirmation that it depends on me to confer being on myself." [8]

Seen in this light, the self appears as the synthesis of the desires and aspirations of the individual as well as of this consciousness of standards; or as a dynamic principle which determines the line of conduct in terms of the individual's fundamental purpose. It is a principle capable of standing back from the various possibilities which suggest themselves, so that the individual concerned may be able not to lose sight of his horizon of highest values. It does not let itself be swayed by successive solicitations but, among the numerous courses of conduct which present themselves, manages to maintain a certain calm and balance. That is what happens, for example, when we say, "Never would *I* stoop to such a thing!" or, "I don't let trifles like that upset me." Actually, this "I" virtually coincides with what we described in the preceding chapter as the "human heart."

Here it might be wise to draw attention to the fairly common error of confusing the "I" with consciousness.

This confusion arises because we cannot define consciousness (having the feeling, having knowledge of, being aware) save in terms of its relationship to the ego. It is always our "I" that is conscious of something, but the sphere of the "I" and the field of consciousness are not identical. This is very apparent from the fact that we are conscious of things outside ourselves, and also that there are obscure regions in ourselves which we do not know because they remain inaccessible to recognition. With his exceptional perspicacity, St. Augustine realized this all those centuries ago when he wrote, in connection with memory, "In fact I cannot totally grasp all that I am." [9] Thus, for example, we retain all kinds of things in our memory even when we think of other things. Sometimes, even, we no longer know whether we know something. That is why we have to distinguish between the latent knowledge of the memory and thought of which one is presently conscious. Man's interior constitutes an immense expanse which we can never completely explore: "Who can reach its uttermost depths?" [10]

The distinction between the "I" and consciousness must be

maintained, particularly if we use Freud's model of ego, superego, and id. Our drives are largely unconscious, of course; on the other hand, we are aware of certain needs and desires in ourselves. Our conscience, fashioned by childhood training, and a product of socialization, as well as our ego-ideal, generally function in an unconscious manner; but our personal perception of values is a conscious process. The self is, of course, conscious of its being, but some of its activities, such as the defense mechanisms, remain unconscious.

We have also to avoid the error of regarding the self or the heart as an autonomous principle, a kind of independent pilot inside us. Such a notion comes from our *reifying* tendency. Instinctively we imagine psychic phenomena as entities, organs, or objects. Sometimes we go so far as to confuse introspection with a microscopic examination designed to catalog substances buried in our inmost being, as though our inner life were a kind of aquarium inhabited by various species of fish. Using abstractions as a little net, we take out a drive, a need, a feeling, a principle, a motivation, a complex, the will, conscience, the defense mechanisms, the "I," one after the other.

The use of substantives to designate these psychic phenomena is, incidentally, a residuum of this tendency to reification, or even an animistic survival. We have to bear in mind that all these names are only symbols to designate the totality of our active being. The intelligence, the "I," or any other faculty cannot really be regarded as parts of the personality. At the psychic and affective level there is neither dissociation nor departmentalization. A desire, a motivation, and consciousness, are not more or less independent entities within the individual; it is the individual in his totality who at certain moments desires, is motivated, or is conscious. My superego, for example, is my whole being insofar as it regulates and restrains my instinctive actions; it is I insofar as I identify myself with the punitive authorities of my childhood. Or, in psychoanalytical language: the superego takes its energy from the id. What we call "principles" in the psychic structure may be compared to registers on which the personality plays successively or simultaneously.

Thus, when our ego is torn in opposing directions between assenting to an instinctive drive and carrying out a duty, it is not a case of a conflict taking place in a particular area between two rival forces, in which the self plays the part of the impartial arbiter. In point of fact, our ego considers various courses of action in turn, then anticipates the possible outcomes and the roads that lead to them. The id and the superego, spontaneous desires and conscience, constitute as it were anticipatory modes of action. They are symbols for a conflict between different interests within the human heart.

We might illustrate the point with an example from life. A survey was conducted in which those interviewed were asked to describe the most difficult decision of their lives. Among the answers was the following:

> One day, someone suggested that we should escape from the reformatory. I had to decide between Christmas and the New Year. I spent all night thinking it over. I found myself faced with the choice of staying there and turning into an upright citizen, or going off into the unknown with my pal and laying myself open to every kind of trouble. I had disliked the school for a long time. The other kids were always teasing me on account of my red hair. And life there was so humdrum and uninspiring. At the same time, I realized that it wouldn't be easy to get away and land on my feet; I realized, too, that I might quite easily go wrong again. Then I thought: I don't care! it will turn out badly anyway! It's better to live outside the law than to be confined here all the time. That's how I finally came to agree . . .

Here we have a conflict between two contrary tendencies, a choice between different possibilities. The young man hesitates between his ego-ideal and the voice of his conscience, on the one hand ("turning into an upright citizen," "I might quite easily go wrong again"), and, on the other hand, the temptation to get out. His hesitations are brought to an end by the sudden thought: "I don't care! things will turn out badly anyway! It's better to live outside the law . . ."

The logic of this argument can be understood only in terms of an attitude to life and an orientation of the will in which the protests of conscience and the desire for amendment are increasingly stifled by the anticipation of freedom. The contrast only accentuates his longing for freedom of movement. The conflict is resolved in the direction of that desire for freedom.

This example shows how reflection and deliberation are anchored in affectivity and in the person's existential purpose (*qualiscumque unusquisque est, talis finis videtur ei prosequendus*). The objections to attempted flight are thus minimized by reason or suppressed. The young man is aware, of course, that his present attitude and his plans for the future are not "upright": he will be living "outside the law." But the importance and force of this voice of conscience are neutralized by the "I don't care!" Thus, the reform school experience is represented as a nonvalue.[11]

My ego, then, or my heart, cannot be regarded as a neutral principle which effects a choice between two courses of conduct without becoming involved itself. We still too often think of free will as a kind of dictator, making arbitrary decisions.

The heart, Pascal writes, is the locus of commitments and decisions. My ego is moved by a disposition; it is oriented; it is structured by its individual purpose in life and its fundamental option. It is not neutral and uncommitted, but rather *prospective* and *propulsive*. The ego, or the heart, is a central principle and an orientation resulting from a number of factors related among themselves by a feedback system. Its main components are the following: the dynamism resulting from needs and vital drives (the id); the demands of the external world; the prohibitions and imperatives of the superego, the knowledge of certain standards and the personal conscience; individual aspirations and the ego-ideal; the rigidity factor and compulsive repetition (*Wiederholungszwang*).

All these factors determine the personal configuration, profile, or character. The individual expresses himself through his over-all conduct or particular style of life, which becomes more or less stable and which maintains itself through the ego, or heart, by means of the defense mechanisms.

We might illustrate the intimate relationship between the factors enumerated by the following very simple case in which we see the operation of the repressive defense mechanism.

A sixteen-year-old is doing his homework one evening. His mother calls him to dinner. He does not hear her, does not want to hear, and does not move. Why? Because he enjoys his reading and his study; he is absorbed; he does not want to be disturbed (the id). He is afraid of not being able to finish his homework and getting a detention (the superego). He is right in the middle of puberty and is developing an ego-ideal or independent existential purpose. Relations between mother and son are somewhat strained. "She can call me again!" Or perhaps, "I'll get even with her and assert myself a bit, and teach her to stop treating me like a child!" This quickly develops into habitual cantankerousness (repetition and rigidity). The repressive energy is thus supplied convergently from a number of different sources.

On the basis of certain propulsive tendencies, precedents, and experiences, a fundamental attitude is prepared, formed, and gradually crystallized in every man; a character or approach to life which might be summed up in general axioms such as "attack is better than defense," "if you fail at the first try, it's best to give up altogether," "everything will turn out all right—you just have to hold fast and try again," "never do today what you can put off until tomorrow, " "honesty is the best policy," "if you're honest, you're bound to be a sucker," "don't trust anyone—you have to do everything yourself if you don't want it to go wrong," "power and prestige are everything!" "it's dangerous and harmful to admit you're wrong," "live and let live—take it easy!"

In each of these cases we have a fundamental attitude or personal style of life. The over-all style of life or individual profile of a person is the climax of his biography. The human being *is* what he has *become*. Our vital needs for affection, security, independent activity, development are canalized by the education we have received. This socialization can take place harmoniously and satisfactorily, but it can also lead to stern repression and frustration. A child who constantly hears his parents saying, "He's a very difficult boy, naughty and disobedient," and who is treated accordingly, eventually says, "I am bad, unlikable" (introjection, identification). In general, we are very much inclined to adopt the views of our fellow men, especially in the case of authorities, or else to adopt the contrary position in protest. Thus, for example, "we have to decide for him" becomes, "I am not capable of making personal decisions." "We expect a great deal of you" becomes "I have to do everything as perfectly as possible," or "it's hopeless anyway, so there's no use in trying." "We are all corrupt through and through and we must systematically repress our instincts" becomes "I have to control myself with an iron hand," or "I don't dare face my own sexuality; I must deny it as something taboo," or again, "if *they* claim I'm bad, then I'll show them they're right!"

The very strictly brought-up child goes out into life inhibited and fearful; he tries to avoid any uncertainties and the demands of every new situation—a process which of course takes place largely in the sphere of the unconscious. His first experiences teach him a very special defense tactic. He escapes into daydreams, avoids contacts, tries to remain a little child (regression), takes shelter behind aggressiveness and falsehood for fear of losing all affection. . . . Gradually this fundamental attitude toward himself and others is consolidated into his own profile, which is characterized by automatic repetition and a stereotyped continuity. It is this last factor especially—compulsive repetition, rigidity, or hardening—which provides the energy for the defense mechanisms of the ego (the hardened heart).

This heaviness of the persistent ego is described by St. Augustine in a striking image. "Conversion and the confession of your sin involves a struggle against yourself. Not only against the devil, but against your bad habits; against the years of your previous bad life, which draw you down into your rut and hold you back from change . . . You are burdened with the load of the past . . ." [12]

To sum up, the defense mechanisms can be described as a psychic activity of the ego, or the heart, which is essentially conditioned by the individual structure of the personality with its past, its present situation, its aspirations, and its future plans as by a rigidity factor (hardening). This structure is nourished by the energy of the instinctual tendencies; it includes both conscious levels and unconscious regions; it functions to set aside disturbing elements and unpleasant factors in order to protect the individual's personal balance.

Shifting responsibility

Long before psychology brought up the problem of the defense mechanisms, the religious man knew that the confession of his sin meant overcoming tenacious resistance and concealment tactics.

The story of Eden in the book of Genesis describes the phenomenon in colorful pages which are undoubtedly among the finest in world literature. Adam and Eve, representing man (Mr.

and Mrs. Everyman), have tasted the forbidden fruit and are guilty of infidelity and rebellion against God. After the fall, they hide from Yahweh, who calls to them to give an account of themselves. They feel naked in His presence, guilty, ashamed, anxious; yet they are not prepared to acknowledge their guilt. Adam at once adduces alibis to establish his innocence. He does not deny his action, but puts the responsibility on his wife—and indirectly on God Himself: if You hadn't given me Eve, I should not have been tempted! Eve, in her turn, tries to clear herself by blaming the serpent which tempted her (see Gn 3). It would be difficult to find a better illustration of man's tendency to "wash his hands among the innocent." [13]

To exonerate ourselves means to seek reasons and point to outside influences to show that the responsibility for some misdeed is not ours, St. Augustine explains.[14] And excuses abound, as he observes in a number of passages. We can plead fate or chance to explain our conduct. We can accuse the devil or make God responsible, since He creates and governs all things. It is even easier to point to our instincts and to personify them in mythological figures: Mars makes me irascible and aggressive, Venus makes me erotic and adulterous, Saturn makes me miserly . . .[15] St. Augustine again, who may be regarded as the Church's authorized spokesman in the matter, continually cautions against the danger of such an attitude. The man who justifies himself and refuses to admit his offense honestly simply cannot be pardoned by God and set free.

Significantly, Augustine constantly sets *defense* against *confession*. "The sinner who perseveres in his sins heaps up sins upon sins. Instead of purifying himself of his sins by self-accusation, he multiplies through his defense what could be removed by confession." [16] In connection with the man who seeks to hide from the divine omnipresence, Augustine quotes Psalm 139: "If I asked darkness to cover me, and light to become night around me, that darkness would not be dark to you, night would be as light as day" (11–12). Like St. John, he uses the notion of darkness in the allegorical sense of sin and hardening of heart.

> Do not darken your darkness; then God will not enshroud you in darkness but in light. Who are those who darken their darkness? Bad and corrupt men. When they sin, they become

darkness. When they refuse to confess the sins they have committed, but instead justify them, then they engulf themselves in still deeper darkness. If you have sinned, you are in darkness. But by confessing your darkness, you deserve to have your darkness lit up. If, on the other hand, you justify your darkness, you make it darker still. And how will you ever extricate yourself from this twofold darkness if you already have so much trouble with a single darkness? [17]

The experience of guilt and the knowledge of his state of sin create an intolerable condition of discomfort in the sinner. Searing remorse puts man to flight, like a house with a leaking roof or a room filled with suffocating smoke.[18] But it is impossible for man to escape his guilty conscience. It follows him as relentlessly as his own shadow. "Where shall I fly? Where shall I find refuge? On top of what mountain? In what cave? In what fortress? To what citadel shall I flee, with what walls shall I surround myself? Wherever I go, I am always myself to myself. You can flee anything but your conscience. Go into your house, go to bed, withdraw into your inmost self . . . There is no inner room where you can escape your conscience when your sins prey on you." [19]

Adam could not hide from God; nor could Jonas:

> Yahweh, you examine me and know me,
> you know if I am standing or sitting,
> you read my thoughts from far away . . .
> you know every detail of my conduct.
> The word is not even on my tongue,
> Yahweh, before you know all about it;
> close behind and close in front you fence me round,
> shielding me with your hand . . .
> Where could I go to escape your spirit?
> Where could I flee from your presence?
>
> (Ps 139:1–7; cf. Ws 1:7–9)

"You can, of course, take refuge in your house, in your most secret chamber and in your own heart," comments St. Augustine. "But God is present in your heart. Wherever you flee, He is there . . . So there is no other way of escaping a wrathful God than by seeking refuge with a reconciled God. Or rather, there is nowhere to flee. You want to flee far from Him? In that case flee right to Him!" [20]

Elsewhere, St. Augustine writes that man can be so bad as to deprive God of the possibility of having pity on him, particularly when he takes the defense of his sins, for in that case he is defending what God hates.[21] And again: "Just as God hates the man who defends his sins, so he raises up the man who confesses them." [22]

By sin, we sever our union with God and refuse to recognize that we were created *servants of Yahweh* and *handmaids of the Lord*. Thus man's deepest and most ineradicable need, for security and peace, remains unsatisfied. His uneasy conscience and sense of sin demonstrate this need to him. As every being fights off its own disintegration, the guilt-ridden individual will defend himself against his negative feelings of shame, of anxiety, of uncertainty, of being out of touch, of alienation, and of loneliness. Instinctively he aims at restructuring his personality and restoring the totality of his being. This tendency may be observed even at the biological level. An impaired and frustrated organism exerts a vital defensive activity and seeks to adapt itself. We have only to consider the natural healing of wounds. But there too the restructuring and the healing process sometimes take pathological forms. Then the cells begin to proliferate at random. A warning signal may activate the defense mechanisms, but in a chaotic and anarchic manner.

That, roughly, is what the sinner does when he tries to allay his anxious conscience by defending himself against accusation. He exonerates himself, uses anesthetics and inappropriate compensations. But this pharisaical self-therapy or self-justification gives him only an artificial relief. Genuine healing can come only with the acceptance of pardon and with absolution. And this presupposes the honest confession of sin. To quote St. Augustine again: "The more a man tries to justify his sins on the basis of his own merits and refusing to recognize his iniquity, the more he undermines his strength and his energy. The strong man is one who relies not on his own strength but on God's." [23] Luther brilliantly elaborates on this theme. When my conscience accuses me, he says, and I confess my guilt, then Jesus Christ becomes my Defender. And because He takes my defense, I need no longer take my own. When I come forth from behind the thick shrubbery (Adam, where are you?) and frankly confess my sin, the God who demands a reckoning becomes my Savior who absolves me.[24]

Consequently, before the *evangelist* comes to announce the good news of God's reconciliation with sinful man, the *prophet* must probe man's receptiveness and, if need be, help him to recognize his guilt and confess his sin. On that condition alone can there be any transition "from refusal to petition," as Gabriel Marcel puts it. This, clearly, is an extremely important aspect of pastoral action and not an easy one.

Gregory the Great, in his pastoral counsels, reminds us that the guilty are reluctant to admit their faults and do everything to excuse them. This self-justification, nurtured by a life style that has become rigid (the hardened and blinded heart), disconcerts the pastor. He is bewildered by the staggering duplicity of the guilty, to the point of doubting what he had previously taken for granted concerning them. In his colorful style, St. Gregory compares the sinner to a hedgehog. First, you see its head, its feet, and its whole body. But as soon as you stretch out your hand to grasp it, it rolls up in a ball, tucks in its feet, and hides its head; at the same time, its quills bristle. That is how the dishonest soul protects itself when confronted by its fault. Let us say that we have discovered the capital sin which has led the sinner to all the other vices. We have uncovered the paths of iniquity which he has followed. But the perfidious sinner hides his head and rolls up in a ball like the hedgehog. He makes all sorts of excuses to conceal his misdeeds and his failings. Rolled up in a ball and turned in on himself, he takes refuge in his impenetrable conscience behind the quills of his self-justification.[25]

The background of exculpation and self-justification

We come, finally, to the question of the dynamic background of the exculpatory tendency. Whence comes our tendency to deny that we have sinned? Why do we so stubbornly resist the confession of our offense? What is the driving force of the defense mechanisms which we deploy to escape a distressing self-accusation?

For a general reply to this question, we refer to the analyses of the structure of the ego, or of the heart, with its power of resistance. Our fundamental option, our existential purpose and our over-all life style determine the profile of our personality; and our personality secures itself against disintegration or self-reformation through the defense mechanisms, and thus maintains its rigidity. It would be interesting to study the application of this principle to the ego structure of the sinner, who regards confession as a threat from which he instinctively recoils. There can be no question here, however, of any such detailed study.[26] We shall confine ourselves to pointing out two factors which in many cases may inspire, nurture, or reinforce the exculpatory tendency. They are among the many components of the ego.

The first, which we might call a genetic element, is the actual experience of the child of a particular form of upbringing which conditions the development of a sense of sin. The second concerns the more deliberate structuring of the adult's moral and religious approach.

Cultural anthropology, or the comparative study of cultures and systems of education, shows that the parent-child relationship in our Western civilization is based on and inculcates a morality of retribution. As always with attractive theories, we have to beware of oversimplification and hasty generalization. Nevertheless, there are many, it would seem, who in their childhood had very exacting parents and teachers: parents who gave their child love and affection exclusively or mainly in exchange for his qualities and what he could give them in return. In such a case, tenderness and acceptance are bestowed only as a reward; and that, too, is how they are experienced. The child has to *deserve* his haven of peace and the warmth of the nest by exemplary behavior, by bringing home good report cards and generally achieving outstanding results. We thus have adults who in their childhood rarely knew what it meant to be unconditionally and totally accepted. They never really experienced what it meant to be loved altogether gratuitously and regardless of many faults and failings. And so they do not realize now that it is possible to be accepted by another even though they may be "unacceptable."

The atmosphere in a good number of families seems to be that a child can deserve love and hope for security only to the extent that there is not the slightest cloud in the sky and that the child's conduct is above criticism. It might even be said, somewhat paradoxically, that self-accusation is punished. For the child who "dares" confess must expiate and pay. Of course, he is punished for misdeeds he really committed, but the fact remains that, had he not confessed, he would not have been punished! That, at least, is how the child "lives" the situation. Confession is not accepted as a sign of repentance, conversion, asking forgiveness, and reconciliation. When parents, through their prohibitions and their accusing presence, become in the child's eyes the personification of the threat of abandonment, withdrawal of love, contempt, and rejection, then the basic human duad becomes that of the accuser and the culprit, of the judge and the convicted malefactor.

In such an atmosphere the child becomes, as it were, panic-stricken when he happens to make a mistake or contravene an order through stubbornness or unruliness. The situation then becomes in practice such that it is really impossible for him to acknowledge his misdeeds and to ask and receive pardon. He never has a chance to experience a freely offered reconciliation. He does not learn that one can be loved despite one's ingratitude, and without having claims to acceptance. In a word, the child grows up in an atmosphere in which he is obliged to defend himself at all costs by concealing or denying his faults. The instinct of self-preservation functions automatically. The panic fear of losing the affection of his parents forever prompts the child to avoid admitting his offense by whatever means he can.

The inculcation of a healthy guilt sense and training in confession of sin begin in the earliest years of a child's life. This, again, is a matter for domestic pastoral action.

One of the most elementary principles of education is that the child should not be forced to disregard or deny his physical and intellectual limitations. This applies *a fortiori* to his moral and religious failings,[27] since the grown man's relation to God is largely conditioned by the relations he had as a child with his parents and teachers. An identical or analogous behavior pattern occurs at either level. The child's first encounter with God is in the family. We might even go so far as to say that he does not yet make any distinction between God and parents. Trust, love, fear, rebellion, gratitude to father and mother, imply the same attitude toward God. Some psychologists claim, indeed, that religion is no more than the projection of the father image and of the parent-child relationship into the universe and the sphere of metaphysics:

man has created God in his own image and likeness. Or rather, man has created God according to the pattern set by his parents and teachers.

This approach actually contains a great truth. Man creates his God in the image of his parents. This individual experience is the starting point and determines the orientation and tone of that creation. Basically, all that we know, is taken from our contact with the reality of the senses. No one has ever seen God. We know Him only indirectly, as through a blurred mirror—although we can and should subsequently correct this representation of God by listening with faith to what He communicates to us through His revelation concerning the inner mystery of His being. That process of refinement becomes particularly difficult, however, when the parent-child relationship has not been harmonious, so that the child's affectivity has been disturbed and he has come to form a distorted notion of God. An unbalanced father-son relationship only too often results in what St. Paul calls exchanging "the glory of the immortal God for a worthless imitation, for the image of mortal man" (Rm 1:23) or, worse still, for a monstrous idol.

Thus it is that the image of God in many people's minds reflects the features of their own fathers: an exacting and pitiless guardian whose affection and esteem must be laboriously merited; or a being in whom a trace of indulgence and clemency is rarely to be found. The words *mercy* and *pardon* remain for them meaningless and without content. These are experiences that they have barely known. "Our Father, who art in heaven" means for them, in practice, "Dreadful Judge, who ruthlessly punishes sin and disobedience . . ."

In this tragic development we recognize the transference mechanism. The habit formed in childhood of at all costs avoiding the admission of guilt is transferred and transposed to the moral and religious sphere and becomes a generalized tendency to protect oneself against any confession of wrongdoing. In such an atmosphere, it becomes impossible to approach God, to see in Him the merciful father of the parable who is overjoyed to recover the son he had lost. "If the young child's guilt sense was so painful and so strong that a protective system totally suppressed it, the subject will refuse to admit any real guilt, even if it is justified, because it will reactivate the anxiety which must at all costs be stifled." [28]

If we bear this substratum in mind, we shall form some understanding of the fact that some people come ultimately to live their guilt in an hermetically closed circle.[29] They feel their guilt, of course, and they are ashamed of their moral insufficiency, but in an egocentric manner. They do not enter into communion with their neighbor or with God. In their eyes no one is prepared to accept them despite their unworthiness; no one is great and merciful enough to grant them his pardon and freely deliver them from sin.

It is hardly surprising, therefore, that this *morbid* guilt sense should produce neurotic forms of behavior activated by the defense mechanisms.[30] The autistic individual will either seek to rid himself of his heavy burden of guilt by denying his responsibility and, in the process, resort to rationalization, minimization, projection, and other maneuvers; or he will feel increasingly crushed under the burden of his guilt, reflect on his shame without prospect of pardon, and *eat his heart out*. He will try to expiate the injustice he has committed and set himself free by his own efforts. He will seek salvation in excessive mortifications or in a masochistic self-punishment as a form of compensation. But it will all be to no avail.

The same principle holds at the purely human level. Our offense can be pardoned only if we are prepared to be delivered from it. But the *sine qua non*, here, is that we should recognize that another is free in relation to our offense: one who is not caught in the false dilemma of conniving in and justifying a wrong on the one hand, or harboring resentment and demanding expiation with pitiless severity on the other; one who permits us to escape from the closed circle of the egocentric experience of guilt; one at whose hands we may experience an objective judgment (censure) as well as limitless compassion.

This applies even more on the moral and religious level. To develop a genuine and healthy Christian sense of guilt means learning to see our sin with the eyes of faith in the light of the revelation of salvation. Only thus can we come to see sin as the attitude of an ungrateful creature who fails to appreciate God's love and who offends his greatest benefactor, while at the same time retaining our confidence in God as in one who is ready for reconciliation and who offers us His grace through Jesus Christ. Thus while our offense remains a real sin, it may also obtain pardon for us if we will only confess it.

Behind the phenomena of psychology and pedagogy, of course, we find the outlines of the fundamental categories of theology. Ultimately everything turns on the essential problem of law and grace, of holiness through works and redemption. Either we opt for a morality of reward and punishment, for a self-justification through our good works and our merits (legalistic religion, pharisaism), or we accept justification as an undeserved grace and a pure gift of God.[31]

Every man progressively forms an image of himself, an idealized representation in which he recognizes himself or to which he endeavors to conform. But what matters to us most is what others, and particularly those in authority, expect of us. We are prisoners of other people's opinion of us. The experience of feelings of shame and guilt unseal our eyes. Pitilessly they remind us of our omissions or transgressions and we feel we are being pilloried. The more exalted the ego-ideal, the more disconcerting is the awakening: the demands are too exacting, the task beyond our powers. There follows a sort of moral and religious megalomania, a type of perfectionism or angelism. But as the old saying goes, it is dangerous to bite off more than we can chew. Utopianism leads sooner or later to discouragement. At first, perhaps, we may grasp at other exalted ideals, equally impossible of achievement, but this only adds to the list of our failures and confirms our feeling of inadequacy. And since there is no prospect of pardon, resistance to the admission of guilt becomes stronger than ever—for at least we must preserve our dignity . . .

This brings us to the second factor which may condition or nurture the exculpatory tendency: the concept of sin in the context of an apersonalist ethic. Is it not true to say that many of our contemporaries conceive of sin as a violation of a law, as a breach or a nonobservance of a principle or a duty?

This occurs when, following perhaps in the footsteps of Kant, we regard the moral law as autonomous. Law and justice then appear as a kind of absolute and irresistible power governing the whole universe (immanent justice). In that context, ethics is dissociated from religion. Obviously in such a case there is no room left for pardon. The law must take its course. How could an impersonal principle or an objective order be merciful? This radical impossibility will subsist even if God is subsequently and artificially reintroduced in the system, since this God will have, as it were, to obey the supreme law in His turn. He becomes the guardian and preserver of the unwavering rule. His office being to ensure respect for the law, He must require payment of compensation in case of infraction. For the law brooks no exception. . . . In other words, God becomes an intermediary figure between the abstract or supreme Good and man. He is given the role of supervisor, of judge. The highest court is the moral law, not God.

Needless to say, this has little in common with the biblical approach, where morality is subordinated to religion and the law is not autonomous, but where God is the absolute sovereign. God can remit sin and pardon the sinner who confesses and is sorry for his offense. There is room for reconciliation. In this view, sin is not primarily a breach of a law but rebellion against God, an act of infidelity or adultery, an act of ingratitude, a breach between the Lord and His servant, between the child and his Father, between bride and bridegroom.

In a word, the exculpatory tendency and the refusal to admit one's guilt become virtually inevitable in a purely juridical, areligious, or humanistic ethics, since the interpersonal relations linking man to his God are lacking. A God can pardon, blot out, reward, writes Simone de Beauvoir, but if God does not exist, man's offenses are inexpiable.[32] And one can understand that the proponents of a "tragic anthropology," who regard all forms of belief or religion as illusion, should maintain that the idea of a God who pardons is but the facile solace which the weak grant to their own sense of guilt.[33]

The parables and the defense mechanisms

Before proceeding to a more detailed investigation of the defensive tactics employed in the service of the exculpatory tendency, we should return briefly to the parables mentioned earlier.

Prophetic preaching aims first and foremost at challenging

man's conscience, so that he may recognize his guilt and come to confess his sin. The method of indirect persuasion, as used in the parables, seems the most effective in this respect. When man is confronted with himself as in a mirror, he may come, despite his blindness and hardness of heart, to pronounce a new value judgment on his own action. This approach opens up abundant possibilities for a pastoral action which emphasizes the value of the prophetic function.

In the first place, we have to announce the parables themselves. Through His prophets and through His Son, Jesus Christ, God speaks to men of all times. In our day, too, the parables hold a message, provided, of course, that they are adapted to our times and updated (*aggiornamento*), so that the listener may existentially feel that they are addressed to him personally. Next, we can try to create new parables and use current situations or events to reformulate the eternal Gospel.[34] In order to help man to judge himself objectively, we may also, instead of telling a parable, *show* and describe his defense mechanisms.

That is why in the present study we deal both with biblical parables and with psychic defense mechanisms, which at first sight would appear to have little in common. Both the parables and the description of defense mechanisms enable us to step back from ourselves and thus, despite our blindness of heart or the rigidity of our personality structure, to adopt a fresh approach.

The concept of a model may serve as a link between the parables and the defense mechanisms.[35]

Through the discovery of the microcosm (electromagnetic phenomena, atoms, etc.) which cannot be made visible to the human eye, the natural sciences found themselves in a position which the philosophers and theologians had encountered before them: they were forced to concede that both our imagination and our conceptual language are inadequate when we seek to present reality adequately. The conclusion is unavoidable that our words are not altogether accurate and univocal, although neither are they altogether devoid of meaning and equivocal. This tension between *not altogether accurate* and at the same time *not completely untrue* means that we must assume an analogous relationship. This is the basic insight, of course, which supports all philosophical and theological speculation.

The natural scientists, and Maxwell in particular, have introduced the *model* category along these lines. They argue that it is possible to make the phenomena of the microcosm intelligible through analogies taken from the macrocosm. The object of these transpositions or analogies is not so much to produce faithful representations of a reality which must forever escape us, but rather theoretical representations or configurations built up from scratch.

At the same time, such models (for example, the atom in the form of a planetary system) are not arbitrarily conceived. They correspond to laws and relationships which may be observed in time and space. The diagram serves as a working hypothesis. It aims at unifying the discoveries made and rendering them a little more intelligible, but it also serves as an excellent research tool, making possible *inter alia* certain calculations (heuristic value). The model thus stands approximately halfway between the symbol and the abstract concept.

Dynamic depth psychology was born in the technological era. It employs the same thought processes. It conceives of the psyche and of man's affective life in terms of a technological device (the ego with its defense mechanisms situated between the superego and the id) displaying causal interactions. Mental and emotional disturbances are described in the manner of conflicts within a disorganized undertaking.

So long as we do not lose sight of the hypothetical and provisional character of a thought model, this method is unobjectionable. But alas, psychoanalysts have not always respected these caveats. And they have felt themselves capable of adequately and fully (but univocally) explaining the human psyche by their mechanistic categories of cause and effect. We have referred to this misunderstanding earlier in the present study. When defense mechanisms are defined as constitutive structures or as behavior configurations, this cannot be understood as representing static realities or spatial figures. They are figures extending into the time dimension and expressing man's historicity, rather as a single melodic theme is recognizable in different variations. We may thus speak of dynamic structures of human behavior to the extent that such behavior is repeated and establishes itself like a persistent melody of action.

This approach has some analogy with certain biblical parables. There, too, an invisible supernatural reality is clarified through a dynamic *event* and not always through a *static* symbol. This is true, for example, of the parables which begin with the stereo-typed introduction: "The kingdom of heaven is like . . ." (an employer who hires laborers for his vineyard, stewards who administer their master's property in different ways, bridesmaids awaiting the opening of the nuptial feast . . .).

We are living in an age of technology and in a world of machines and devices. It is scarcely surprising, then, that a mode of thinking which takes account of *defense mechanisms* to clarify the operations of our interior life should suit us better than images taken from nature or situations familiar to the East.

In the parables, the sinner recognizes himself as in a mirror; he is helped to become aware of his sin and to confess it. Our aim in the chapters that follow is to achieve the same result through a description and an analysis of the defense mechanisms. Confronted with these personality structures, man is made capable of recognizing himself, understanding his own position, and accepting his responsibility. By two different roads we arrive at a method of clarification which makes it possible to discover a latent fault by lifting to the level of consciousness what had previously lain buried and in darkness.

Notes

1. *Enarr. Ps.*, C.C.L., 39, 1410.
2. Aristotle, *Nicomachean Ethics*, VII, 5, 1147. *"Concupiscentia quaerit latebras et dolose subintrat,"* writes St. Thomas Aquinas, in *Summa Theologiae*, II–II, 156,4.
3. See I. Caruso, *Soziale Aspekte der Psychoanalyse*, Stuttgart, E. Klett, 1962, p. 13.
4. See J. Brehm, "Postdecision Changes in the Desirability of Alternatives," in *Journal of Abnormal and Social Psychology*, Washington, D.C., 1956, and L. Festinger, "Some Attitudinal Consequences of Forced Decisions," in *Proceedings of the Fifteenth International Congress of Psychology*, Brussels, 1957.
5. A. Goerres, *Methode und Erfahrung der Psychoanalyse*, Munich, Kösel, 1958.
6. See H. Reiner, *Pflicht und Neigung*, Meisenheim Glan, West-kultur–Verlag A. Hain, 1951, p. 122; H. Ey, *La conscience*, Paris, Presses universitaires de France, 1963; D. Rapaport, "La théorie de

l'autonomie du Moi," *Revue française de psychoanalyse*, Paris, G. Doin, 1964, p. 344.

7. L. Lavelle, *Les puissances du Moi*, Paris, Flammarion, 1948, p. 12.
8. G. Madinier, *Conscience et signification*, Paris, Presses universitaires de France, 1953, p. 61.
9. St. Augustine, *Confessions* (tr. F. J. Sheed), New York, Sheed & Ward, 1951, book VIII, p. 220.
10. *Ibid.*
11. H. Thomae, *Der Mensch in der Entscheidung*, Munich, Barth, 1960.
12. *Enarr. Ps.*, C.C.L., 38, 1039.
13. This expression, which has passed into many languages, also comes from the Bible (see Dt 21:6; Ps 26:6 and 73:13; Is 1:16; Mt 27:24). It is based on a Jewish practice symbolizing that a man is innocent, that he declines all responsibility in a matter, and that he places the consequences of an action at the door of another. Originally, the expression probably signified purifying one's hands of the blood of a slain man.
14. *Sermo 29 de V.T.*, C.C.L., 41, 374.
15. *Enarr. Ps.*, C.C.L., 38, 236.453; 39, 740.1280; 40, 1887.
16. *Ibid.*, C.C.L., 40, 2017.
17. *Ibid.*, C.C.L., 40, 2000.
18. *Ibid.*, 39, 1410.
19. *Ibid.*, 38, 196.
20. *Ibid.*, 39, 1031.
21. *Ibid.*, 39, 740.
22. *Ibid.*, 40, 2106.
23. *Ibid.*, 383, 232.
24. *Cor defensor, Deus accusator;*
    Cor accusator, Deus defensor.
25. *Liber Regulae Pastoralis*, XI (see note 14 to chapter 1).
26. The reader who desires a fuller treatment of the question can consult works of moral theology and psychology on the problem of sin and guilt. Among the best recent works, we might mention J. G. McKenzie, *Guilt, Its Meaning and Significance*, New York–Nashville, Abingdon Press, 1962.
27. This is not an argument in favor of the elimination of all punishment or all disciplinary action in education.
28. C. Nodet, in *Monde moderne et sens du péché*, Paris, P. Horay, 1956, p. 171.
29. J. Pohier, "La pénitence, vertu de la culpabilité chrétienne," in *La vie spirituelle, Supplément*, 1962, p. 377.
30. "It might be preferable not to have a sense of sin if it is not offset by grace" (P. Simon in *Monde moderne et sens du péché*, Paris, P. Horay, 1956, p. 212).
31. Two more examples of a fundamental attitude (see p. 141, as indicated above) are the following: "Better to be always unfortunate

than to have to live with a conscience seared with remorse or guilt sentiments" (result of an education in contradiction with 1 Jn 3:19–20: "By this we shall know that we are of the truth, and reassure our hearts before him whenever our hearts condemn us; for God is greater than our hearts"); "You don't really begin to be a Christian until duty becomes difficult" (as though *virtue* were synonymous with *sacrifice*).

32. S. de Beauvoir, *Ethics of Ambiguity*, New York, Citadel, 1962.
33. L. Flam, *L'Homme et la conscience tragique*, Paris, Presses universitaires de France, 1964. But there are also those who become atheists because they cling fiercely to their innocence. "Atheism, as far as I am concerned, has no other meaning than the refusal to accept guilt" (F. Jeanson, "Athéisme et liberté," in *Lumière et Vie*, 1954, no. 13, p. 93).
34. This corresponds by and large to what takes place unconsciously in certain very significant dreams.

It is a generally accepted belief, and the Bible is no exception to it, that dreams often have an important message for us. Depth psychology has reminded us of this once more. In colorful language, accompanied by intense feeling, the dream portrays, retrospectively or prospectively, something in our personal life. Its message is presented in the form of symbols and offers us, as in a mirror, a revelation of ourselves. We are confronted with our past, informed concerning our present condition, instructed concerning future possibilities. Dreams can play an important part in the exploration of the secret sources of our action.

We should not dismiss a dream as an illusion or as unimportant (the deceitfulness of dreams!), since it is capable of clarifying and orienting our existence. An old rabbinical saying has it that a dream that we do not take to heart is like a letter that we receive and refuse to read. A dream is "the encounter of the dreamer with his inner self." Its purpose is "to bring us to experience what has as yet been incompletely experienced" (I. Caruso, *Bios, Psyche, Person*, Freiburg, Alber, 1957, p. 202; an important study of the dream is presented on pages 162–201). Other interesting works on the subject are: M. Boss, *Der Traum und seine Auslegung*, Bern, 1953; W. Wolff, *Dream, Mirror of Conscience*, New York, Grune and Stratton, 1952; A. Resch, *Der Traum im Heilsplan Gottes*, Freiburg, Herder, 1964.
35. Cf. *The Concept and Role of the Model in Mathematics and Natural and Social Sciences*, ed. Hans Freudenthal, New York, Gordon and Breach, 1961; J. Auer, *Die Bedeutung der Modell-Theorie für die Hilfsbegriffe des katholischen Dogmas*, in Festschrift Soehngen, Freiburg, Herder, 1962, p. 259.

6

Repression

Repression, rejection, oblivion

The most elementary means of defense is to ignore a danger, to protect oneself by repressing it. Freud's great contribution is to have shown that this mechanism is the mainspring of all subsequent defensive tactics. By repression or inhibition, psychoanalysts mean an activity whereby we banish certain perceptions from our consciousness because they conflict with an evaluative principle in our personality. The aim of such defensive action is to protect the structure of the ego against psychic factors incompatible with our concepts of values and standards. The superego and the ego-ideal unconsciously exercise a certain censorship.

Considerable emphasis has recently, and justifiably, been placed on the need for situating this phenomenon in a broader perspective.[1]

Repression presents an undeniable analogy with rejection and oblivion. An emotion, a desire, an idea, or an experience can absorb us to the point where everything else is excluded from the field of consciousness. This phenomenon is bound up with the limitation of our being. It is impossible for us to be intensely preoccupied with several things at once. Thus, an act of the will or some intellectual activity can be thrust aside by emotion; or again, a biological need can be superseded by a spiritual factor. As a general rule, working out ideas, listening to music, suffering with a toothache, or dealing with some plan that must be urgently carried out are all mutually exclusive occupations. This is sometimes referred to as a *shrinking of consciousness*.[2]

This kind of repression has some analogy with a revolving door. Perception and automotion are interdependent: by moving, I make a new perception possible; and in observing, I involuntarily move in order to see the object better, to hear it or to feel it. We cannot see the inside of a house without going in, but we no longer see it once we are outside. The principle here is that of *mutual invisibility*.

With oblivion we go further. Forgetting something means that a psychic content eludes our field of consciousness. Here the time factor plays a part. A phenomenon of erosion or disintegration takes place. But more is involved than duration. Forgetting fulfills an economic function in our existence. If everything that we had ever experienced, felt, or thought always remained present to our minds, life would become impossible. Anything that overloads the consciousness and asks too much of the memory is instinctively set aside. We automatically forget whatever is momentarily unimportant, unnecessary, or uninteresting. An element which has lost its usefulness and become superfluous for a person pales and falls into oblivion. Its place is taken by others. There is a kind of rivalry between our experiences, so that one has to vacate the premises to make room for the next.

Unpleasant experiences especially are obliterated. Time heals every wound, the saying goes. On the other hand, there are persons who like to recall the difficult days of their past.

Nevertheless, we are able to recall at will a good part of what had been forgotten. Here we are dealing with the *latent unconscious*. Many events or names are in this category. That is why memory is both the faculty of retention and that of forgetting.

But there are also affective factors at work which do not coincide with the *important-harmful* duad. For example, at the moment of appearing before the examiner, a candidate suddenly forgets what he knew by heart a moment before; and he remembers it again immediately after failing his examination. Under the dominion of anxiety, our consciousness can thus be deprived of its most useful content. But the contrary also occurs. Thus we are capable of recalling at will quite unimportant episodes of our childhood—for example, a Sunday afternoon under a cherry-blossom tree. Yet the recollection evokes no more than sunlight, the humming of bees, and an inexpressible state of mind. Why do such experiences have such a tenacious hold on the memory? Perhaps they are important after all?

Repression presents striking analogies with rejection and oblivion. In each case, we have a spontaneous and unconscious activity. A selection takes place by which preference is given to certain psychic contents rather than others. This choice is individual and differs from person to person. It is conditioned by the individual's style of life. Nevertheless, a characteristic of repression is the rejection of unpleasant experiences. We repress when we reject and suppress feelings, perceptions, desires, and thoughts which give rise to some painful emotion. The following case, described by Freud, illustrates the point.

A young woman was much drawn to her brother-in-law, her older sister's husband. Suddenly her sister died. The young woman, quite unprepared, was brought in to view the body. For an instant only, the thought crossed her mind: now he is free and can marry me. Her ardent desire for her brother-in-law, which she had previously harbored unconsciously and inarticulately, had suddenly risen to the level of consciousness. But it was immediately and violently suppressed. Shortly thereafter, the young woman began to exhibit symptoms of hysteria.[3]

Here we have a typical inner conflict. On the one hand, the frightful, selfish desire to take the place of her sister; on the other, the spontaneous indignation of a conscience which will not tolerate adultery.

According to psychoanalytical theory, the process of repression consists in violently suppressing instinctive drives and keeping them away from the field of consciousness, without first examining them calmly and admitting to the concomitant emotions in one's heart. "I am too virtuous, too noble, too chaste, too intelligent, to old, too virile to permit such emotions, desires, hopes! Therefore this sensation is not mine! I am such that I cannot experience this desire!"

Repression and self-control

We repress what we cannot bear to look at and what we cannot accept because it is incompatible with some fundamental attitude of ours. Nevertheless, the essence of repression is not protest or reaction against a feeling or a desire, for that is characteristic of self-control too. Repression consists primarily in refusing to recognize the existence of the unpleasant element and relegating it to the unconscious. We simply do not want the thing to be true. We look the other way in order not to see it. We adopt the ostrich policy. Repression, therefore, is a game of hide-and-go-seek; it involves encasing ourselves in armor and closing ourselves up.

We exercise self-control, on the other hand, when we take the incipient tendency seriously and recognize it for what it is. We realize that a particular desire is incompatible with our moral and religious principles. We know that it is senseless, that we could not remain true to ourselves or happy were we to give in to it. We might find ourselves wishing, for instance, that another should fail in his endeavor, or even that he should die. The person with self-control will honestly admit that he has this desire. But he will think better of it and consider how he wants others to treat him (the golden rule) and what God demands of him through the voice of his conscience. In this way, he will come to understand why he cannot assent to this wish. His refusal thereby becomes meaningful. This is a reasoned and personal stand on a matter. In such a way we can set aside not only unpleasant and painful fantasies and desires, but even agreeable ones, and turn instead to the performance of an important and necessary, albeit disagreeable task. For man is an animal capable of sacrifice.

The Greeks noted long ago that a man who is tortured for his convictions is certainly not happy in the hedonistic and materialistic sense of the word, yet he would rather obey his conscience and suffer the consequences of his fidelity than enjoy the advantages or pleasures which would be the reward of his betrayal. He realizes that such betrayal of his better self would make him even more wretched than he is now.

The principal differences between repression and self-control might be summarized as follows: [4]

1. The content and object:
    We repress what is painful, unpleasant, disturbing, shameful and humiliating.
    We control that which, after careful examination, we find incompatible with our own personal value experience.
2. The motive and reason:

We repress out of uncertainty and fear of punishment; out of shame, fear, vanity, and pride.

We control ourselves because of respect for values perceived, because we want to be just, and because we realize that love of neighbor and of God requires this sacrifice.

3. The manner:

Repression takes place automatically and unconsciously and without mature reflection; it is the tense reaction of the man who does not have the courage to give in to temptation but who does not succeed, either, in clarifying the problem; he avoids a confrontation.

We exercise self-control in full awareness of what we are doing, freely and deliberately; we recognize that a problem exists and that there is an inner conflict; we come to a decision calmly.

4. The result:

Even after the troubling element has been repressed the anxiety and tension associated with it remain, as well as the sense of dissatisfaction and depression; the forbidden drive retains its dynamic force, but instead of being resolved in broad daylight, it seeks an outlet by provoking all kinds of symptoms.

Self-control leaves little or no bitterness; the renunciation has been decided level-headedly and produces a sense of freedom and autonomy; tendencies which had previously been contradictory and anarchical are unified more and more harmoniously and increasingly brought under control.

Forms of repression

As we said earlier, the central element of the phenomenon of repression must be sought in the refusal to confront the painful reality which is the cause of the anxiety. That, indeed, is why the complete term for the process is *repression into the unconscious.* We can drive unpleasant experiences as far from the field of consciousness as possible by simply denying them. That is the most extreme form of the mechanism of repression. We learn it prematurely, incidentally, as children. "You'll see how good it is," the adult tells the child as he gives him the bitter-tasting medicine. Or again, "Look, Mother will blow on your hurt hand and the pain will fly away!"

If this method of suggestion is used too often, a habit is formed of categorically denying a fact or an experience which had been clearly perceived. We teach the child to resort to magical formulas, developing an attitude which lends mysterious force to the word or to the simulated denial. This is why some adults think they can blot out an unpleasant experience by denying it categorically or persuasively. Such an approach is catastrophic not only for individuals but also for groups and even for whole nations, which may find themselves on the road to collective suicide because they have stubbornly ignored self-evident dangers.

There is yet another and more subtle form of repression, which is to make oneself immune to unpleasant perceptions. We nip them in the bud by refusing to recognize them. Even if we cannot always succeed in forgetting unpleasant or repulsive things, we can try to prevent any light falling on them. Our thought is clarified when it is articulated, even in our own minds; whence the tendency of excluding from our attention whatever is contrary to our desires and avoiding *conceptualization* or *verbalization*. We can be cowardly even in the realm of ideas, and "set them aside by closing our eyes" (Goethe).

This tactic of repression is applied to whatever is allegedly *not talked about*. The subjects are awkward ones, they are taboo. Either there is no appropriate term or, if we know it, we do not want to use it. This remarkable phenomenon of subtle repression, by which we do not permit certain contents to penetrate to clear consciousness, is well reflected in such expressions as "What the eye does not see, the heart cannot grieve for." Thus we protect ourselves with blinkers so as to avoid seeing our frightening surroundings. So often, in a group discussion, one of the participants will suddenly interrupt the train of thought with an outburst, a criticism, a reminder of the subject of the debate ("We're going off at a tangent!"). In the language of group dynamics, such a person is known as a blocker. The subject treated arouses feelings in him of anxiety, embarrassment, guilt, or shame. He realizes more or less clearly that any more thorough discussion of it might shed a painful light on the problem, and the threat must be warded off. This is negative repression: preventing a thing from being clarified through conceptualization and verbalization. If the moderator then draws the group's attention to the concealment tactic by asking, "What are we doing right now?" the person concerned will at once put forward several "valid" reasons for his conduct: the set program should be completed, or again, the conversation was on the point of becoming too painful for some other participant . . .

In the preceding Chapter we showed that the defense mechanisms operate in the service of the ego. We shall carry the discussion a little further in its particular application to repression.

We repress unpleasant experiences from the field of consciousness because they conflict with a normative principle. That principle is not, of course, the personal and adult conscience; when we listen to the voice of conscience, which reflects the voice of God, we control our instinctual drives, we do not repress them. The normative principle which causes this relegation must therefore be sought in the unconscious, in the two earlier phases of the not-yet-adult consciousness: the superego and the ego-ideal.

The superego is the ego identifying itself in enduring fashion with its first teachers. This regulatory system, operating unconsciously and automatically, is a product of the process of socialization by which the child gradually adopts and incorporates the imperatives and prohibitions of authority (introjection, internalization). This authoritarian and heteronomous aspect of the ego erects a barrier against the forces surging up from below which are experienced as inappropriate or threatening, since to give free rein to them would place the individual in conflict with the external world and with authority. Sexual and aggressive drives are repressed in this manner; but past experiences of our lives may be similarly repressed.

There is probably some connection, as psychoanalytical theory maintains, between this mechanism of repression and the anal phase of life, during which the child gradually learns to control himself and to discipline the sphincters. There is indeed a striking analogy between such terms as repress, inhibit, block, contract, etc., and the terms used to express the regulation of the organs of evacuation.

In addition to the superego, the child, but especially the adolescent, gradually develops an ego-ideal—an attractive model which constitutes as it were an autonomous and humanistic consciousness favorable to the structuring and development of the individual. This rather egocentric controlling image results from the identification of the young man with persons whom he admires. He wants to be like them; to be as brave, as powerful, as deserving of envy. Unlike the superego, which gives rise mainly to fear of punishment and guilt complexes, the ego-ideal arouses sentiments of shame and inferiority. One causes us to tremble, gives us the shivers, depresses us; the other makes us blush, for shame is a combination of anger and fear.

Just as the superego instinctively and unconsciously vetoes forbidden desires, so the ego-ideal resists whatever might compromise the individual's dignity and his tendency to make the most of himself. Whatever happens, the individual must not be lowered in his own eyes or lose the esteem of another. Nothing is so terrible at this phase of development as humiliation and scorn. "I can't bear to be made a laughing stock. I cannot accept these humiliating facts, therefore they do not exist!"

As Nietzsche put it in unforgettable, if somewhat theatrical, language: " 'I have done that,' says my memory. 'I cannot have done that,' says my pride, and remains inexorable. Eventually—memory yields." [5]

Whenever we have a chance to look at ourselves in a mirror and to see ourselves as we really are, we can measure the extent of this process of self-idealization for the sake of maintaining one's self-esteem. A very mild analogy would be a recording of our own voice on tape, revealing to us personal traits of which we had hitherto been unaware. Yet it not unfrequently happens that a person will refuse to use this acoustical mirror, because the image it reflects is too unflattering. We do not want to come down from our pedestal or to lose the halo we had bestowed upon ourselves. This overvaluation of self is a form of repression.

The question arises: what is the driving force of this inhibiting action? It is obviously very difficult, if not impossible, to give a universally valid answer to this question. Each individual case differs with the biographical background of the person concerned. But some general observations may throw a little light on the subject.

It would seem that the repressive energy is really supplied by a form of anxiety. Fear prevents us from looking truth in the face. If repression takes place mainly under the influence of the superego, the fear will be one of punishment or of losing security or the affection of the authorities. This is a fundamental uncertainty accompanied by a lack of confidence and courage. If, on the other hand, the inhibition is a product of the ego-ideal, the fear will be rather a panic fear of suffering contempt and humiliation. Here one is concerned first and foremost to preserve and develop his prestige. But the ego-ideal may also, and not infrequently, be set too high, and give rise to complacency, vanity, narcissism, or a kind of perfectionist complex. Repression comes into play as a defensive reflex against a threatened disintegration which generates anxiety. Anxiety is the emotion we experience when the internal balance of the psyche appears to be disturbed. The anxiety-gripped individual attempts to resolve the crisis engendered by the conflict in a radical but regressive manner, suppressing one of the elements of the conflict instead of integrating them both.

In many cases, the driving force of the dynamism of repression is probably concealed in an attitude which absolutizes some relative value. For man is so constituted that he cannot live without acknowledging and pursuing a supreme and absolute value. Our hearts are restless, made for the infinite, as St. Augustine puts it. This capacity, or hunger, should normally be directed toward God, the only being objectively able to satisfy it, if He is recognized as the supreme principle and value. But original sin describes a situation in which man has turned away from God. It follows that man gives himself over altogether to a relative and limited value, which is promoted to a virtually absolute value. "They have given up divine truth for a lie and have worshipped and served creatures instead of the Creator" (Rm 1:25).[6]

In saying this, St. Paul describes the universal situation of sinful man in every age who allows himself to be completely absorbed by created values and neglects God. Our substitute for God is concretized in one of our instincts with its correlative value of usefulness or pleasure, or in one of our fellow men, in society, in authority, in the ego itself. There is no dimension of our existence which has not been the subject of a pseudo-cult. This worship of a relative value means selling ourselves to an idol; it is not a matter of the intelligence as much as of the heart. We are prepared to sacrifice everything to it and become its slaves. Where our treasure is, there will our hearts be too (Mt 6:21). For no one can serve two masters (Mt 6:24).

Needless to say, in this area we are particularly open to delusion. Our existential god may be very different indeed from the God we explicitly claim to revere and serve.

In absolutizing a relative value, we lose contact with reality. We do not see objective reality as it really is. The center of gravity is displaced, with the fatal consequence that reality is twisted and falsified. Everything comes to be considered in a false light in terms of the idol to which we have attached ourselves. Facts which cannot be reconciled with the demands of what has been absolutized are simply not tolerated. We deny and repress distressing evidence. Our perception is itself disturbed and the famous "blind spots" make their appearance. Only if we are reconciled with God and give Him the place in our personal lives to which He is entitled can we be reconciled with the whole of reality.[7]

Repressed guilt

Freud and the first psychoanalysts were particularly concerned to examine inhibition as directed against the instinctual drives (the id) and the neurotic phenomena which occur in its wake. It has been claimed that they were thereby advocating the unbridled indulgence of sexual and aggressive passions and preaching libertinage as the sole solution. Such a generalization is a product of ignorance or bad faith. Modern depth psychologists are fundamentally consistent with their predecessors when they point out that repression can also operate in a contrary direction: man can also repress his conscience or his principles and reject the experience of guilt. In other words, he can repress the higher values just as well as the so-called inferior ones.[8]

This conclusion of contemporary psychology has of course uncovered nothing new. At best, it has given renewed currency to an age-old truth. One need only recall such expressions as "resisting the call to do good," "turning deaf ears to conscience or God," "stifling one's better impulses," "hardening one's heart." St. Paul speaks of the "flesh"—selfishness—warring against the Spirit (Ga 5:17). This may be compared with "everyone who does evil hates the light" (Jn 3:20). The Bible, of course, is full of prophetic appeals such as "consider!" "remember!" etc., based on the assumption that man is inclined deliberately to forget the truth or to keep God's Word far from his mind and heart.[9]

In this connection, theologians have developed a concept which broadly corresponds to repression: *ignorantia affectata*. This is ignorance resulting from self-interest: it is to our advantage not to know something. We deliberately remain ignorant of a fact or an obligation and refuse to seek information or ask advice through fear of having to revise our conduct or being tormented with remorse.[10]

Much of what has been said about the repression of instinctual drives applies directly to the repression of conscience. Here too we begin with an experience of displeasure and discomfort. It is humiliating to conclude that we are guilty, that we should and could have acted better than we did. Our sense of pride is offended. Our instinctive desire for harmony within ourselves rebels against whatever is the cause of our distress. To acknowledge that we have failed in our duty means a diminished satisfaction for the ego and frustration with its life-style and present aspirations.[11]

This applies in the first place to the retrospective guilty conscience, which accuses and reproaches us (*conscientia mala consequens*); but also to the prospective conscience, which raises its voice to forbid or to command (*conscientia antecedens*).

A closer examination will show that there is actually a connection between the repression of "inferior" values and the refusal of higher values. It might even be asserted, almost paradoxically, that the man who represses his instinctual drives at the same time implicitly and indirectly represses his conscience. For when we relegate unpleasant experiences to the unconscious in the name of the superego or the ego-ideal, we are refusing to recognize reality for what it is. We shirk our fundamental existential duty, which is to assume our responsibilities and take our own lives in hand. "Man is an animal with precepts," says Renouvier, after Kant. As men, it is incumbent upon us to become conscious and free, to attain to an adult plenitude of acceptance and love. This challenge to become ourselves by transcending our basic egotism is the genuine voice of our prospective conscience; it is God's invitation to us.[12]

From that point of view, all repression or inauthenticity is a retreat, an existential deficit and an omission: a life not lived but wasted, or self-alienation. Our deepest aspiration remains frustrated; our condition is one of sterility and infidelity to our own being, a kind of flight from ourselves. That is why we call this *existential culpability*, or failing in our duty to build up our own lives; we have not become what we could and should have become. Being unfaithful to our own nature, we thereby become unfaithful to God's plan. This wasted existence engenders dissatisfaction with oneself, a sense of frustration and remorse, generally formless and unconscious. "The man I am sadly salutes the man I might have been," says Hebbel. But when this latent experience of anxiety and culpability is repressed in its turn, an endless vicious circle is set up, an infernal chain of anxiety constantly renewed by repeated endeavors at repression. Stifling the mandatory summons in order to escape discomfort is a radical but illusory solution; its price is another wave of anxiety and guilt.[13]

Some forms of repression of conscience

Guilt is obviously repressed out of vanity, pride, and self-complacency: I simply cannot recognize and acknowledge myself to be what I now am, for that would mean a radical conversion and the restructuring of myself, which I do not want.

However, as we suggested earlier, this basic bad will may in part be the result of an inadequate knowledge of God. If there is no prospect of grace, the confession of sin and the actual experience of pardon become virtually impossible.

The negative confession formularies of ancient Egyptian burial literature provide a typical example of the refusal to assume one's culpability. The deceased, standing before Osiris, god of the underworld, enumerates all the misdeeds he has not committed. There is no question of confession of sin. The deceased even denies ever having regretted anything, or having *consumed* or *swallowed* his heart. "Oh my heart from my mother, oh my breast from the days I was on earth, do not rise up against me as a witness in the presence of the Lords of all things. Do not betray me by saying, 'he really did it,' about what I have done. Do not cause any trouble for me in the presence of the great god, the lord of the West [Osiris]."

The total absence of prayers or confession of sin in the texts on the pyramids is very striking. We find hymns of adoration and thanksgiving, but there is never any question of repentance or asking pardon.

The magic virtue of incantatory formulas is regarded as rendering superfluous any prayer for pardon. Because of the dynamic background of anxiety and belief in salvation through works, without prospect of a generous pity, man is driven to deny his sin. The smooth scarab, the heart of stone, poignantly symbolizes the tragic hardening of the Egyptian conscience.[14]

A similar attitude seems to have inspired certain Bantu prayers in which declarations of innocence also predominate. "Lord God, may my goods continue to prosper! For I am not a thief, I have never attempted to seduce another's wife, nor to assail a maiden's virtue. So if anyone looks upon me with an evil eye, do you, my God, look upon him in the same way." "Lord God, I have never stolen, never put a spell on anyone. What then, is this evil eye that dogs my house?" [15]

Sheer denial is the most radical way of repressing guilt. Refusing to admit the existence of a problem, we render our consciousness deaf to the voice of conscience.

At every stage in his life, man is confronted with certain duties. History is irreversible and cannot be halted. We have to keep pace with the development of our lives on the moral and religious levels too, if we are not to succumb to infantilism. Healthy maturing implies the positive integration of each new situation.[16]

A critical point of this kind for the adult is, for instance, the attainment of middle age—between thirty-five and forty. The man who refuses to admit that at that point approximately half of his life has gone by, that many of his hopes and plans have remained unfulfilled, is guilty of repressing his conscience. He will not recognize that he should revise his style of life and he refuses to adopt some other, perhaps more modest program. The problem arises again, more acutely, in old age in the desperate efforts made by some elderly persons to remain young at all costs, it is no exaggeration to speak of repression.

Another example. We should certainly collect material for a fascinating thesis were we to study the numerous exculpation tactics (especially projection and rationalization) employed by Catholic theologians and historians during the past four centuries with a view to rejecting all responsibility for the schism of the Western Church. (The same applies naturally, *mutatis mutandis,* to the representatives of the Protestants.) That is why the self-criticism and the request for pardon with which Paul VI opened the second session of the Vatican Council had such spectacular resonance; it has been referred to as constituting a turning point in history. "If any fault can be imputed to us in connection with this schism, we humbly ask God's pardon for it, and we also ask pardon of those brothers who might feel in any way offended by us" (September 29, 1963). In these words—although certain commentators admit disappointment at the use of the conditional mood—we hear once more tones which had long been scrupulously stifled among high ecclesiastical dignitaries. They echo the energetic terms of Adrian VI in 1522, at the height of the Reformation: "All of us, prelates and ecclesiastics, have strayed from the path of justice . . . That is why we must all give glory to God and humble ourselves before Him. Each of us must examine the cause of his decline and condemn himself rather than have himself condemned by God, on the day of wrath." [17]

But the repression of conscience can take place in other ways than by sheer negation, and may be disguised, for example, in the subtler form of *escape*. For we can cautiously avoid, or pass by what we perceive, see, or understand; we can shirk a disagreeable obligation; we can remove annoying things from our field of vision; we can avoid touching on certain problems. We pay no attention to warnings but indulge in quibbling and then change the subject. This is a form of negative omission rather than a deliberate attempt to set problems aside. We repress our conscience in this discreet manner (with gloved hands) when we do not resolutely embark upon a task but instead close our eyes and put off the needed structural reform *sine die*; or when we fail to revise an indefensible pattern of living; or when we refuse to draw the conclusions from new findings.

The parable of the good Samaritan suggests such a discreet form of repression. The priest and the Levite see the suffering man at the side of the road, of course, but they pass by on the other side (Lk 10:31). This shows that their attempt at silencing their consciences had not been altogether successful. There is a grinding in the gears of the defense mechanism. They draw to the other side of the road so as not to have to see the wounded man since the mere sight of him is an accusation. It is probably for the same reason that the rich man in the parable leaves the destitute Lazarus outside. He forbids him access to his house not so much through fear of catching his fleas, or contracting a skin disease or tuberculosis, as because he simply cannot endure the sight of such wretchedness. He does not want to see him. And this is true of us all. We do not want to look misery in the face, with its entreating eyes. For to look at our fellow men is the first act of fraternal charity and assistance. Love is ingenious. It mobilizes our eyes first, and only then our hands. If we close our eyes or turn them away, then our hands, too, will remain inactive. Finally our conscience will go to sleep, for the disturbing element has vanished from our field of vision.

Perhaps that is why, at the last judgment, our eyes will be examined first. When Jesus tells us, "It was I who came to you in the features of the suppliant starving, of the homeless, of the prisoners and the sick, but you did not help me," the accused will promptly reply, "Lord, when did we *see* you in need?" And the priest and the Levite might also say and, if need be, prove that their steps had taken them in a wide circle around the wounded man, so that they could not have noticed that he was their neighbor and their Savior. But they deceive themselves cruelly. They confuse cause and effect. They did not fail to come to the help of the victim because their steps took them too far away from him; they passed by on the other side precisely because they did not want to see him.

It is not so hard, after all, to make detours so as not to have to see; to turn off the radio or the T.V. set when tales of disaster challenge our generosity; to juggle with poverty statistics through fear of the disagreeable consequences. We are all experts in this kind of repression. We are outraged at the attitude of the multi-millionaire toward Lazarus, reminding ourselves that we do not live in a mansion or possess a large bank account. Right away, the parable has been rendered innocuous, like a time-bomb that has been defused. We think of the rich man as asocial, as a monster, so that we can murmur complacently, "*I'm* not so selfish!" Meanwhile we forget that we all belong to the category of the brothers of the rich man, still refusing to listen to the prophets (Lk 16:28). For that is the truth which the Lord wants to teach us: each of us is rich and well-provided for in some area. We all have a Lazarus seated somewhere behind our houses. Our wealth, perhaps, consists in being loved: we enjoy much affection and friendship. But in our midst there lives a person who does not have the good fortune to be so well liked. He, or she, passes through life with lips compressed in bitterness. Such a person is avoided, left outside in the cold. Without even realizing it, we are repressing Lazarus from our lives.

Consequences of repression: complexes

The consequences of repression are not long delayed. Reality cannot be disregarded with impunity.

The content of consciousness which is repressed is not thereby destroyed. The conflict is not resolved. Emotions and desires which have been violently rejected continue to proliferate and to carve out a way for themselves. The disturbing element, temporarily stifled, continues to exert its influence from the depths of the unconscious. Psychoanalysts compare the process to the formation of air bubbles in the folds of a sheet dipped in a tub: the bubbles have only to be submerged at one point to reappear on the surface at others. Or again, to the action of the waters of a river contained by the construction of a dam; the river seeks to flow out through another channel and rises out of its bed.

Unresolved conflicts and unintegrated drives retain their dynamic potency.[18] But this energy, instead of being harnessed in the full light of consciousness (self-control), tends to be released in all kinds of symptoms. The repressed element poisons human life and throws it out of gear, reintroducing itself in the form of new and ultimately irrepressible kinds of distress—frightening dreams, for example, and nightmares. For reality insists on being taken seriously.

Complexes originate in repression. As the term suggests, the complex constitutes a combination of representations, situations, emotions, and actions with a strong emotional charge for the person concerned and which influence his conduct. A sexual or aggressive drive, expelled from the field of consciousness, develops to the point of becoming a more or less independent entity in which perceptions, aspirations, and energy are interwoven. It begins to lead a life of its own and to threaten the integrity of the person concerned. That is why complexes are often compared to bacteria, to animal or vegetable parasites, to cancerous tissues or to snipers.

Complexes should not, of course, be regarded as "things" or residues deposited deep down in the human being and liable periodically to rise to the surface. Through the accumulation of poorly integrated memories, charged with affectivity, certain types of reaction set in—rigid structures which engender constant and anachronistic behavior patterns.

Because the repressed elements have become unusable, the complexes are reactivated in every circumstance which recalls the original tragedy or trauma.

For example, if a person reacts with a violence disproportionate to the objective stimulus, we conclude that there is hyperesthesia in this area. The disproportion between the stimulus and the reaction betrays the presence of a form of complex. One of the first examples noted by Freud was that of a young woman with an insuperable physical aversion to drinking from a well-washed glass. It turned out that the cause lay in a repressed traumatism: she had once seen a dog touch a glass.

An unjustified or panic fear (phobia) of certain objects, places, animals, or persons that are in themselves quite harmless is based on a complex which associates a variety of perceptions and emotions. Confronted with fact B, the person reacts as though he were simultaneously faced with both B and disagreeable fact A, which had previously been repressed. A now automatic behavior pattern is set in motion and gives rise to reactions which are not adapted to the real situation. Thus we speak, for instance, of the Oedipus and Electra complexes, in connection with representations and relationships heavily charged with affectivity on the part of the child toward his parents, which have their repercussions in later life. The father or the mother is felt to be a rival who must be eliminated. But this wish, violently repressed, is accompanied by some other form of distress: the Diana or Amazon complex based on a protest against one's own nature as a woman; the Cain complex of unconscious jealousy on the part of the older child who fears to lose his parents' affection on the birth of a rival; the Samson complex, of seeking to destroy others together with oneself; the Polycrates complex, which is the agonizing conviction that success and happiness arouse the envy of the gods and must be paid for subsequently by some compensatory failure; the Icarus or angelism complex of the man who wants to fly too high and transcend his own physical being, but perishes lamentably; the Cyrano complex, the inferiority complex, the scapegoat complex, etc.

It is especially important to note that the complexes are "burdened" with affectivity and charged with dynamic force. Operating on the level of the unconscious, they influence the conduct of their victim, at least in certain circumstances. They generate anxiety feelings. Just as we experience pain and suffering as a danger signal when the integrity of our organism is threatened, so anxiety is aroused whenever the integrity of the ego-structure is in jeopardy.

For some psychologists, anxiety, and particularly a vague anxiety which lacks any specific content, is simply stifled libido or aggressiveness. Repression, according to this theory, acts as a transformer of primitive energy; anxiety is the sour vinegar produced from the good wine by a process of acidification. Others find this image too crude and believe that the experience of anxiety is the result of emotions which have been expelled from the zone of consciousness. Whatever the case, it seems to be a fact that all repression produces some feelings of anxiety and culpability.

We have already shown that man is capable of repressing almost anything: his physical being, his sexuality, his age, and his antecedents; his failures and his limitations; his grief, his aggressivity, and his affection; the voice of his conscience, his responsibility and his duties, his failings, and his culpability; his need for a meaning to existence; his need for God. If a man fails to incorporate one or other essential factor in his existential purpose, he finds himself in the position of a traveler missing an important encounter or connection. And the result is that his personality remains underdeveloped.

Existential anxiety, or a nameless sense of guilt,[19] is the spontaneous reaction of our being, which confusedly feels that something is lacking to it and that it is failing. The price of betrayal of truth or of infidelity to reality is the loss of interior peace and excruciating frustration. It is a kind of horror in the face of the existential vacuum (Frankl). A vague metaphysical threat sets off anxiety. The danger signals are on: your being is threatened! Not without cause, some speak of this as *Trennungsangst*—terror of separation.

Repression means degeneration and atrophy, compromising all

communion with the order of nature, with our neighbor, with God our Creator, and with our destiny. "Those who choose another god multiply their sorrows," warns the psalmist (16:4). And if it is true that repression is ultimately the absolutizing of a relative value, it is logical that it should be followed by bitter disillusionment. The idol is ultimately revealed as a Moloch which devours its own servants and children. When a man resorts to falsehood and hides behind deceit, he concludes a covenant with death. But he will learn to grasp the meaning of the saying, "The bed is too short to stretch in, the blanket too narrow for covering" (Is 28:20).

Mounier writes in this connection: "Culpability develops in us unconsciously and without identifying itself. Once repressed, it turns into a diffused sentiment, an obscure, nameless uneasiness, intolerable because it is nameless. It contracts our action in a sort of generalized phobia which spills over from situations involving a moral responsibility onto all those which solicit the individual. Every other person appears to the guilt-ridden as a potential judge, every misfortune as a punishment . . . The world becomes an immense court of law." [20]

A Kafka parable on repression

The deep impression made in our day by Kafka's *The Trial* is not primarily attributable, it seems, to the strange details of a somewhat tortuous plot. Joseph K., an upright but rather insignificant bank clerk, is unaware of having committed any offense, although he is stubbornly pursued and accused by mysterious legal authorities. He is awoke one morning by an individual who has come into his bedroom to announce his arrest. The remainder of the work is a haunting description of the vain attempts made by the accused to discover what he is accused of. The mesh of vague accusations tightens, and from the accused that he was he feels himself becoming more and more the culprit. He dies of a knife wound, with the unanswered question on his lips: for what crime?

This tale, so fascinating for so many readers even if they do not understand its full import, has been variously interpreted. Some have seen it as a warning against the arbitrary processes of dictatorship and the tyranny of an all-powerful police state. Others regard it as the prophetic portrayal of an increasingly automatized world, in which technology deprives man of all personal initiative. Psychoanalysts reduce the "Kafka complex" to a morbid culpability, engendered by the atmosphere of the family in which he grew up. They see Kafka as the son of an authoritarian father, who prevented him from becoming a virile adult, tortured by the temptation to parricide and the fear of castration. Others, again, think that Kafka was describing the fate of a man assailed by violent remorse as a result of his many omissions in regard to his neighbor and himself: a fate of self-punishment brought about by an obsession with boundless culpability and total damnation which no human authority can allay.

While it is of course true that a poet can operate simultaneously on several levels and invest a single symbol with various analogous meanings, the last of these interpretations seems to us to come closest to fact.

Kafka inserted a Jewish legend in his novel which takes on the significance of a hieratic parable. K. hears it in the cathedral from the mouth of a priest, just as his trial has reached its decisive stage.[21]

What emerges so strikingly from this parable is that modern man has lost the Law, lost the God who communicates Himself. In Nietzsche's words, God is dead; He is absent, He has disappeared from many men's hearts and thoughts. But Kafka could not reconcile himself with such a conclusion. It seemed to him impossible to surmount the alienation from God, and the resulting anxiety and sense of guilt, by assigning oneself, on one's own authority, a new goal in life, and finding salvation outside the "kingdom." In point of fact, all Kafka's writings turn on the problem of "having forgotten." God's revelation has disappeared from man's memory. But the absence of this contact, which is needful to life, weighs heavily on him, creating an excruciating anxiety and a painful uncertainty. That is man's tragedy: he remains oriented toward God and linked to Him, although he no longer knows or recognizes Him. But it is also a final convulsion of life, making possible a chance of salvation.

Against this backdrop of loss of God, conscience and culpability take on a new and sinister significance. God has been repressed to an inaccessible distance, but He continues to govern the world.

When He and His Law are no longer known, it becomes impossible to give any significance to culpability, to sin, and to free pardon. The only thing remaining to the man alienated from God is to deduce indirectly from his punishment what it is that constitutes his culpability. This idea is based on the typically Jewish axiom (we may refer to Job's friends) that the nature and malice of the sin (the X factor) may be deduced from the rate of the penalty and from the form of the retribution. This is horribly illustrated in the short story "In the Penal Colony." The commandant has invented an apparatus of torture in the form of a harrow with sharp spikes, which inscribes the prisoner's offense on his body. "Does he know his sentence?" asks the visitor. "No," the officer replies, "he'll learn it on his body." [22]

What Kafka, with his extraordinary gift for expression, manages to suggest in *The Trial* is man's culpability as such: a vague, fluid, apparently unmotivated anxiety. He brings out the existential realization of those who do not know why and to whom they are responsible and who do not know what it is they fear, precisely because God and His revelation have been forgotten and repressed. Joseph K. belongs to the category of the accused. And because he does not know and does not want to recognize his guilt, that guilt progressively condenses. His situation remains hopelessly mysterious and refractory to any rational explanation, because his existential religious culpability cannot be defined in legal or ethical categories. If Joseph K. could assume and recognize his real guilt (cross the threshold of the Law despite the fear with which the doorkeeper inspires him), he would be able to know his sin and confess it. Then he would be freely justified and saved. But he is punished with death, with the loss of life. For, as Kafka writes in *The Castle*, the man who does not seek will nevertheless be found.

The wisdom of mythology

To wind up this Chapter on repression, here is a very ancient tale from Greek mythology.

Young Persephone, Demeter's daughter, is listening in ecstasy to the song of the sirens and picking flowers in a smiling meadow. She comes upon some marvelous narcissi. Just as she stretches out her hands to grasp this treasure, the ground opens under her feet and Hades, son of Cronos and lord of the underworld, carries her off. She becomes Hades' wife and the children born of their union are the Erinyes—the daughters of the night, the Furies who pursue the guilty. Their names are Alecto (unceasing in anger), Tisiphone (avenger of murder), and Megaera (anger and jealousy). [23]

In Persephone we may see the personification of man (the Latin word *persona* is probably related to the names Perseus-Persephone); the human person carried away by his vertiginous, foolish covetousness. The narcissus symbolizes the vanity of the ego, in love with itself. This basic self-love is repressed and descends to Hades, the infernal world of the unconscious. The result is remorse, anxiety, and a sense of guilt. These also reside in the nether regions. The man who has become a prey to relentless guilt has only one refuge: the temple of Apollo, the god of harmony and perfect order. On the frieze of Apollo's sanctuary we read the device: *know thyself!* It is an exhortation to modesty and humility. Do not exalt yourself above your own nature; recognize and confess what you are.

Notes

1. Among others: G. Gusdorf, *Mémoire et personne*, Paris, Presses universitaires de France, 1951, vol. II, p. 344; I. Caruso, *Bios, Psyche, Person*, Freiburg, Alber, 1957, pp. 113, 129; D. Wyss, *Die tiefenpsychologischen Schulen von den Anfängen bis zur Gegenwart*, Göttingen, 1961, pp. 343, 399.
2. See our remarks on scotoma, chapter 4 above.
3. S. Freud, *Gesammelte Werke*, London, 1952, vol. VII, p. 21.
4. Cf. C. Odier, *Les deux sources, consciente et inconsciente, de la vie morale*, Neuchâtel, Editions de la Baconnière, 1947, p. 231; A. Goerres, *Methode und Erfahrung der Psychoanalyse*, Munich, Kösel, 1958, p. 151.
5. F. Nietzsche, *Beyond Good and Evil* (tr. W. Kaufmann), New York, Vintage Books, 1966, no. 68, p. 80.
6. Were it not anachronistic, we might even say that St. Paul is using the technical term "repression" in this context. Cf. Rm 1:18: "men who by their wickedness *suppress* the truth" (the Greek word *katechein* means to stifle, to overwhelm, to hold captive). To sin is to refuse to *recognize* God, to deny the truth of our human con-

dition, the fact that we have been created by Him. And right away it becomes impossible for us to *know* God: we are blinded. The punishment consists in alienation from God, freely chosen by us. Thus the sinner punishes himself.

7. On this point, see the following important works by W. Daim: *Umwertung der Psychoanalyse*, Vienna, Herold, 1951, and *Tiefenpsychologie und Erlösung*, Vienna, Herold, 1954.

8. Valuable studies in this area have been made by the following authorities: Baruk, Caruso, Frankl, Daim, Haefner, Wolff, Siebenthal, Von Gebsattel, Tournier, Zarncke.

9. Especially in Deuteronomy and the prophets, e.g., Is 46:8. The pastor who wrote the second epistle of St. Peter regards *recalling* as his principal pastoral duty: "Therefore I intend always to remind you of these things, though you know them . . . I think it right . . . to arouse you by way of reminder" (2 P 1:12–13).

10. The person we are most concerned to deceive is ourselves, writes Father Faber. And he adds: how fortunate are the mists for the man who does not want to be seen! (F. Faber, *Spiritual Conferences*, London, Burns & Oates, 1858.) He writes further that we go on our way with half a dozen important matters needing to be clarified, but which we let lie like documents in the endless filing cabinets of a high court of justice. This, he says, is another way of deceiving ourselves, for fear of having to buckle down to work, or because we suspect that a good look at ourselves would leave us no alternative but to abandon ourselves to God or flatly to refuse what He asks, and we do not want to do either.

11. See the previous chapter on the structure of the ego and its efforts to maintain and protect itself.

12. We might recall, here, the Gospel parables of the talents and the vine or fig tree from which the Lord sought fruit.

13. In his critique of anthropocentric humanism and atheist Marxism, H. de Lubac has some magnificent pages elaborating on this central theme. See *Sur les chemins de Dieu*, Paris, Aubier, 1956, p. 228.

14. According to Barucq, such a view should be somewhat attenuated. While the Egyptian confronting death was concerned only to protest his innocence and virtue (burial texts), he sometimes, in cases of sickness or other distress, accused himself and confessed his guilt in order to be relieved of his sufferings. Cf. A. Barucq, *L'expression de la louange divine et de la prière dans la Bible et en Égypte*, Cairo, French Institute of Oriental Archeology, 1962, pp. 315–319.

15. Cf. R. van Caeneghem, *La notion de Dieu chez les Baluba du Kasai*, Brussels, Académie royale des sciences coloniales, 1956, pp. 84, 97.

16. See R. Guardini, *Les âges de la vie*, Paris, Editions du Cerf, 1956.

17. Instruction to Cardinal Chieregati, deputy to the Diet of Nuremberg. The historical details have been assembled by K. Blockx, *Si quae culpa . . .* , Ephemerides Theologicae Lovanienses, Louvain-Bruges, 1964, p. 474.

18. That, of course, is why repression cannot be regarded as a transitory and unique action with permanent consequences—an action, for instance, like the killing of a living creature, which from that instant would have been definitively eliminated. Repression requires a constant effort, a sustained defense, and a considerable expenditure of energy. That is why it is correct to speak of an inhibited *attitude* or of a personality *structure*.

19. We are certainly not suggesting that all anxiety and guilt feelings are the result of repression. There can also be organic causes: pathological melancholia, or endogenous depression. It is also a fact that neurotic phenomena of anxiety and guilt can ccur without any responsibility on the part of the affected person. But it is always easier to formulate general distinctions than to establish a correct diagnosis in an individual case.

20. E. Mounier, *Traité du caractère*, Paris, Editions du Seuil, 1947, p. 722.

21. Franz Kafka, *The Trial*, New York, Alfred A. Knopf, 1963, pp. 267–269.

22. *Id.*, "In the Penal Colony," in *Selected Short Stories*, New York, Random House, 1952, p. 96.

23. See K. Kerenyi, *La mythologie des Grecs*, Paris, Payot, 1952; also P. Diel, *Le symbolisme dans la mythologie grecque*, Paris, Payot, 1952. In an excellent introduction, each of these authors draws attention to the relationship between depth psychology and mythology.

7

Rationalization

The psychological phenomenon of rationalization

Rationalization seems to be contemporary Western man's favorite defense mechanism for the repression of painful conflicts. What it really comes to is making use of arguments and explanations to avoid having to accept some truth which conflicts with our basic approach.

McDougall's classic experiment admirably illustrates this procedure. An individual is hypnotized and ordered to tie a knot in the handkerchief of one of the persons present. When he comes out of the hypnosis, he finds himself in an embarrassing state of conflict. On the one hand, he has a definite urge to carry out the order; on the other hand, his sense of propriety restrains him from so doing. He therefore looks for a plausible motive to justify his conduct, and a host of arguments cross his mind at lightning speed: for example, that the person in whose handkerchief he wants to tie the knot has an appointment that evening and must be reminded of it. He is of course unaware of the true reason (the hypnotist's order), yet that reason nevertheless determines his conduct. At the same time, he feels impelled to give a satisfactory explanation of his curious action. And he does find a reason which could be genuine, but which in fact he has fabricated out of whole cloth: it is a pseudo-motive invented *for the occasion*.

We know that every living being instinctively defends himself against dangers that threaten him: this is unconditioned reflex action. But the human being possesses the specific property of being endowed with a reasoning faculty whereby he can regulate and motivate his conduct. He thus instinctively tries to understand and explain what happens to him. Nevertheless, he is not always logical in his reasoning; indeed, far from it. Though *rational*, our considerations are often far from logical, objectively accurate, and in harmony with the truth. Whence the term *rationalization*, with its pejorative connotation, to indicate that a person has some ulterior motive for arguing in a particular manner.

Making excuses is indeed so widespread a practice that each one of us can at any time catch himself in the act of adducing specious arguments to defend or justify himself, even if we are trying to be truthful and honest with ourselves. Rationalization thus appears to be a psychic mechanism which is automatically set in motion to protect some deeper orientation. Thought is placed at the service of the heart. Just as the wish is father to the thought, so fear is the mother of argument. The motive force which triggers the mechanism is man's fundamental attitude or his ego structure, which he seeks to maintain. This is especially so when our sense of dignity, our prestige, or our social standing is involved. It is intolerable to our honor and our pride that we should be despised by others, or that we should be lowered in our own estimation. The ego-ideal exercises a kind of constraint upon us to keep up our position.

When a man does not manage to attain the goal he is pursuing, he feels he has failed and is overcome by a sense of dissatisfaction. He then seeks instinctively to escape from this distressing situation. Experience teaches us that if, as a result of external circumstances independent of our own will, we find ourselves virtually forced to recognize a fact or to perform an action repugnant to us, we are capable in such a case of easily adducing a multitude of reasonable motives for so doing, even though in fact we had no other choice. Reasons come afterward, as justifications, remarked Pascal. They are explanations made *post factum*, which had either little or no influence at all on our action. But they may appear so convincing and reasonable that we speedily begin to think that they really motivated our decision. This is what Lessing called a *Sinngebung des Sinnlosen:* giving a meaning to what has none.

Such posthumous motivation on ideal grounds is very common

in our everyday life: in our social relations, in our professional activity, in connection with expenditures on dress and housing, in politics, etc. The general attitude and the action in this case precede the thought. The individual instinctively and unconsciously seeks excuses to justify a decision that has already been taken for other reasons which he does not like to have revealed. They are shock-absorbers intended to reduce the painful contact with brutal reality. We try to make a virtue of necessity through disguises in the shape of idealizations.

The two principal forms of such rationalization are the "sour-grapes" reaction and the "sweet-lemons" reaction.

According to a very ancient fable, the fox maintains that the grapes which he is unable to reach are sour. What we like, but remains unattainable, we claim to be less beautiful and not very interesting. Thus when a young man is jilted, he suddenly finds that his erstwhile fiancée had a thousand faults. Better a broken romance than an unhappy marriage! As the Congolese proverb has it, "The man who has no bracelet claims that a bracelet smells bad."

The sweet-lemons reaction is just the contrary. The unpleasant but inevitable factor is painted in bright colors and embellished. Thus the man who cannot afford a car will assert that it is much healthier to ride a bicycle or that the train enables him to save precious time. We find an echo of this rationalized resignation in certain dictums of popular wisdom: the secret of happiness consists not in doing what one likes but in liking what one does; a bird in the hand is worth two in the bush, etc.

The dynamism of the rationalization mechanism is thus provided by affectivity. And this presents a broad spectrum of shapes and colors: desire, appetite, love, aversion, fear, anxiety, anger. Necessity stimulates man to research, to work, to reflection. Love makes him ingenious, and anxiety in particular can cause even a man of modest intelligence to elaborate very cogent arguments, to establish relationships between things, and to draw conclusions.

Fundamentally, rationalization is the consequence of anxiety repressed into the realm of the unconscious. We notice something distressing or humiliating. We do not feel able to admit it, or we do not want to recognize it. We drive it away and reject it. The result is partial blindness or scotoma. We subsequently advance an acceptable explanation in lieu of the repressed cause. Usually the reasons given are ones that flatter the ego. In this way systematic errors are born and fallacies skillfully constructed. A teacher, for instance, will be unfair to a child whom he happens to dislike for some obscure reason; if this is pointed out to him, he will not readily admit it, but will undoubtedly be able to find in the child's behavior a dozen reasons for his own reaction. Minor failings and transgressions which he does not even notice in students he likes are ruthlessly exposed and emphasized. However wrong he is, he feels absolutely justified in what he is doing.

Rationalization often bears a great resemblance to *concretization*. When we do not know what it is we fear, and when we neither dare nor desire to recognize our fear (repression), an anxiety without content and without apparent foundation makes its appearance. To escape this anxiety, we set about looking for an object which is really frightening. Thus the nameless anxiety is transformed into a well-founded and definite fear. In this way, our distress is explained and we are better placed to defend ourselves.

In the Bible, this defense mechanism is illustrated by an amusing maxim: "'There is a lion outside,' says the idler, 'I shall be killed in the street!'" (Pr 22:13; cf. 26:13). Under the prevailing conditions of the time, the indolent man could justify his anxiety on the grounds that prowling beasts constituted a threat to life. The same pretext, transposed into the modern idiom, would point to the heavy traffic which causes so many serious accidents, or to the possibility of a fainting spell or a heart attack in the street.

This mechanism is probably at the root of certain phobias and obsessional actions. Some people have an obsessional fear of certain objects, actions, or situations. Impressive Greek terms have been invented to describe them. They recall the ten plagues of Egypt, says Freud, except that they are far more numerous. The best known are agoraphobia, claustrophobia, nosophobia, nyctophobia, mysophobia, and phobophobia. A diffuse sentiment (compounded largely of anxiety and guilt), unrelated to any specific object and whose cause is either unknown or unrecognized, emerges from the realm of the irrational and suddenly bursts into our life, like an avalanche. We are panic-stricken, like an army when elusive guerrillas perpetrate acts of sabotage behind the firing line. But as soon as a mysterious, omnipresent danger has been pinpointed, localized, and identified, it can be opposed and there is relief, at least, in having found a sufficient reason. The fear of an object or of a situation serves as a protective mechanism. We attempt to overcome or hide the real fear by enormously exaggerating some threat or possible danger. On looking closer, we find that, paradoxically, we are often *minimizing* our existential culpability by *exaggerating* something else.[1]

One of the features of rationalization is that its mechanics are located in the twilight regions of our personality and that we are only half aware of it, if at all. In this respect it differs from cynical or conscious falsehood and from deliberate deceit and hypocrisy. Examples of the latter are Herod's instruction to the wise men, "Go and search diligently for the child, and when you have found him bring me word, that I too may come and worship him" (Mt 2:8), or Judas' indignation at the waste of the precious ointment to anoint the Lord's feet: "This he said, not that he cared for the poor but because he was a thief, and as he had the money box he used to take what was put into it" (Jn 12:6).

The man who rationalizes is scarcely aware of his inauthenticity. The sophisms of justification are what Pascal calls the reasons of the heart which the reason does not know. He unconsciously deludes and deceives himself. He will believe ever more firmly in his apparent motivations and in the arguments which he constructs *post factum*. These are manifestations of a deeper mendacious existence.[2] That is why, when there is rationalization, arguments will generally be advanced with violence and passion. For the mechanism functions effectively as a means of protection only so long as the individual concerned is himself convinced of the force and value of his reasoning. This is particularly necessary since others easily see through the illusion and do not let themselves be taken in.

If rationalization takes place largely or wholly unconsciously, the question of responsibility naturally arises.

To avoid an answer that fails to take due account of individuating factors, we have as always to realize that human freedom is not a question of all or nothing but of more or less. Freedom presupposes that we act in full knowledge of our action and deliberately. We have, on the one hand, the complete opaqueness of the unconscious or of the marginal consciousness and, on the other hand, explicit self-knowledge; but the transition from one to the other is as fluid as that between light, twilight, and darkness. Moreover, it is possible that what is taking place perhaps unconsciously is the result of some earlier and deliberate decision, for there also exist culpable forms of blindness and insensibility. We have to ask ourselves whether the present darkness is not the consequence of a refusal of light in the past; if we do not really approve of the screen set up between the good and ourselves, by refusing to see clearly. Selfishness, insincerity, lack of frankness are the principal architects of the blindness and dullness of the conscience. In Montaigne's phrase, if we cannot practice what we preach, we preach what we practice.

Rationalization at the service of the repression of conscience

After these rather general considerations on the existence and modes of operation of this defense mechanism, let us look a little more closely at the way in which a guilty man uses it.

A survey conducted recently of a number of asocial or delinquent young people showed that certain excuses frequently recur. These excuses are rationalizations; for example: "everyone steals and cheats sometimes, but most people don't get caught"; "others get away with much more than I do"; "once is not a habit"; "so what, anyway"; "people who have a lot can give up something, after all, to those who haven't enough; and if they don't, then we just have to take it ourselves!" [3]

Without claiming that they are complete, we would classify the main tactics for escaping from a sense of guilt under the following headings: generalization, denial of responsibility, indefinite postponement of execution, label-faking, theological rationalization, rationalization in the priestly life.

Generalization

This phenomenon is bound up with the deeply ingrained desire to disappear in the anonymous mass. I will pass unnoticed! I'm so unimportant in the midst of so many others!

The Old Testament cautions us against this minimizing generalization:

> "Do not say, 'I will hide from the Lord,
>   who will remember me up there?
> I shall certainly not be noticed among so many;
>   what am I in the immensity of creation?' "
>
> (Si 16:17)

"But everyone does it!" "The others are no better than I!" That is certainly the most common and the most facile of all excuses. Why worry about these many faults of everyday life, which are not really so important? Most of the time we commit them without really thinking: like using the public transportation system without paying the fare, or evading taxes, or little deceits, petty thefts . . . What driver does not sometimes exceed the speed limit or take unjustified risks on curves where the visibility is limited? Who does not sometimes leave dangerous objects lying about, poisons, for instance, within the reach of children or incompetent persons who might take them to their own harm or that of others? Who does not sometimes forget to turn the gas off carefully or to put out a match before throwing it away?

Fortunately such carelessness does not always have catastrophic results. It would be *bad luck* if some accident resulted; sheer bad luck, again, if I was the one to be caught, punished, and fined.

This kind of hedging for the sake of providing oneself with an alibi is mainly used when some thoughtless omission or carelessness brings about unfortunate consequences. "These things happen . . ."

What we are actually doing, when we take this position, is to combine two types of defensive tactics: generalization and projection. We generalize and we put the blame on something else—bad luck, fate. This procedure is supported by the fact that the legal sphere (*forum externum*) and the moral and religious sphere (*forum internum*) do not altogether coincide. The law requires an accounting only from those who through their carelessness in fact provoke an accident. Yet they are no worse than the many others who also neglect their duty and act just as carelessly. In their view, it would be purely pharisaical to consider those who did not get away with it as the only ones responsible, and to acquit the others who behave in the same way, simply because they have been *lucky*.

Yet if we go into the matter a little more deeply, we see that this rationalization is flagrantly illogical. To exculpate ourselves, we cannot point to the impunity of those who have not been caught, or whose thoughtlessness has not gravely injured those around them. That is not the problem. Even a deception which remains concealed, or a foolish action which causes no accident, are deserving of censure, for the person concerned is acting immorally and culpably. It is true that the law provides no sanctions for such cases; that is the only difference. The antitheses set out in the Sermon on the Mount (Mt 5:2–48) make this very clear.

A striking illustration of this defense mechanism applied on a large scale is still engraved in the memory of many. After the collapse of the Nazi regime, a violent tide of shame and guilt swept through wide sectors of the German population. It was expressed, *inter alia*, in literature and many films. But the tide soon abated. The reflex of self-defense went into operation automatically. "In time of war and emergency everyone acts like that . . . The Russians and the French are no better than we are. They use torture too . . . Obviously it's the loser who pays for the others . . ."

We are not free!

With this assertion, man moves a step forward: he denies his responsibility and tries to show that the fault cannot be imputed to him. The Bible warns him against this shelving of responsibility:

> "Do not say, 'The Lord was responsible for my sinning,'
>   for he is never the cause of what he hates.
> Do not say, 'It was he who led me astray,'
>   for he has no use for a sinner"
>
> (Si 15:11–12).

The great attraction which the youthful Augustine found in Manicheanism was its grandiose endeavor to shift man's guilt from his shoulders: God, not man himself, is responsible for evil (see *Confessions,* book VII, 3 and 4).

The authors of this kind of anthropology are astute enough not to deny the fact of sin. But they empty it of its content: malice is indeed present in us, but it is to be imputed to another's will. It is impossible for us not to sin.[4]

The history of humanity is sometimes compared to an age-long progress along a road whose sides are strewn with the debris of outmoded philosophical systems. Many of these deal with the vital problem of our freedom and responsibility. For the Christian, who bases his view on divine revelation and therefore believes that man really is free to choose and to act responsibly, it is clear that philosophical theories which attempt to prove the contrary are a product of the mechanism of rationalization, with its goal of self-exculpation.

The favorite method of shifting responsibility is to appeal to astrology. This is still true in our own day. It is quite horrifying to see how many people consult horoscopes, people who at the same time flatter themselves on their rational and scientific attitudes. It is so reassuring to think that the planets and the zodiac determine the orientation of men's lives and therefore bear the responsibility for them, for then I am no longer responsible for what happens! Shakespeare's sarcastic comments have lost none of their relevance: "Villains on necessity; fools by heavenly compulsion; knaves, thieves, and treachers by spherical predominance, drunkards, liars and adulters by an enforc'd obedience of planetary influence; and all that we are evil in, by a divine thrusting on. An admirable evasion of whoremaster man, to lay his goatish disposition to the charge of a star!" [5]

This tendency to deny personal freedom and self-determination is expressed in a more dignified way in *reductive theories* concerning man. Whenever we experience defeat or give way to some failing, we quickly find a satisfactory explanation by adducing factors which irresistibly determine our personalities: hereditary dispositions, hormones and instincts, temperament, education, social environment. And of course there is some truth in the argument. We are in fact free only within our own specific situation. Our freedom is a *human* freedom, that is, limited, relative, and conditioned. But we are not wholly or solely the product of impersonal forces. Our basic existential option is to some extent determined by ourselves.

In a number of cases this rationalization is based on an oversimplification of scientific or philosophical theories. Jung, Von Gebsattel, and many of their colleagues note that people nowadays tend to go to a psychoanalyst rather than to a confessor. The phenomenon is of course related to the slackening of the ties to

organized religion or the Church. But it is far more the consequence of the desire of many to unburden themselves of the anxiety and the culpability to which they are a prey, without having to
revise a reprehensible fundamental option. The people concerned
are seeking an alibi, whereas the pastor generally points out the
role of our personal responsibility in the emergence of our psychic
difficulties. He tells us that we are sinners and that we are on the
wrong road, that we must be reconciled with God and be converted. He does not justify our sin. (Or at least he used not to do
so. For nowadays some spiritual directors profess quite disconcerting theories.) He offers us hope of free pardon provided that
we recognize our sin, that we ask forgiveness, and that we are
prepared to change our attitude. From the psychiatrist, the patient
expects just the contrary. He hopes to learn that he is not at fault
at all. He wants to be able to remain passive and to have the
doctor cure him as a *patient*. He hopes to receive the assurance of
an accredited scientific authority that his symptoms and troubles
are due to circumstances beyond his control: to atavism, to nerves,
to a trauma, to complexes, to organic disorders, etc. In a word,
everything is reduced to complications which can be treated without the basic existential purpose having to be modified. Gertrud
von Le Fort has one of her characters embody this approach:

> I, who had always clung so nervously to my own soul that I
> could never quite open myself to the divine Love, I now in my
> fear unlocked myself to mortal man—not however to man in his
> compassion, but to man in his presumption. To this presump-
> tion I exposed those deeps of my soul which God alone has
> reserved to Himself the power to adjust. Instead of flying to the
> Sacrament, I fled to science; I confessed to the doctor, and I
> received from him the only absolution which the world has the
> power to give, namely, the absolution of the psychiatrist, in the
> eyes of whom there is no sin that cannot be forgiven, because,
> there being no such thing as the soul, it cannot refuse itself to
> God. And this absolution conferred on me the terrible peace in
> which thousands live today whose disease is simply this, that
> they have despised the peace of God! [6]

Men will find ever more subtle rationalizations to explain away
their responsibility. Thus they will claim that the argument for
human freedom based on reflection on our own experience is a

delusion, of the same order as that of the sun turning around the earth. Or they will assert that the notion of human freedom is simply a hoax that society wants to put over us in its own interests. Groups which believe in their freedom are apparently stronger than fatalists which do not share this conviction. Hence the assertion that man is free and responsible is no more than an axiom inspired by the collective instinct of self-preservation . . .

In the last Chapter we saw that it is not only instinctual drives which are sometimes repressed and lead to neurotic behavior, but also that which is highest in man, his value judgment and his conscience, can be repressed, and that this absence of veracity leads to affective disorders.

These two forms of repression may be empirically observed. For the first, Freud adduces irrefutable proofs. A number of contemporary psychoanalysts pay more attention to the second. Persons who in time of war found themselves obliged to commit actions which their conscience reproved may be placed in the latter category. The disregard and repression of their conscience may lead, even many years later, to disorders in the form of searing remorse and all kinds of traumatism. One is reminded of Cain, the man marked with a sign, who travels to the land of Nod, to the east of Eden (Gn 4): a journey to the land of unrest, to a dead end.

But the proponents of a down-to-earth materialism and a hedonistic view of man have an answer to this too. These conscientious objectors in retrospect, they coolly maintain, are in fact weighed down by an inordinately swollen superego. It is their infantile conscience which prevents them from satisfying their instincts, their innate aggressiveness, for example, in the extermination of the innocent! In other words, the fact that they cannot accept their past actions without a neurotic reaction indicates that they are repressing their healthy aggressivity. The normal reaction, according to this theory, would be to carry out orders with no inner resistance and not to be tormented by one's conscience later . . .

The indefinite postponement of execution

Speech, like man himself, is essentially ambiguous. The human being uses it not only to think and to express himself but also to lie and deceive. For words may be used not only to reveal, explain, and express something (to communicate a sentiment, proffer information, establish a relationship), but also to conceal and obscure. Language, Talleyrand said, was given to man to veil his thought.

Chatter very often conceals a need to misrepresent certain situations, to disguise oneself, and to mislead others. In some people, this habit takes the form of a deliberate mannerism. Thus people will often turn a conventional scientific language into a jargon whose complex prolixity borders on the esoteric. The magic sound of learned terms gives the talkative man a sense of superiority and raises him above the level of the uninitiate.

We often resort to chatter in order to still the whisper of conscience, both the conscience which points out the course to be followed and the conscience which experiences shame and guilt. Among those who like to discuss religious questions and the great problems of life, there are not a few for whom such talk is simply a way of hiding in the thick bushes of speculation, as Kierkegaard puts it, behind which, like Adam, they seek shelter. All the stratagems of their endless arguments are aimed only at proving to others, and even more to themselves, that all this is mere absurdity; that the indefinite series of *pro* and *contra*, of objections and replies, can lead to no result. The flood of words is intended to heal the wound of conscience and to anesthetize inner disquiet.

The theologian whom we see questioning Jesus, in the tenth chapter of St. Luke's Gospel, undoubtedly belongs to this category of persons.[7] By his question (what should he do to attain eternal life?), he wants to "disconcert" Jesus and put Him to the test. Fundamentally, he is not well disposed toward Jesus. He wants to get the Master into a tight corner. Like a chess-player, he has doubtless foreseen his opponent's moves. If Jesus answers, for instance, "To fulfill your destiny, you must believe," he has his rejoinder ready: "Why, then, did God prescribe so many liturgical rites?" This can lead to a good *debate*, to exceptional oratorical jousting. He is jubilant beforehand at his own shrewdness and quick-wittedness.

But to his amazement, the Nazarean does not fall into the trap. Jesus' reply disconcerts him. The theologian is referred back to what he was taught as a child: You must love the Lord your God with all your heart . . . and your neighbor as yourself! In other words, don't waste time speculating on the meaning of existence: act!

But at the last moment another thought crosses his mind which might get him out of his predicament: Yes, but who *is* my neighbor? Perhaps he can after all succeed in involving the Master in a debate, and thereby avoid the awkward question of putting the commandment into practice. By his skeptical question, he seeks to *justify* himself, St. Luke observes (10:29). The word implies a concern to exculpate oneself, to prove one's innocence, to prove that one is right. We have to gain time. As long as we can go on raising problems, we are not obliged to take action and we get a stay of execution. We can peacefully linger in the realm of theory and abstraction, in the zone of noncommitment.

"Love my neighbor? I agree, and as a lawyer I know of course that I have to love my companions, the people around me. But there is absolutely no agreement as to who does and does not come under this heading. Is it only my fellow countrymen and the proselytes? Or the non-Pharisees too, and the half-pagan dwellers of the countryside? Do sinners come under it? Can *you* perhaps draw any precise limits to charity? How far should it go? How far does this famous commandment extend? I can't help everyone, after all! Who has priority? That is the whole point!"

Having formulated his question, he feels better. The shaft which has so painfully wounded him can be removed without much difficulty. It is up to the other side now to clarify the terms neighbor, human community, nearness, distance, order, social duty, etc.

But he has miscalculated again. Jesus tells him the story of the good Samaritan.

What we have here is the classic tactic for circumventing an injunction of conscience: "deliberately to maintain confusion in discussions from which we do not want a clear decision to emerge." [8] We wrap ourselves in a smokescreen of lofty speculation. To justify inaction, we withdraw into an artificial fog made up of a plethora of problems. If we want to postpone an unpleasant decision or action indefinitely, we talk about conflicts of conscience; we claim that we are faced with contradictory commands and obligations. We talk of bewilderment. "So many people need my help. Where should I start if I want to love? The

hierarchy of values is not at all clear. Suppose I took this delinquent youngster under my care and he later became a criminal? Or
suppose I gave money to a beggar, and he used it to get drunk?"

In a word, we are filled, or so we believe, with feelings of benev-
olence toward our neighbor, but we are afraid of one day regret-
ting a good action; we fear the unfortunate consequences for
which we might have to bear the responsibility.

Very often our religious or moral disengagement is thus disguised behind a *conflict of duties.*

An inner conflict leads to an examination of conscience. The
longer a decision is postponed, the more impressive the unpleasant
consequences connected with the performance of the duty become. But the deliberation is often attended by the secret hope
that a consequence will be discovered which is not only unpleasant
but also to be avoided as dangerous and illicit. Then we can with
good conscience refrain from making a decision or suspend action
and settle down in a comfortable quietism. We are safe. We have
justified the omission in our own eyes and in those of others.

It would appear, then, that to weigh the pros and cons is often a
useful way to confuse a clear issue, to make believe that things are
not so simple. We still our consciences with the idea that we are
failing in our duty not because of its disagreeable nature but because of its problematical results: we might sully our hands. What
was at first sight a clear invitation or command is so thoroughly
dissected that we finally succeed in discovering a directly contrary
duty.[9]

We thus throw dust in our own eyes. A long and subtle deliberation can increase the danger of delusion when it is a sympton of too
little generosity and of reluctance to take action. To quote Saint-
Just, "mistakenly he calls virtue the muted crime clothed in
sophistry." When people who pride themselves on having religious
and moral convictions nevertheless do evil, they attempt to do so
with the conviction that it is legitimate. Only the cynically immoral will commit crimes openly. Hypocrisy is the sorry privilege
of the conscientious. The insincere man is not necessarily a man
without faith or scruples. The reason he dissimulates is precisely in
order to silence his uneasy or accusing conscience.

A variation of this rationalization is *paralyzing self-criticism.* In
our conscience, we hear God's call to spend ourselves in the service

of higher values and our neighbor. This invitation, however, crosses our personal plans. If, then, we go on deliberating long enough, it will become possible to remain attentive to conscience without having to do anything. Especially if we concentrate on our motives and our approach. This preoccupation provides a distraction. The sifting of our motives saps their vital energy. And to the degree that our intentions begin to appear uncertain or suspect, our activity is paralyzed. As the Latin saying has it, *deliberando saepe perit occasio*. For in the process of constantly analyzing our motives, we turn aside from objective values and hypnotize ourselves. The moral and religious imperative is replaced by psychological introspection. Instead of taking decisions, we become spectators. We can act only once we stop searching our own motives in regard to the judgment of our conscience and resolutely turn our attention to what is required of us and to the one who is appealing to our conscience.

Let us go back for a moment to the story of the good Samaritan. St. Luke does not indicate the motives which prompted the priest and the Levite to pass by on the other side. Without forcing the evangelical text, we may suppose that the ministers of religion could put forward all kinds of pious sophisms and excuses. At least once they came home. Thus, for example, that the unfortunate man was probably dead—or almost dead, and that contact with a corpse would render them ritually impure, so that they would be unable to carry out their liturgical functions in the Temple . . . And do not duties of state have priority? In any case, it would have been imprudent to remain in that dangerous area any longer; it would have meant heedlessly jeopardizing their own safety. And it would have benefited no one had they fallen victim to robbers in their turn. As the breadwinners for their families, they must think of their responsibilities. Moreover, their modest incomes did not allow them to take on the care of a gravely wounded man. (For according to Palestinian custom, the person who gave first aid in case of accident must continue to support the patient.)

Rembrandt, in his famous picture of the scene, portrays the ministers of the Temple absorbed in the recitation of their prayer books. As a representative of a religious community which proposes to concern itself with the welfare of souls, a man may turn his eyes away from material and social distress. He says his prayers and specializes in theological and ecclesiastical problems. One cannot do everything at once, after all! Looking after the sick and social work come under some other jurisdiction. And anyway, is not the interior life most important of all? If someone is lying half dead on the side of the road, well, yes, that's just a part of the reality of this world . . .

Such arguments to avoid getting one's hands dirty, while at the same time maintaining a good conscience, may appear somewhat farfetched. Yet they are not pure invention, as we may see from the rationalizations of the clergy not only in the past but also in our own day. To justify their silence in the face of widespread and large-scale social injustice (oppression of minorities, institutionalized violence, war) which offends God in the humble, they point out that tensions in this sinful world are unavoidable, that eternal life is so much more important than biological life, that politics must be kept separate from religion—or again, that church and state cannot in fact be separated.

We have been dealing, so far, mainly with rationalizations designed to postpone indefinitely the performance of some action which we know to be incumbent upon us. But man uses the same defense mechanism to protect himself from his *retrospective conscience*, which accuses him of some misdeed or omission. Even a detailed self-analysis, which at first sight appears to include a confession of guilt, may in fact be an attempt to self-exculpation. For concepts can also serve as shelters. Bernanos' country priest begins his diary with the following pertinent warning: "I considered very carefully before making up my mind to write [my diary]. But that is not much comfort to me now. For those who have the habit of prayer, thought is too often a mere alibi, a sly way of deciding to do what one wants to do. Reason will always obscure what we wish to keep in the shadows." [10]

The following passage is perhaps clearer still:

Petty lies can slowly form a crust around the consciousness, of evasion and subterfuge. The outer shell retains the vague shape of what it covers, but that is all. In time, by sheer force of habit, the least "gifted" end by evolving their own particular idiom, which still remains incredibly abstract. They don't hide much, but their sly candor reminds one of a dirty window pane, so blurred that light has to struggle through it, and nothing can be clearly seen. What then remains of confession? It barely skims the surface of conscience. I don't say dry rot has set in underneath; it seems more like petrifaction.[11]

Here Bernanos really gets to the root of the problem. Rationalization is the substitution of a conflict of abstract entities for an experiential tension. It is an explanation or interpretation which reduces our personal problem to general considerations of a psychological, philosophical, or theological nature. This is the direct antithesis of a genuine self-confrontation which both enables us to recognize our basic motivations and gives us the courage to revise them if need be.[12]

When we rationalize, we are trying to justify our conduct, our approach. A genuinely Christian sense of guilt will lead us to confess our misdeeds without looking for explanations to excuse them. "Confession of sin is the clearest confirmation of the mysterious character of sin in the Biblical sense; it implies the rejection of any valid explanation." [13]

We realize that the study of defense mechanisms may also degenerate into an abstract rationalization which we place as a screen in front of the mirror of genuine self-confrontation. This would be the case were we simply to indicate and identify the mechanisms which play an active part in a person's behavior (our own or someone else's). But if we illustrate the exculpation tactics by sufficiently practical examples in which the person concerned can as it were read his autobiography, perhaps this danger may be averted.

Label-faking

Under this heading we may list rationalizations in which slogans are juggled in order to lull the conscience.

Take, for example, the problem of lying. In his *Histories*, Herodotus tells how a usurper, claiming to be Cyrus' son, had seized the throne of Egypt. Once the imposture was discovered, the legitimate successor, Darius, decided to put the usurper to death. But the execution of that design proved difficult, as the usurper never left his strongly guarded palace. Darius held a council of war with his friends and suggested that he should pass himself off as a personal envoy from Cyrus, commissioned to transmit a most secret message to him. His refutation of his friends' objections and scruples in the matter proceeds as follows: The man who lies and the man who tells the truth ultimately pursue the same end. The first lies in order to have something accepted as the truth and to derive an advantage therefrom. The second tells the truth in order to safeguard his own interests and to rally people to his side. Both, therefore, taking different paths, are trying to achieve the same end. Their conduct is dictated by self-interest. If that motivation were not at issue, they would be little enough concerned whether they lied or told the truth.[14]

The theory that the end justifies the means, which Darius was somewhat clumsily putting forward here, has since been defended by ever more subtle arguments. For instance, lying is permissible provided one is not expressly intending to deceive. Or again, lying is forbidden only if its purpose is malicious. Lying, thus, is an indifferent or neutral act, and therefore licit in a case of just compensation or by reason of human frailty; it is also licit as a means of legitimate self-defense. Some situations warrant falsehood, just as "stealing" is permissible in case of extreme necessity. This also applies when contrary obligations conflict with each other. Language and speech are man's free invention. Consequently, lying is simply a matter of contravening human conventions. We may resort to lying when there is no genuine communication and confidence among the parties concerned, since in that case there is no right to truth . . .[15]

The axiom, no punishment without fault, is a fundamental principle of natural law and is basic to the human conscience. It is self-evident for everyone (synderesis) that an innocent person must not be penalized. This instinctive awareness of values also presupposes the conviction that the human person is able to act freely and thus responsibly.[16]

If we want to escape this principle of culpability, we have to find all kinds of excuses to placate our conscience. Thus in Nazi Germany the killing of "tainted" races or individuals, of Jews and of persons hostile to the regime, was no longer presented as a punitive measure: such euphemisms were employed as security, preservation of racial purity, protection of the public health, elimination of dangerous elements.

In time of war and enemy occupation, common law criminals find it perfectly natural to identify their own cause with their country's. They make it their business to disguise their egotism and to pass off their anti-social ventures as heroic acts of patriotism or of sabotage against the enemy. How could a thing be immoral if it was done in the name of a higher cause? History provides plenty of examples of such humbug under cover of a great ideal.

The exploitation of defenseless persons, aggressive wars, and colonialization policies, etc., are frequently justified by *humanitarian* considerations. The pretext is given that the victims are too weak to manage for themselves, that they are not ready for independence, that they have to be given prosperity, culture, etc. Molière has something to say on this point in *Tartuffe:*

> "Yes, now there is a science that succeeds
> In stretching consciences to meet our needs,
> And can correct, by a sublime invention,
> An evil deed just by a pure intention." [17]

Theological rationalizations

Closely related to the preceding category are other labels of a more specifically religious character. In his first epistle, St. Peter addresses a warning against "using your freedom as a pretext for evil" (1 P 2:16). He was probably thinking of the faithful who forgot that the redeemed Christian must be a servant of the Lord (see Rm 6:22; 1 Co 7:22), people who flourished the slogan of liberty to justify loose, slothful, and self-indulgent mores. We read, incidentally, that people took advantage of St. Paul's teachings (see 2 P 3:16); perhaps of statements such as those in 2 Corinthians 3:17 or Galations 5:13.

This is certainly a danger which remains present in our own day. God is a merciful Father. From the parable of the prodigal son (Lk 15), we know that He presses us to His heart as long-lost sons, notwithstanding our rags and our leprosy. His liberality and grace are infinitely more powerful than sin (Rm 5:20). At which point our reasoning may go off at a tangent. God loves us with a boundless love. Therefore it may not be so very important, after all, whether we are a little more or a little less defiled. If we stay abroad a few years longer, leading a life of sin, it will still be all right. The Father is not resentful, but indulgent . . . We have, as it were, an entrance ticket to heaven in our pockets. We are insured against everlasting death. There will always be more joy in the rescue of a black sheep *in extremis* than in the perseverance of a large number of docile believers. So we can safely be that single sinner. The others can be the ninety-nine just . . .[18]

In some MSS of the Gospel according to St. Luke, we find a remarkable saying of Jesus (6:5). "On the same Sabbath day, Jesus saw a man working. Then He said: man, blessed are you if you know what you are doing. But if you do not know, then you are cursed and you transgress the Law."

This episode certainly does not teach us that the Sabbath rest has been abolished. The emphasis is clearly on the end of the passage, which carries a grave warning. The man is probably carrying a load. The Lord allows for the possibility that he is doing this in order to help someone. We may paraphrase His words as follows: If you understand why I did not observe the Sabbath rest when I was helping the needy (e.g., Lk 13:10; 14:1; Mk 3:1), if you transgress the Sabbath laws in order to help another, because you know that the obligation to love the children of God is paramount over all the other commandments and prohibitions, then I declare you blessed. But if you think that I give you permission lightly to profane the prescribed holy day, if you are acting through indifference or cynicism, then you deserve the death penalty according to the Mosaic Law.

What Jesus is emphasizing here is the twofold freedom we possess in relation to the divine order and to the sacred laws. On the one hand, there is the liberty of the children of God who know they are bound by charity (free positively, for the sake of something and someone). On the other hand, there is the liberty of the rebellious who live out their lives in untrammelled egotism (negatively free of troublesome obligations). Everything turns on our dispositions and intentions.[19]

Luther's famous dictum has been flourished too: *pecca fortiter, crede fortius*, as a kind of safe-conduct for sinning without restraint. In fact, of course, Luther meant that it was possible and permissible for sinful man to take heart, because God assures us of His grace. It was an exhortation to preserve faith and trust in the divine mercy.

In Catholic circles, we are more familiar with the skirmishes over various moral systems. Extreme *laxism* has been officially condemned. *Probabilism*, however, is quite acceptable and provides a splendid solution to many conflicts of conscience. It permits the discovery of new lines of conduct and does not do violence to freedom because, in case of doubt, it makes action possible even, if need be, in contravention of existing positive laws. In times of radical social changes (as in the sixteenth and even more in the twentieth century), this is the only position which takes account of a new situation as such and allows for the taking of justified risks.[20] At the same time, probabilism is sometimes used as a selfish alibi in order to evade annoying rules of conduct, and it may open the door to selfish caprice.[21]

Another appalling instance of theological rationalization is that of the various ingenious attempts made to resolve the problem: can the Sermon on the Mount be put into practice?

Reading St. Matthew, Chapters 5 to 7, one is crushed under the Lord's weighty condemnations, which appear not to take account of the modest possibilities of sinful man. Whereupon sinful man organizes an opposition to these impracticable laws. If we do not want to revise our way of life by a complete transvaluation of all our values, then we must find a loophole through which to escape the fundamental experience of conscience: "you can, because you ought."

Some deny the Sermon on the Mount the force of universal law on the grounds that it was addressed only to a limited group. On this theory, it is a kind of optional program, intended either for the Apostles on their missionary journeys, or for a select group of the ecclesial community: the prefect, the monks, the Christian élite. All Jesus' disciples do not have the same vocation nor receive an equal measure of grace. The evangelical counsels are addressed to volunteers and are not binding on everyone.

Others refer to an *interim morality*. According to this view, Jesus' demands were so exorbitant because of the extreme gravity of the times. The final eschatological crisis was imminent. The time for decision was now or never. God was giving men one last chance of conversion and salvation before the final flood swept over the earth, or a rain of fire and brimstone descended upon it. As John the Baptist put it, the axe was already laid to the roots of the tree. The Sermon on the Mount proclaimed a state of siege. Christians must understand that at any moment everything could collapse. And just as a state of political and military emergency will induce citizens and parties to call a halt to feuding and to join forces, so the faithful of the last times must set aside all hostility and all preoccupation with special interests. However, since the final catastrophe has been so long coming, the eschatological fever has subsided, and the Sermon on the Mount can no longer be proposed to us as a universally valid rule of life, which we have to establish in this world on a permanent basis.

Others, again, will *historicize* the Sermon on the Mount, interpreting it as linked to a special place and time and conditioned by singular circumstances. Such radical demands can no longer be valid for us, who live in quite different circumstances. Jesus' bald statements must be seen in terms of his polemic against the Pharisees and the rabbis. He was reacting against a piety congealed in ritualism and casuistry; against people who tried to discharge their duties to God by means of formalities without any conversion of heart. Since this was what Jesus was protesting against, He emphasized total and personal abandonment to God as the only healthy religious approach. Thus it was not at all His intention to establish absolute, universally valid positions, but rather to formulate contrary positions. Since the front against which He was defending Himself is not ours, we are not bound by His radical demands. To grasp what He really expects of us, we have first to purge the Sermon on the Mount of its polemical overtones, make it relevant, and adapt it to our times.

Still another argument, related to the preceding one, is that based on a *morality of intention*. According to this view, we do not have to convert specific directives into practical action, but rather to transpose the Oriental imagery into contemporary terms. We have to act according to the spirit of the Sermon on the Mount and let our inner disposition be ruled according to the principles of Jesus. But in our practical dealings, we must use our common sense and be capable of making realistic compromises.

Finally, according to orthodox Lutheranism, the Lord deliberately proposed a program that was impossible of achievement. He was well aware that His demands were superhuman, that it is not in our power to extirpate every impure sentiment, anger, insincerity, resentment, hardness of heart. He set such requirements in order to strike at our self-sufficiency. The Sermon on the Mount must be understood in the Pauline context as interpreted by Luther. Thus the Law was promulgated not to bring us life, but to make us conscious of our sin. It is not the Law that saves, but faith in the God of mercy. Through the unattainable goals He set, Jesus wished to rid us for good of any grounds for boasting of our good works and merits, and to teach us to despair of ourselves, so that we might be permeable to the good news that the Father would grant us His free pardon nonetheless. The Sermon on the Mount was thus a preparation for the prayer, "Forgive us our trespasses," intended to help us to arrive at the attitude of the humble publican.

Rationalization in the priestly life

Rationalizations related to the apostolate and to pastoral care deserve particular attention.

The Bible refers constantly, almost to the point of monotony, to the refusal of the people to listen to the prophets. One good way of neutralizing the prophets' alarming warnings was that of *insinuation*.

Amos, for example, was accused of rebelling against constituted authority; consequently no credit should be given to his words (7:10). Hosea was treated as a madman who should not, therefore, be taken seriously (9:7). Isaiah was arrogant and was hatching a plot against the Temple. Jeremiah was guilty of high treason; his defeatist attitude was discouraging the army and leading to the ruin of the country (38:4). Ezekiel was rejected because he used incomprehensible language and spoke in riddles . . .

Jesus' contemporaries used the same tactics to deny Him the right to speak and to defend themselves against the guilt feelings which He aroused in them: He did not observe the law of the Sabbath, He criticized Moses, He associated with persons of doubtful morals, He did not live as an ascetic, He was seducing the people, He was mad or possessed by the devil, He was in league with Satan . . .

If we can cast doubt on the competence or veracity of the prophet, his warnings immediately cease to apply. In our day, we vilify the speaker by calling him a leftist, a crypto-Marxist, a pacifist, a reactionary, a progressive, an innovator, a disguised modernist, a Jansenist, a pessimist, or a rigorist.

In Chapter 2, we noted that the themes of sin, of guilt sense, of contrition, and of repentance were not very popular with many preachers and listeners of our day. One of the reasons averred is that contemporary theology and pastoral care is concerned mainly with essentials. An authentically Christian life, according to the Gospels, is communion with God and our neighbor through faith, hope, and love. We have to stress the theological virtues and preach a positive Christianity; this means a return to the Sermon on the Mount and the first epistle of St. John. There we can find a program with tasks and obligations to fulfill. Let us not waste precious energy in the negative business of "experiencing guilt and avoiding sin." What counts is not the evil that is forbidden but the good we can and should do. Omission is far more serious than transgression. Why should we constantly explore our guilt feelings? This morbid introspection should be left to psychoanalysis, which is symptomatic of our cultural degeneracy. Technological man of the modern era needs a Christian horizon for his Promethean impulse and his earthly mission . . .[23]

In his interesting study of the problem of the worker-priests, Siefer looks for the real reason why the experiment was suspended, and finds it in the fact that it represented a threat to Church unity. It was feared that a deep class division would be created between the worker-priests and the rest of the clergy. French Catholics of the establishment were apparently not yet prepared to welcome workers with their own way of life, their own culture, and their own combativeness into *their* Church. According to this view, then, the impetus of the spirited *avant-garde* was halted by a general absence of missionary spirit and universality. Had the majority of the French clergy and laity been less identified with the middle class, the experiment would not have had to be suspended. But the arguments advanced to justify this unfortunate step were quite different: the circumstances in industrial plants, the impossibility of combining priestly life with the life of the workers, the personal failure of certain of the worker-priests . . .[24]

Conversely, priests and laymen engaged in apostolic work will sometimes use theological rationalizations when they come up against misunderstanding and resistance. They will console themselves, perhaps a little too quickly, with Christ's missionary directives, such as "Happy are you when people hate you, drive you out, abuse you, denounce your name as criminal, on account of the Son of Man" (Lk 6:22; Mt 5:11), or "Alas for you when the world speaks well of you!" (Lk 6:26). And they will recall the tragic experience of the great prophets and the example of Jesus, whose success in His apostolic activity was meager too. Yet it not infrequently happens that they are shunned not for acting in the name of Jesus but because of their paternalistic and dictatorial attitudes, their legalism, fanaticism, and triumphalism. In other words, their failure, which they would attribute to the depravity of the "world," is in fact the result of their own clericalism. And because of this rationalization, they will persist even more obstinately in their mistaken approach, while anticlericalism hardens in its turn.

It is therefore essential that all those involved in missionary activity of any kind should become conscious of their sin, like the prophet Isaiah at the time of his calling: "What a wretched state I am in! I am lost, for I am a man of unclean lips!" (6:5). The pastor must be conscious of his sin too, and feel the need for purification. We have to begin by recognizing, for instance, that while our desire for the apostolate is certainly inspired by God, it is frequently mingled with all-too-human considerations. Love of God, love of neighbor, and self-conceit are intimately bound up with one another. And as is only too often our habit, we give this mixture the name of its noblest component: apostolic zeal.

The intense desire to do good, to succeed, to achieve more and greater things than others arises not only out of concern for the well-being of our neighbor, but also out of a need for success and admiration. This is clearly apparent in our concern to display our results before authority. Our disappointment at a failure, or our severity with a colleague when he makes a mistake, are motivated not only by a feeling of responsibility but also by fear of ridicule.

How difficult it is, when a man dedicates himself heart and soul to some objective (a parish, a group), when he identifies himself with it and in fact makes it move, not to try to advance himself with it at the same time! Personal ambition, the desire to be the

pioneer who arouses admiration, mingles with legitimate concern
for the welfare of those for whom we are responsible. And we
unconsciously deceive ourselves when we seek our own advantage
under the alibi of serving the common interest. Moreover, to the
extent that we selfishly seek our own advancement, we become
useless to God and our neighbor, because we are no longer wholly
open and receptive. We follow our own notions, we are distracted
from essentials. When a pastor with such an approach listens to
anyone, he is already concerned to win him over to his own views
and plans. He no longer has the necessary openness and patience
to respect the slow burgeoning of grace in the other, or his halting
progress. Or again, we find the will to power and the spirit of
domination giving rise to mutual jealousy, envy, and criticism
among pastors, apostolic associations, and religious congregations.

Notes

1. See below, chapter 10.
2. "It is a far cry, indeed, from direct falsehood to a deluded conscience. Nevertheless, it is in terms of such falsehood that we shall
   be able to reach and throw light upon the strange power which
   liberty possesses to deceive itself, to hide itself to itself by losing
   the key to its own stratagems" (P. Ricoeur, *Philosophie de la
   volonté: le volontaire et l'involontaire*, Paris, 1960, p. 351).
3. G. Dietrich, *Untersuchungen über die Motivationsstruktur sozial
   auffälliger Jugendlicher*, Erlangen, 1958.
4. See below, chapter 8.
5. *King Lear*, act I, scene II.
6. G. von Le Fort, *The Veil of Veronica*, New York, Sheed & Ward,
   1934, p. 298.
7. See H. Thielicke, *Das Bilderbuch Gottes*, Stuttgart, 1957, p. 239;
   H. Gollwitzer, *Das Gleichnis vom barmherzigen Samariter*, Neun-
   kirchen, 1962.
8. E. Mounier, *Traité du caractère*, Paris, Editions du Seuil, 1947, p.
   747.
9. Cf. Hesnard, *Morale sans péché*, Paris, Presses universitaires de
   France, 1954, p. 91, on fear of responsibility: "It is the moral
   abdication of the respectable, esteemed by them as a virtue because
   it derives, ultimately, from some inner constraint, but which
   eventually turns their moral life into a vast, sterile and even dangerous endeavor to shut off all accusation."

10. G. Bernanos, *The Diary of a Country Priest*, New York, Macmillan, 1937, p. 5.

11. *Ibid.*, pp. 86–87.

12. We should like, here, to point in passing to the real difference between existential philosophy and the other philosophical schools. The latter tend to study man in general as an object among others. But it is only by speaking in the first person singular that a man will feel himself involved, as subject, in the enigma of life. Kierkegaard, Heidegger, Jaspers, and others caution against the dangers and potential errors inherent in the objectifying approach. By draping ourselves in the mantle of abstract man and hiding behind his mask, we avoid any personal confrontation with ourselves. We are then very easily able to delude ourselves as to our real selves, since we have every interest in so doing. The authors named emphasize the need for a sincere confrontation with ourselves, in which we look at ourselves not from without, but from within, so that an illumination of our existence (*Existenzerhellung*) is produced. This existentialist position is of course a direct extension of the Christian message of salvation addressed to each individual person as such.

13. G. Berkouwer, *De zonde*, I, Kampen, 1958, p. 151.

14. *Histories*, book III, no. 71.

15. See the historical inquiry by G. Müller, *Die Wahrhaftigkeitspflicht und die Problematik der Lüge*, Freiburg, Herder, 1962. Our purpose here is merely to note certain rationalizations to which we sometimes resort to justify lying. We certainly do not claim that there can never be real conflicts of conscience for a person who is concerned to preserve values other than those of veracity and honesty.

16. See A. Kaufmann, *Das Schuldprinzip*, Heidelberg, C. Winter, 1961.

17. Molière, *Tartuffe*, in *Tartuffe and Other Plays* (tr. Donald Frame), New York, The New American Library, 1967, p. 294.

18. Just as he tempted Jesus Christ with scriptural quotations, so the wily demon seeks to lull the conscience of the sinner with all kinds of specious arguments, writes St. Gregory the Great: "He speaks at one time of the graver deeds of others, at another time that the ill done was of no account, then of the mercy of God, and gives assurance that there is time for repentance later on . . ." (*Liber Regulae Pastoralis*, p. 201; see note 14 to chapter 1 above).

According to St. Augustine, we must beware both of rash confidence and of premature despair. "Listen to the man without hope: 'I'm damned anyway, so why shouldn't I do what I like?' Listen to the confident man: 'God's mercy is great; when I am converted, he will forgive me everything; so why shouldn't I do what I like?' Man despairs in order to be able to sin, and man hopes in order to be able to sin" (*Enarr. Ps.*, C.C.L., 40, 2096).

19. See J. Jeremias, *Unbekannte Jesusworte*, Zurich, Zwingli-Verlag, 1948.

20. See W. Schoellgen, *Konkrete Ethik*, Düsseldorf, Patmos-Verlag, 1961, p. 11.
21. Minimalist legalism is expressed even more clearly in the doubtful maxim *caritas non obligat cum tanto incommodo.* See the explanation by A. Van Kol in the periodical *Bijdragen*, 1953. The notion of a two-edged action is also sometimes exploited for the sake of procuring an alibi. We know we are covered and we theoretically deplore secondary consequences injurious to others. Fundamentally, however, we rejoice over them, especially if they include some personal advantage to ourselves.
22. However, some of these attempts to grasp the real significance of the Sermon on the Mount contain some portion of truth. For a balanced discussion of the matter, see *inter alia:* J. Jeremias, *Die Bergpredigt*, Stuttgart, Calwer Verlag, 1959. Here we are simply concerned to point to the danger of delusion and rationalization.
23. Some priests tend somewhat lightly to settle complex problems by saying, "We have to make sure not to make of his material sin a formal sin." In other words, we should not correct the objectively mistaken conscience of a person who subjectively is well intentioned and sincere. This principle, however, is too easily generalized, so that it leads to laxism and indifferentism. We forget in such a case that the first duty of the conscience is assiduously to seek truth and rectitude. We have a fundamental obligation to conform to the objective demands of morality and honestly to seek God's will, as it is made known through an upright conscience. The duty of the Church and of its pastors is precisely to "teach them to observe all the commands I gave you" (Mt 28:20).
24. See G. Siefer, *La mission des prêtres ouvriers*, Paris, l'Epi, 1963.

8

Projection

Selective perception

At a round-table conference of leaders of various youth organizations, the question came up as to the cause of the current difficulties of the youth movements. How was it that these movements no longer reached more than a minute proportion of the under-twenty group, and why was it increasingly hard to find good leaders?

An obvious answer was that the responsibility often lay with the chaplain. Examples were cited of groups which had been extremely active but which had disintegrated and disbanded within barely a year after their chaplains' departure. Either the chaplain took on too much or else he did too little and left everything to Providence . . . But after a further exchange of views, it became apparent that this explanation was not altogether satisfactory. Soon a more plausible explanation was found: youth centers and under-twenty clubs were more attractive to the young. A drink, playing the jukebox, dancing, and other pastimes were naturally more fun than disciplined action within a youth movement. It was unfair competition; it was taking advantage of the indolence of youth! And so the discussion went on until finally one of the participants diffidently suggested that perhaps the leaders might examine themselves as to their methods of work, their plans, and their organization; perhaps that might reveal another causal link . . .

Here we have a very commonplace example of the projection mechanism operating in the service of self-exculpation.

Before looking more closely into this all-too-human tactic to avoid the admission of error, let us take a look at the general psychological background.

Our idea of the world about us is necessarily dependent upon our senses, but the physiological structure of our eyes or ears is a limiting factor in itself: we can hear only sound vibrations of a certain frequency or intensity; we cannot see the ultraviolet or the infrared components of the spectrum.

We can compare our senses to perceptive devices which select a single aspect of reality. The maxim *"quidquid recipitur ad modum recipientis recipitur"* applies here too. Modern psychology shows us, moreoever, that we perceive only what is meaningful to us. The hunter, the forester, the geologist, and the painter will look at one and the same landscape in very different ways. Three persons walking along the same road in a big city will each notice different things, or will pass by certain displays or incidents without paying attention to them.

What we remark and select from the virtually unlimited quantity of objective data which the world offers us is determined by the *theme* of our investigations. Our perceptive field (*Merkwelt*) and our operative field (*Werkwelt*) coincide. Our individual disposition or our personality structure, in which our past and our existential purpose exert a major influence, delimits the profile and the relief of our perceptive field. Our affective life and our disposition at a particular moment play an important part in this matter. If I am out of temper, I see the clouds or the sea in a somber and oppressive light. If I am depressed, a well-lit room is too bright and flashy. Our surroundings appear different to us according to our moods.

It is therefore quite true to say that human perception and knowledge are never wholly receptive and passive, but active and generative of forms and structures, even creative. That is why it is perfectly correct to emphasize the subjective character of our sensory and intellectual knowledge. An objective foundation exists, of course, in the reality outside us, but our idea of it is largely influenced by our own nature. It is we who provide the lighting. This is the background against which we have to consider the delicate problem of religious projection: to what extent is our anthropomorphic conception of God a subjective projection? We do not intend to go into that question here; some reference, however, was made to it in the latter part of Chapter 5 above.

This universal psychic phenomenon of projection is a normal human activity, inherent in our nature. It means organizing a given disparate multitude of objects; endeavoring to understand the unknown through the agency of certain apperceptive and operational schemes.

But it is also undeniable that projective activity often extends so far that, instead of conferring meaning on the reality perceived, it tendentiously distorts it. Objective perception is then interrupted by subjective elements to the point of becoming inaccurate.

If we are impatiently waiting for someone to come, or for something to happen, we will interpret the least sound as indicating the fulfillment of our wish. We will constantly imagine a noise of steps or a knocking at the door. The intensity of our desire has the effect of suggestion. It gives everything a special significance. The same thing happens with fright. At the least rustling or movement, we *see* in the mysterious darkness the robber who is not there. In extreme cases this leads to delusions, hallucinations, and fixed ideas. Through such projection we fill a vacuum: something which is absent from the objective reality, but of which we feel a need (whether we ardently desire it or fear it), is invented and created. This brings us to pathological phenomena. Delirium will lead to fantasies expressing subjective needs.

Normal thematic apperception confers meaning; tendentious apperception distorts meaning. The area between the two naturally greatly resembles a no-man's-land and cannot be clearly defined.

An example will bring this mechanism home to us. How do we represent to ourselves a person whom we know only fragmentarily? We complete the image through associations colored by our expectations. We relate it to that of someone we have once met. After listening to a reporter on the radio, we are sometimes astonished when we see him on the T.V. screen or in person: I had not expected him to look like that! Where did I get my picture of him?

It is because of this error, in favor or to the detriment of the person concerned, that the psychoanalyst remains outside the visual field of his patient. He sits behind the couch, preferably in semidarkness, to facilitate the projective activity of the patient, who thus has a chance to attribute a number of unreal qualities to him. He thus becomes a kind of screen on which the patient can at will project the father or mother image or the image of other persons of importance in his life (transference).

Projection is thus accompanied by externalization. It is a form of self-expression in spite of oneself. "The man who rents and furnishes a house, projects his inner self in forms and colors. And when he has finished, he can tell what his inner self looks like" (A. Strindberg). In one of his novels, Strindberg describes a character who decorates his house to his taste. First, he subdues the light by means of drapes. He hides the nudity of the walls by placing furniture in front of them. He gets rid of the irritating whiteness of the table by covering it with a cloth. And finally he tries to harmonize the colors of everyday objects. In this way, the author has indirectly portrayed the tenant of the room himself: anxious, slightly unbalanced, desirous of order, peace, and harmony; a man who is trying to overcome his horror of emptiness.

Projection is significant in relation to the subject on which it throws light and it refers back to the person who projects himself. Each of us has his own world of projections and transposes his inner self on the external world. Man projects himself in games, in dreams and daydreams, in errors or failures. Whence the immense importance which psychoanalysis attaches to these spontaneous revelations, with their great diagnostic significance.[1]

The danger of bias in the reading or interpretation of a text is universally recognized. Historical documents or statistics can be made to say almost anything you like. The same is true of the Bible. Either we read too much into a text or we minimize it, emptying it of its objective content because we do not like what it says. None so deaf, indeed, as he who will not hear.

Jung drew attention to the fact that projection uses archetypes as a pre-established sensory-motor equipment. Lovers, for example, see each other in a very special light. Their intense feeling imparts an aura of fascination to what is often an insignificant reality. They do not see each other as they are in fact, nor even as they may or should become, but as each wants the other to be. Their apperceptive apparatus seems provided with a creative force which adorns the other, as though by magic, with perfection. But experience shows that, after the honeymoon, a crack soon appears in the fragile crystal. The weight of humdrum reality breaks down the illusion. The magical effect dissolves like a morning mist. The time of disenchantment comes; then each begins to see the other in his or her true light, with eyes from which the scales have fallen. Eros projects on the loved one the image of the ideal spouse (*animus* or *anima*). Under the effect of a certain stimulus, chords of sensibility are touched and harmonies aroused; archetypes or basic collective structures are set in motion and impose themselves with authority. The archetypes (*inter alia:* the hero, the king, the sage, the friend, the enemy, the doctor, the savior, the giant, the priest, the female counselor) give a positive or negative value to our actual experiences and concretize our desires in imaginary figures. This explains why the primary images of fairy tales, myths, and parables touch us to the very depths of our being. They arouse a thousand echoes in us in the form of motor responses.[2]

Projection as a defense mechanism

What we experience and sense about ourselves (our motives, our character, our conduct) may sometimes be so disagreeable that we cannot resolve to attribute it to ourselves. We more or less deliberately refuse to identify ourselves with it. We repress the unpleasant fact and banish it beyond the realm of consciousness. Our conscience speaks to us in the second person singular, but we do not react by an admission of guilt.

An effective weapon here is externalization: we attribute the unacceptable fact to others: these feelings, ideas, plans, or way of life belong to other things, or preferably, to other persons. For depth psychology it is of the utmost importance to see projection as a consequence of repression. When an inner perception is repressed, writes Freud, its content, after undergoing certain changes, eventually reaches consciousness as a perception coming from outside.[3] That is why we so easily attribute some inner censure, following upon an illicit action, to others, preferably to formidable figures or anonymous powers. This externalization or displacement of remorse makes the conflict less painful. Thus a woman who has vilified her neighbors and feels guilty about it will worry instead about the possibility that her neighbors may trace the slander back to her. Or an employee who has not carried out his assignment in accordance with his own standards will fear a reprimand from his boss. Or again, there is the fear which grips certain people after some transgression: fear of a car or plane accident, of an explosion, of being struck by lightning . . . Moreover, such anxiety in anticipation (*Erwartungsangst*) often leads to provocative action. So many guilty persons seem unconsciously to want to be caught by making foolish mistakes or slips of the tongue.

Man forms as it were a symbiotic unity with his surroundings. When he finds distrust or suspicion in his heart, he attributes his feelings of hatred and envy to others and accuses them of aggressiveness. People with a happy and vivacious disposition, on the other hand, attribute a similar disposition to their fellows. We tend to see the world around us as mirroring our features and we feel that our image of ourselves is the face of others. Self-complacency and our ego-ideal make us sing the praises of our own qualities, while at the same time we feel superior to others, whom we despise. That brilliant moralist and psychologist St. Augustine put it this way: "A man is inclined to suspect of another what he feels in himself. As long as he refuses to turn his eyes away from the vanities he finds in himself [see Ps 119:37], he suspects them in others. Thus he believes that the reason why he reveres God and does good works is the one which inspires other men." Similarly, Satan rashly suspects Job of serving God through greed for gain.[4] St. Augustine adds that such repression and projection are accompanied by rivalry and jealousy.

Objective reality is distorted, subjectively interpreted and arranged; it is egocentrically adapted to the person projecting it. A young woman, for example, is driving a sports car on a busy road at moderate speed. She is in no particular hurry. But along comes a Volkswagen which tries to pass her. Immediately the young woman steps on the accelerator. Questioned subsequently about her crazy driving, she explains: "I won't let a wretched little car overtake me!" Her pride and her dignity cannot bear it. She wants to be the more powerful and to maintain her prestige. And this need is apparently stronger than her desire to act courteously and reasonably. Drivers do indeed have a tendency to identify themselves with the mechanical properties of their vehicles. The man at the wheel of the small car is instinctively classified as lower. In puerile fashion, our young woman thinks that he wishes to humiliate her. Although the other driver has neither the desire nor the means to do so, she is determined to interpret the facts egocentrically and uncritically in defense of her prestige.

Projection is thus a consequence of infatuation or idealization and of repression. We suspect others of being what we are ourselves, but without realizing it or without admitting it, because then we would be admitting to difficulties, failings, and faults in ourselves. That is why we will accuse our neighbor (colleague, inferior, superior) of cupidity, intolerance, selfishness, sexual aggressiveness, etc., even if these faults are in no way characteristic of him.

Accurate self-knowledge and healthy self-criticism make us less inclined to indulge in projection. Such a stepping back from oneself is extremely important for anyone in a position of having to give advice—as a spiritual director, social worker, personnel chief, neighborhood organizer, psychotherapist. That is why there is such insistence in psychotherapy on thorough self-criticism. The individual concerned becomes capable of dealing with the problem of his own ego structure, his antecedents, his character, and his existential purpose.

In the pastoral context which concerns us here we have to be particularly careful not to give way to an obsession with guilt; we must not turn into prophets who project their own faults on others and ferret them out among those around them. As regards the connatural danger of illusion to which we are all exposed, it is good not to forget that there is a close link between rationalization and projection. Most of the time, men's decisions and actions are simultaneously inspired by several motives which intersect, complement, or conflict with one another. But when we act, we tend to simplify this complex datum and reduce it to a single motive. This partial explanation is based on repression and insincerity: on the system of half-truths. The mixture is named after one element. But we have two systems of measurement. In connection with our own conduct, we generally overemphasize our noble intentions and underestimate our selfish motives (rationalization and idealization). In connection with the conduct of others, we tend to reduce all other motives to the main selfish one and to soft-pedal the secondary good intentions (projection and minimization).

In his *Vipers' Tangle*, Mauriac shows how tragically prejudice against another can falsify and distort perception. Louis, the rich old landowner, has nurtured feelings of resentment, bitterness, and hatred toward his wife throughout his married life. In a moment of distress, his wife confides to him that she has constantly desired him during all those years when he had believed her to be utterly indifferent to him. And suddenly he realizes that his negative bias has prevented him from seeing her as she really was.

> I gazed at the vineyard without answering. A doubt came to me, at that moment. Is it possible for us, for nearly half a century, to observe only one side of the person who shares our life? Can it be that, out of habit, we pick and choose among the things they say and the things they do, retaining only that which nurtures our grievances and perpetuates our resentment? Have we a fatal tendency to simplify other people—to eliminate all those features which might be regarded as extenuating, which might render more human the caricature of them which our hatred needs for its justification? [5]

But as his wife appears unduly anxious to exploit this long-delayed thaw, he immediately returns to his isolation.

Morgenstern has a striking formula for the use of projection and externalization in the service of self-exoneration; man, he says, is a prisoner locked up in a dungeon of mirrors. When man suffers, he attributes his suffering to things, to conditions, to his fellow men, to God. He projects. He stubbornly resists any possibility of awareness of unpalatable truths, especially of humiliating facts which might wound his dignity. He prefers to ignore and repress the real cause and takes consolation in the thought that his suffering has been brought on by external factors. He remains enclosed in his prison hung with mirrors and he places the responsibility for what he should seek within himself on the figures reflected therein. Only honest admission can break down the glass walls and set him free. "You will know the truth, and the truth will make you free" (Jn 8:32).

Our hearts are warped and twisted, says St. Augustine. That is why they must first be broken and crushed. That is what we indicate symbolically when we strike our breasts. Only then can God heal our hearts and make them upright. As long as the human heart is twisted, it cannot delight in what God says and enjoins. "The man whose heart is twisted believes that all God says and does is wrong. Every judgment of God displeases him, especially when it censures him. He refuses to correct himself according to God's standards, and seeks instead to mould God to his own standard." [6] "I am twisted under the weight of my own iniquity. But your word is the right rule of truth. Straighten me, therefore, twisted as I am, according to your rule." [7]

The scapegoat complex, or transculpation

In the Bible, and among most peoples, sin is represented as a painful burden: man is bowed down under the crushing weight of the disastrous consequences of his sin. This image probably explains why the ancient Babylonians believed that they could rid themselves of the burden by placing it on the back of an animal, which could then carry it off. We find an echo of this primitive rite of exculpation in Leviticus 16:20. At a religious solemnity, all the accumulated faults of the community are unloaded upon a goat, which is then driven out into the desert.[8] A similar custom exists in India. A canoe is symbolically laden with all the faults of the members of the community, then taken out to sea. In this way the group and the individual hope to be purified of their sins and to escape punishment.

The colorful image of the proverbial scapegoat strikingly illustrates the process of projection. We might draw attention to a significant example of the process in recent contemporary history.

In 1963, when the Italian Communist party was spectacularly successful at the polls, the neo-Fascist and liberal press, and also some of the clergy, imputed the fact to Pope John XXIII, who, they claimed, had initiated a kind of moral disarmament as regards the leftists. Whereas in point of fact is was precisely the people of those social and economic groupings—whether or not they were themselves morally responsible—who objectively bore the responsibility for the great increase in the membership of the Communist party through their appalling procrastination in the area of social thought and action.

One is constantly meeting Christians who have left the Church. They say they have had enough of God and of the Church. Years ago, Fr. X passed them without a greeting; or such and such individuals, pillars of the church, cheated them. So they have stopped going to church. But in many cases a more intimate conversation, in which they really pour out their hearts, shows that the alleged grievances simply provided a good opportunity for a break with God which in fact existed before. Their anticlericalism and hostility to the Church are often no more than a pretext, covering a much deeper problem, sometimes searing remorse, which had been repressed.

Repressed guilt cannot be whittled down. The law of survival applies here too: the unutilized repressed material, finding no outlet, simply accumulates. It cannot be wished away, but only diverted—diverted onto any scapegoat that comes to hand.

The projective structure may be recognized in the jealous and sulky child. The child wants to be loved more than the others, to be given preferential treatment. When he finds to his bitter disappointment that he is not given more affection or care than his little brothers and sisters, he becomes jealous. He is told that he is jealous, unfair, selfish. If he cannot identify himself with this painful charge and recognize that he is in fact envious of the others, then he represses the guilt experience from consciousness. The characteristic is then externalized: my parents are unfair. I have been injured and therefore my attitude of protest is justified. It is their fault.

Aggressiveness plays an important part in the exculpation process. This is particularly true in the case of what are known as difficult characters—individuals who constantly behave unpleasantly toward those around them and remain impermeable to any recognition of their culpability. The origin of this attitude, or its inner dynamism, is often the following. Violent (infantile) guilt feelings, induced by an authoritarian superego, are aroused when aggressive drives are experienced. In order to defend the ego against this feeling of anxiety and guilt, the aggressiveness which is really present is banished from consciousness and stifled. But the primitive energies which have not been constructively integrated, but simply repressed, continue to seek an outlet. To eliminate this tension, the subject needs a real aggressiveness which he can justify in his own eyes. He has to be able to act in legitimate self-defense. He has a vital urge to be able to behave obnoxiously while still believing that he is deserving of no reproach. So he has to discover a satisfactory reason for putting up resistance or passing to the attack. What he wants is not a stick to be able to hit the dog, but rather a dog so that he can use the stick. His repressed aggressiveness forces him, as it were, to create situations in which he can legitimately and at will give free rein to his aggressive dynamism: abreaction with a good conscience. He will thus feel both relieved and covered. He can torment those around him without admitting his guilt. His impossible behavior, he feels, is in fact a legitimate reaction and a well-deserved punishment for the injustice which others commit toward him. Once more the old axiom is confirmed: attack is the best defense!

When this personality structure becomes neurotic, the individual concerned will come to live as the persecuted persecutor, avenging his own bitterness by making life miserable for others. Paradoxically, he turns executioner in order to strengthen his own conviction that he is the victim.

That is why it is so hard to persuade sado-masochistic couples to separate. The courts and the family counselling services know these cases only too well. The two partners cannot do without each other to satisfy their respective needs for being the executioner and the victim. They neither wish nor are able to agree— with all the resulting injury to the children.

A less-complex example of projection is regularly to be seen in the criminal courts. The public self-righteously decries the man who has been found guilty of a crime. But this indignation, vented in primitive fashion, is generally not the effect of unadulterated righteousness. We tend, especially in a group, to belch up our inner accusations against ourselves onto a substitute victim, a scapegoat. We are thus relieved of the feelings of shame and guilt which have been repressed or are barely conscious. These feelings are transferred to a cynical malefactor, so that we may ourselves take our places among the righteous. We cannot but recall here the Gospel scene of the woman taken in adultery and the virtuous men demanding that she be stoned to death.

Among the most spectacular illustrations of this defense method is the famous *Malleus maleficarum* ("Witches' Hammer") by two late medieval theologians, Sprenger and Institor (1487), in which they sought to justify the cruel tortures inflicted by the Inquisition on alleged witches accused principally of having sexual relations with the devil. This was clearly a projection of repressed sexuality and probably of incestuous desires against which the individuals concerned protected themselves by a morbid misogyny.[9]

The *intolerant moralizer* is one who attempts to avoid a conflict between his sexual instincts and religious and moral precepts by identifying himself with the code of laws and attributing to others his own desire which has not been harmoniously integrated: *they* are perverse and live in impurity. He is scandalized by the most innocent things, and even what is healthy appears to him suspect and diabolical.

The same problem is apparent, although in a more attenuated form, in the *celibate* (priest or religious) who constantly fears for himself. He fears his own weakness and his imperfect self-control. He has a panic fear lest his innate inclination lead him to paths which he does not wish to tread; lest he be engulfed in his longing for a feminine presence, an *alter ego* and a partner, without whom it is so hard to go through life. Fundamentally, this is an anxiety produced by his own vulnerability and ineradicable sexuality. But this fear of self and obsession with sin can easily be projected outside, on a woman, resulting in a terror of the opposite sex. Woman comes to be treated as the proximate occasion of sin, as a stumbling block, as a being who for safety's sake must be avoided. The celibate is thus using woman as a scapegoat, although he is himself the real or potential sinner.

Ill-natured gossip is another instance of the same phenomenon. Why do we so readily speak of our neighbor's failings? Why do we take so much pleasure in exposing every detail of the weaknesses and less-savory aspects, the escapades and the romances of other people's private lives? Outwardly we show great indignation, whereas inwardly we are delighted. At such moments, however indignant we may be, we enjoy our superiority. We feel our own worth to be infinitely enhanced when we can utterly demolish others.

Slander and calumny, under which heading we may also place the revelations and scandals of the press, are governed by the idealization of the self and the mechanism of projection. Apparently we are unable to shake off our own guilt so long as we believe in the virtue of others. We want to stay on the pedestal of our own superiority. And shock and indignation about others lend themselves excellently to this enterprise. We raise ourselves up above them. Like the Pharisee in the Temple, we orient ourselves downward, taking as our standard of comparison someone who is still worse than we are (the publican). But when we measure our worth against the shortcomings of others rather than against the holiness of God, we at once become arrogant. Even if we are not concerned to vilify others, we nevertheless try to give the impression that we are on a higher level by debasing them.

Jesus Christ shows us in His parable (Lk 18:9–14) that prayer and examination of conscience are a matter between God and man. The man who appears before the Lord in the consciousness of his guilt does not compare himself with his neighbor; God is his only standard and point of reference. He recognizes his own error and is aware of the abyss that separates the Most High from the sinner that he is. The publican is a wrongdoer. But his humility and his awareness of his sin prevent him from saying: that Pharisee may have more moral and religious qualities than I, but he has his failings, too! Such an assertion would be objectively accurate, but it would be beside the point. The reason why the publican returns home "justified" is because he does not compare himself with those who are worse than he is, but keeps his gaze fixed solely on God and his own unworthiness. He probably had not even noticed the Pharisee praying in the Temple at the same time.

The same considerations apply to the indignation—real or feigned—surrounding resignations from the priesthood. We expect a great deal of those in uniform, in public office, in the professions, in Roman collars, and we tend to judge their lapses very harshly. And rightly so, up to a point; for the individual who sets himself up as a defender of law, of the truth, of health, or of morals must assume his responsibilities and shoulder the consequences. But there is more to it than that. Through our severe demands on such persons, the rest of us feel covered, relieved, and excused. But the practice of not facing our own guilt or taking to heart the warnings of our own conscience is gravely threatened when the professional representatives of responsibility declare bankruptcy. "The less people attend to their own sins, the more curiously they look upon those of others," writes St. Augustine. "For they are concerned not to correct but to devour. And since they cannot excuse themselves, they are always ready to accuse others." [10]

The tendency to proclaim others responsible for our own failures becomes especially virulent in times of economic crisis, depression, famine, and war. After-effects and disappointments whose exact cause it is hard to establish lead to aggressive reaction against those allegedly responsible. The hunt for scapegoats is on, on stereotyped lines. Frustration generates anxiety and a sense of guilt. It gives rise to an exacerbated sense of self and culminates in explosions of aggressiveness. To this is added a tendency to simplify complex phenomena and reduce to a few threads a tangled skein of causes. This makes the situation easier to handle, and the suppressed fury can be more effectively discharged. Such action is rendered particularly easy when a victim is close to hand in the form of a minority group, readily distinguishable by its language, dress, color, or way of life. In such cases, projection closely resembles collective neurosis and mass psychosis. In a group, and especially in time of emergency, a man will easily abdicate his freedom and responsibility, and lose all self-control. Then we get the sickening cases of man-hunts: heretics, witches, Jews, Negroes, dissidents, etc.

Twinning: a variation of the scapegoat tactic

This tactic consists in representing (that is, rendering present) our own problems to ourselves in a partner. The substitute is called upon to experience certain feelings, to exercise certain functions, or to perform certain actions in my place, as a kind of auxiliary self.

When her father and mother go out in the evening, six-year-old Mary starts telling her younger sister scary stories, to make her feel afraid and then to be able to console and protect her. The child is probably trying to shake off her own fear by inducing fear in another. She can then assume the role of her parents and thus overcome her own fear of being abandoned. This detour to protect herself against fear is not a straightforward form of projection but a complex maneuver in which objectification, externalization, and stepping back from oneself combine to create a real bearer of this externalized sentiment.

Psychoanalysts speak in this connection of an *altruistic cession of drives.* This tactic consists in having another fulfill the desires which a man denies himself, so that he may take part in his satisfaction; or again in contriving to obtain for the benefit of another what he does not have the courage to claim for himself.

In his *Othello,* Shakespeare describes how Iago assuages his intolerable jealousy by bringing Othello to the same condition. In the same way, lovers and homosexuals will often incite their partners to jealousy or infidelity in order to escape the same emotions themselves. In some families, husband and wife succeed in arousing in the other his or her own anxiety about the child or anger with the child, so that he or she may remain calm and if necessary intervene as a peacemaker. Or again, we have David contriving to get rid of Uriah through the agency of Joab and the warriors of Rabba (2 S 11). There is also the type of person who tries to pervert others in order to be able to accuse them afterward or, adding insult to injury, to stage a solemn expiation or reparation, or even to attempt to convert the guilty person. A more common tactic is that of calumniators and backbiters who go and tell the authorities that *others* dare criticize them, whereas they themselves are loyally upholding law and order.

We might perhaps relate all this to the phenomenon of gang formation, particularly among young delinquents, as an endeavor to share their anxieties and guilt experience with others.

Such a mobilization of a twin substitute is clearly more satisfactory as a method than ordinary projection. For by acting in this manner, we have the impression of respecting reality. The other person is really frightened, really angry, jealous, or guilty. It is not a matter of mere simulation. The fact of knowing this and especially of circulating it is reassuring. Our self-confidence is strengthened and our self-control facilitated. We succeed in effectively unloading our fault on another and in having this confirmed by objective observers; rather as a liar or a visionary ultimately convince themselves of the truth of their own assertions, once they have succeeded in convincing another.

Abdication

It is also possible to transfer to others our superego or our conscience, the principle which harbors sentiments of anxiety and culpability. This very common self-defensive tactic has already been referred to under the heading of rationalization; it is the appeal to custom and public opinion: but everybody does it! For example, a person realizes that he is harboring some malicious or criminal design. To escape the inner tension of self-reproach, he tries to lull his conscience and absolve himself of responsibility. Only an old-fashioned notion forbids this! It is a remnant of infantile prudery, a holdover from the severe upbringing which my parents gave me. Or again: only a narrow social environment, an outmoded code of laws, the authority of the Church, an institution unaware of the realities of life, reprove this action. Responsible people see nothing wrong with it! Depending on circumstances, these "responsible people" turn out to be movie stars, novelists, psychologists, primitive peoples, etc. They possess more competence, knowledge, or breadth of view than my conscience, which forbids divorce, euthanasia, deceit, masturbation, abortion. Nowadays *they* are much more broadminded about all these issues.

The hidden mainspring governing this projective activity is not only the love of comfort and the selfishness of an ego structure unprepared to put out any effort or make any sacrifice. Another element which very often appears to be involved is the fear of "what will people say?"—in other words, human respect. Thus, a person may feel that he should help some unfortunate individual, or that he should undertake some action in favor of social justice. But what will the others say, those who set the tone? Hesnard writes in this connection: "The social machinery of accusation expands family censure into the mute, icy, or mocking disapproval of friends or colleagues, the man in the street, the public, everyone . . . Finally, the generous—or simply human—idea is banished and turned, as it were, against its author. And thus a person who considers himself virtuous will act as though he really believed that the others were right, although he knows that in fact they are wrong." [11]

This is the radar-man, the other-directed type whose primary characteristic is the importance that *others* take in his life. His style of life is determined by the desire to become and to be like his contemporaries. Strongly motivated by conformism, such persons have an extraordinary feeling for the attitude and expectations of their environment; they resemble a compass or a radar post. They live their lives in a state of permanent and diffuse fear of doing the wrong thing.[12] The experience of living safely in the anonymous mass compensates for the feeling of shame or guilt which comes from a personal deficiency. Very closely related to this personality structure is that of the man subjected to the tyranny of social pressures or of an infantile superego.

Psychologists have devoted a great deal of research to the dismal problem of war crimes. How are such crimes to be explained? Most of the Nazi mass killers had originally been upright members of their families or professions. They had been neither better nor worse than most of us. Real criminals and asocial individuals constituted only a very small fraction of the personnel of the concentration camps. These people, who had been gentle and sensitive at home or among their friends, now turned into sadistic torturers, rather like those ladies who pitilessly exterminate vermin but pamper their cats or lap-dogs. We are reminded of the Pharisees who scrupulously paid their miserable tithes but were unjust and harsh to the poor. How, then, do such upright persons turn into fiendish criminals? The capital factor seems to be moral and religious immaturity, or again, dependence on others: the conscious or unconscious striving for nonautonomy. The man who obeys and conforms to the commands of commonly recognized authority puts himself out of reach of all conflict. He is covered.

This tendency toward abdication is not only found among those incapable of critical thought. Even a very intelligent person is capable of stubbornly barricading his inner self against any self-criticism. He will insert himself unconditionally in another and greater self: a superego. He will then feel automatically dispensed from taking personal decisions of conscience.

The problem whether the authority which is regarded as legitimate can justify its plans and orders simply does not arise. It is unnecessary to think critically. Any personal opinion or value judgment has been given up beforehand. The only thing that counts is that this superego should provide protection and safety, peace and reassurance. Any attempts at an autonomous fulfillment of one's life are confined to working and fighting at the side of authority, or the leader, in a spirit of blind obedience. His opinions, his friends and enemies are also mine. "I have no conscience; my conscience is named Adolf Hitler!" Marshall Goering proudly proclaimed.

Any order from above, in such an ego structure, is automatically valid. Because of this absolutizing, all standards become relative. Crime is no longer crime; in some still hidden sense it is justified. The only crime is to resist authority. To do so is to draw down upon oneself the wrath of one's *god*, with the agonizing sense of being delivered over to nothingness. There is no longer a center from which one can subsequently judge or act oneself. The constantly repeated excuse of the war criminals: "I carried out orders; I did my duty and obeyed; therefore I am innocent" was more than a cheap excuse; it contained a good deal of sincere indignation. They simply did not understand the accusations. Everything imputed to them was outside the sphere of their superego. "Orders are orders!" Eichmann remained unmoved as his abominable crimes were enumerated. But when the judge requested him to stand up for the reading of the indictment, he jumped up and began to mumble excuses and blush with shame. For he had transgressed against the supreme law of his conduct: unconditional respect for authority.[13]

No one, not even a believing Christian, is immune against such blind submission at the risk of losing his self. We are constantly in danger of being drawn into totalitarianism, either by clinging to the formalistic morality of our childhood (fixation), or by unreflectingly adopting new authoritarian norms or slogans which are not based on a personal value experience, and thus remaining at the phase of the infantile superego (regression). We should therefore not be too hasty in rejecting the warning of nonbelievers that our obedience to the Church is often little different from servile docility.

Abdication of conscience can sometimes be cloaked under

action on behalf of another person or group. This happens when the shame and the fear experienced are dissociated from their real source, the forbidden action. We manage to isolate the guilt by allegedly committing the sin to the advantage of another, not of ourselves.

Various consciences, or phases in the development of conscience may be distinguished; these phases continue to function in the adult in a more or less independent manner. They are: the super-ego, or the conscience which is the product of a strict upbringing and of the process of socialization; the ego-ideal, or the conscience structured in terms of the autonomous and individual fulfillment of the ego; the personal conscience as such, responsive to objective values recognized as binding.

In any attempt to exculpate ourselves, these components are set up against one another. This happens, for example, when we give up clearly recognized values for the sake of a priority known as *development of the personality* (the ego-ideal). We claim, then, to be following our *vocation*, or our biological, artistic, or scientific *urge*, in order to get out of our family, social, or religious obligations.

We find a sorry illustration of the point in the diary of the German poet Hebbel. After living in concubinage with Elise Lensing for ten years and having two children with her, he married the well known actress Christine Enghaus. Shortly after, on New Year's Eve, he made the following entry in his diary:

> I've got married, but not to Elise. That says everything . . . It is my conviction, and will remain my conviction to all eternity, that man is delivered over wholly to that power in his being which is the most important. For from that power alone flows his own happiness, as well as anything that he can give the world. In me that power is poetry. How could I ever have kept it alive in the miserable struggle for a living? And how could I ever have pursued that struggle without that power, since there was never any chance of winning? If peace of mind is the guarantee of the quality of my action, then I never did a better thing than when I took the step which Elise calls a mortal sin . . . Naturally I shall do my duty to the children I have had with Elise . . . Can I help it, and have I been a scoundrel, if today my heart overflows, whereas previously it was frozen? [14]

This profoundly human passage very clearly reflects the endeavor to excuse oneself on esthetic grounds: only the development of his poetic talent could make him happy and useful to society. Other defense mechanisms are apparent too: the negation of responsibility (can I help it?); the assertion that his decision is good and his conscience serene, to cover the voice of his remorse; the assurance that he will not neglect his children, in guise of compensation.

When conscience nags us, therefore, we can appeal both to the superego and to the ego-ideal. Paradoxically, however, we sometimes attempt to set our conscience in conflict with itself. For instance, a man feels a desire to change the course of his life and to devote himself to some new task with greater love and self-sacrifice. Or he will begin to doubt the wisdom of a previous decision and re-examine a way of life which had hitherto appeared quite reasonable. Such conflicts occur, for instance, among persons preparing for the priesthood or for perpetually binding vows. And such persons will sometimes categorically banish the idea, reject it, and repress it as a *temptation*. No, they say, we must not be changeable, weak, or faithless! We must not listen to the world, the flesh, or the devil!

So they silence the whisperings of conscience by pinning a pejorative label to the issue. And in this way, they are dispensed from having to examine the issue seriously. They give themselves good marks for faithfulness or generosity and thus skillfully stifle a lack of daring, of self-criticism, and of readiness to follow God's providential hints. In this way, the lazy, immature, or cowardly ego prevents the conscience from calling its existential purpose into question, and it justifies this conduct by reference to the conscience itself.

Such an attitude greatly resembles that of the scribes and Pharisees who silenced God in the name of what He had previously revealed when He spoke to them in and through Jesus Christ. Salvation history is halted. And that is the way the obdurate man acts when he decides what God can and should say, denying Him the right to explain Himself further or to manifest His further designs. And so we come to the phenomenon of projection onto God.

Projection onto God

Herodotus, living over 2,000 years ago, tells the following story: Cyrus, king of Persia, had commissioned his general Mazares to capture the rebel Paktyes alive. The latter, however, had had word of the plan and asked asylum of the city of Kyme. Mazares drew near with his troops to lay siege to the city, and called upon the Kymeans to hand over the refugee. The Kymeans decided to consult their god first. The oracle replied that the man should be handed over. Just as they were about to carry out the order, a citizen of noble rank, Aristodikos, requested that no action should be taken for the time being: he still had his doubts concerning the matter. Perhaps, he suggested, the messengers had misunderstood the oracle or distorted its words. He obtained permission to go to the sanctuary himself and to put the question again. But he received the same reply. Aristodikos then proceeded to destroy the nests of the birds which inhabited the sacred precepts of the temple. Immediately an angry voice resounded from the sanctuary: "Impious man, how dare you lay hands on creatures that are under my protection!" Unabashed, Aristodikos replied: "Lord, you come to the help of those that are under your protection; should we, Kymeans, hand over a man who has fled to ours?" The god replied: "Yes, so that your destruction may be the speedier, in punishment of your sin. For you desired an answer from the oracle as to whether it was permissible to hand over those under your protection!"

It matters little whether this is a legend or an historical event; in either case, it conceals a profound truth which is valid for all times.

What Herodotus has shown in so masterly a fashion is the conflict in man's conscience. The Kymeans hesitate between two attitudes: to respect the sacrosanct law of asylum and, if need be, to brave Cyrus' vengeance, or, in cowardly fashion, to prefer their own safety and disregard an obvious right. Fear triumphs. But in order to escape a gnawing guilt feeling, they try to shelter behind a higher authority. They try to extract an acquittal for themselves and project their responsibility onto the divine legislator. But the conscience of a single individual rises up against this attempt at self-exculpation. He knows the value of the right of political asylum. His desire to respect that right to the full triumphs over his own interests. God who speaks in conscience cannot contradict Himself in an oracle. And the oracle proves Him right; when we hear the voice of conscience clearly, then it is sinful to go on putting questions as though the issue were in doubt and to seek an alibi.

Herodotus presents us here with a kind of parable which unmasks the mechanism of projection.

St. James the Apostle earnestly exhorts us in his epistle to avoid all projection on to God: "Let no one say when he is tempted, 'I am tempted by God,' for God cannot be tempted with evil and he himself tempts no one; but each person is tempted when he is lured and enticed by his own desire . . . Do not be deceived, my beloved brethren . . ." (1:13–16).

The reference to being tempted by God is to the more distant origin of the temptation, not to the immediate cause. It is an attempt to shelve all personal responsibility. It is the alibi which runs throughout man's history: it's not my fault if I sin. Indeed, if God created me as I am, how can I be held responsible when I act according to my nature? Sin comes from God, not from myself (determinism). Such an argument is based on an altogether false image of God. Evil has no attraction whatsoever for God; therefore it is utterly impossible that He should want to incite us to sin. To quote Ecclesiasticus: "Do not say, 'The Lord was responsible for my sinning,' for he is never the cause of what he hates. Do not say, 'It was he who led me astray,' for he has no use for a sinner" (Si 15:11–12). To seek an explanation or an excuse for sin in God amounts to high treason. Only one causal explanation is possible: sin comes solely from man's heart (cf. Jm 4:1).

St. James warns us very clearly against misusing the Genesis story of the fall. There is a danger, as Ricoeur points out, in overemphasizing the external element in temptation, as symbolized by the serpent. "We seek to exculpate ourselves by accusing another . . . The trick in exculpation is to place outside ourselves the temptation which was hovering on the border between inside and outside." [15] Ricoeur also contrasts the biblical idea of sinful man confessing his transgressions with the theogonic myths which reflect a tragic view of existence. But perhaps the Germanic story of creation is even clearer than the examples cited by Ricoeur.

The gist of the story is as follows. The world was made from the corpse of the giant Ymir: the sea of his blood, the firmament of his skull, the clouds of his brain. The giant had been murdered by Odin and his brother, who were related to him. Thus our world originated with an appalling crime. Through this cosmogony the ancient Germans sought to explain that our world was made of poor materials, laden with malediction. If, therefore, all kinds of horror take place in the course of history—infidelities, betrayals, hatred, despotisms (as in the *Nibelungenlied*)—this is simply an expression of hereditary defects. In suffering and in guilt we taste the fatal poison which was injected into our world in those far-off primitive times.

The inventors of this myth sought to understand and explain life in terms of its beginnings. They were exercised by the problem: why are we so unhappy? Why is there so much cruelty, so little pity in the world? Why these innumerable murders and victims? Whence comes this anxiety, this guilt sense? But they did not answer: yes, *I* am like that too. In me, too, there is concealed a potential murderer, adulterer, thief. In me, too, evil is constantly on the alert. No, they sighed resignedly, this is the world we live in; man is made of vile and corrupted stuff. That is why it is inevitable (*Schicksal*) that we should be inhuman and cruel. It is a case of atavism. *We*, therefore, are exempt from guilt. It is the cosmos that is responsible. What can we do, if we have been fashioned of Ymir's corpse?

Our contemporaries echo the argument: can we change our chromosomes, our instincts, our upbringing, our environment? There lies the tragedy. Men do not *do* evil; evil *happens* to us. Or we transform the biblical image to create a new projection: all this would not have happened if *Adam* had not committed sin . . .

In a demythologized form, this tragic view of existence is reflected in the attempt to find causes in the past which will explain, and therefore excuse, our own evils.

After the collapse of the Nazi regime in 1945, Germany was confronted with the painful question: who was responsible for the extermination of millions of Jews, and for all the atrocities committed at Dachau, Oradour, etc.? Are not the people whence so criminal a government could emerge gravely implicated? Is it not the fault of all if such a thing could happen in our country? But after the first hesitations, the system of exculpation went into effect with the question: how did this evil come to take root in our people? And the replies succeeded one another as in a chain reaction.

The unjust Versailles Treaty was at the origin of the unemployment and economic depression. So that was where all the evil came from! And before that there was the military arrogance of the empire which led to war. And then there were the others who were jealous of us because we were energetic and hardworking. And before that there was the real or supposed imperialism of Bismarck's time. And going still further back, there was the Prussian tradition, and the Reformation with its theology of lords and slaves and its doctrine of predestination. Hitler, William II, Bismarck, Frederick the Great, Luther constituted the genealogical tree and the backbone of the system of exculpation. The historians probed ever further into the past, searching for the causes of the tragic development of events, to conclude, wringing their hands: it could not have been otherwise; we are but the unfortunate victims, not the principal culprits! [16]

At the beginning of his novel *Where Were You, Adam?*, Heinrich Böll quotes these lines of Haecker: "A world cataclysm can serve many purposes. It can also serve as a means for finding an alibi in the sight of God. Where were you, Adam? I was in the world war!" The anonymous war operates like an independent entity, ruthlessly grinding everything in the mill wheels of death. *It* bears the responsibility and the fault for all our suffering, for all our evils. *We*, men, are powerless cogs in this monstrous machinery . . . But in his stories Böll shows that malice is hidden in man himself; it is man who is guilty and who causes his neighbor to suffer.

In its infinitely varied forms, the projection mechanism is sparked by the search for justification. The fact of raising the question of the origin and cause of our sin is in itself suspect. When we accuse others, even if those accusations are well founded, we turn our eyes away from ourselves and thereby refuse to accept all evidence that would point to our own responsibility.

Yet there is only one possible solution: to beat our breasts and acknowledge our fault; then we no longer attempt to explain and to deny sin, but are prepared to recognize it as such and to confess it.

Notes

1. See J. van Lennep, "Projektion und Persönlichkeit," in von Bracken-David, *Perspektiven der Persönlichkeitstheorie*, Bern, Schwabe, 1959, p. 206.
2. On the dangers related thereto, especially in pastoral work, see J. Goldbrunner, *Personale Seelsorge*, Freiburg, Herder, 1954.
3. *Gesammelte Werke*, vol. VII, p. 417.
4. *Enarr. Ps.*, C.C.L., 40, 1704.
5. François Mauriac, *Vipers' Tangle*, New York, Sheed & Ward, 1932.
6. *Enarr. Ps.*, C.C.L., 40, 2126.
7. *Sermo 30 in V.T.*, C.C.L., 41, 383.
8. In what sense, according to Catholic theology, does Jesus Christ, as the Lamb of God and the Servant of Yahweh (Is 53:11), take our sins upon Himself and carry them away in our place? See L. Sabourin, "Le bouc émissaire, figure du Christ?" in *Sciences ecclésiastiques*, Montreal, 1959, p. 45.
9. Cf. K. Baschwitz, *Hexen und Hexenprozesse. Die Geschichte eines Massenwahns und seiner Bekämpfung*, Munich, Rütten & Loening, 1965.
10. *Sermo 19 de V.T.*, C.C.L., 41, 252.
11. A. Hesnard, *Morale sans péché*, Paris, Presses universitaires de France, 1954, p. 90.
12. See D. Riesman, *The Lonely Crowd*, New Haven, Yale University Press, 1950.
13. On the relation between individual and collective guilt, see the very interesting study by I. Caruso, *Soziale Aspekte der Psychoanalyse*, Stuttgart, E. Klett, 1962.
14. Quoted by H. Lückert, *Konfliktspsychologie*, Munich, Reinhardt, 1957.
15. P. Ricoeur, *Finitude et Culpabilité*, Paris, Aubier, 1960, p. 240.
16. See H. Thielicke, *Wie die Welt begann*, Stuttgart, Patmos-Verlag, 1959.

9

The mechanism
of compensation

Positive and negative compensation

We owe the demonstration of the existence of this defensive reflex to Alfred Adler. His first great work, A *Study of Organ Inferiority and Its Psychical Compensation: A Contribution to Clinical Medicine?* published by the N.Y. Nervous and Mental Disease Publishing Company in 1917, devoted primarily to a description of the physiological background of the phenomenon. It draws attention, for example, to the fact that, when an organ is lacking or is removed, others obligingly take its place. The living creature is thus equipped with what might be termed a biological regulatory system. If one leg is shorter than the other, the body has to bend to that side. But that position is tiring, and the individual will automatically seek a better balance by straightening the spine by way of compensation. The blind man seeks to make up for his blindness by his senses of touch and hearing. The suppression of some functions automatically triggers compensatory activities in the organism. When one gland is atrophied, another takes over its functions. Hypertrophy of a part of the stomach, a lung, the heart, etc., are characteristic in this connection.

Compensation, in this sense, is the contribution made by other organs and by the organism as a whole once a function has been partially inhibited or wholly suppressed. According to the law of dynamic equilibrium, physiological disorders and deviations are regulated as far as possible through the coordination and interaction of the different functions. The feedback system of certain modern devices is based on the same principle of automatic self-regulation.

This model from the physiological sphere throws light on certain psychic phenomena. The various psychic functions, like the physiological organs, are dynamically linked and, under the influence of an organizational center, set off in search of a new equilibrium.

Two categories are to be distinguished in this compensatory activity.

One is direct compensation, or triumphant performance in the very area where an inhibition or a threat of inhibition has occurred. Such was the case of Demosthenes, who became a peerless orator in spite of a speech defect.

The other is indirect compensation, whereby a person seeks to distinguish himself in an area other than the one in which he is handicapped. The hunchback cannot get rid of his deformity, but he can become powerful and act behind the scenes through tenacity and cunning. Such is the figure of Tom Thumb; if you can't be strong, be smart! A physical handicap will often lead to intellectual prowess. Immanuel Kant, for example, suffered much in his youth from pigeon-chestedness, which obstructed the functioning of his heart and lungs. Gradually, however, he adjusted himself to this handicap and concentrated on his studies; his aim, he said, was to have a clear head even if his chest was constricted.

These two historical examples show that the inferiority complex plays a considerable part in the compensation mechanism. It is not unusual for a physical handicap to generate a sense of powerlessness, restriction, and depreciation in the corresponding psychic area. Adler's "individual psychology" points in that connection to certain characteristic inadequacies in different categories of persons: for example, the sense of littleness and dependence in the child in relation to adults; the sense of subordination in the woman in relation to the stronger sex; the sense of inferiority of certain social or ethnic groups in relation to others.

To understand the dynamic background of the phenomenon of

compensation, we have to take account of man's fundamental need to become and to be "someone": the instinct of self-preservation and self-realization. This implies the desire for recognition and appreciation. If for some reason this urge is frustrated, a sense of dissatisfaction is generated. No one likes to admit that he is not normal, that he has not really succeeded, or that he is inferior to others. A contrary drive comes into play to eliminate the sense of inferiority. This explains why compensation should be included among the defense mechanisms: its dynamic energy takes its origin in the experience of conflict.

The constituent mechanisms of the unconscious develop as it were on two levels: by retreat in repression and by expansion in projection. When self-protection takes the form of compensation, the tendency to self-affirmation is activated. The energy expended in the conflict is not frustrated or used to repress the distressing experience but instead is directed outward. Repression says no; compensation says yes.[1] Here, however, we find two possibilities: that of positive and that of negative compensation.

It is undeniable that in many cases the experience of inferiority results in an enrichment of the personality. Innumerable outstanding achievements in every field are to be attributed to some defect which the individual concerned has overcome. Such compensation (as witness Demosthenes) is generally constructive and prospective. Conflict forces the elaboration of new projects, the search for a real solution and an adequate adaptation. In other cases, on the contrary, we find morbid and neurotic forms of compensation with destructive consequences. Here there is no expansion and enrichment of the personality, but rather an extension and intensification of the conflict. This negative form of compensation actually differs little from repression: the acceptance is purely fictitious. It is confined to perpetual planning, blustering, daydreaming. This is the famous inferiority complex which generates what Adler calls arrangement, prestige politics, the tendency to ostentation, protestations of virility, will to power. It is an attitude which makes the conflict even more apparent. And in fact it does not lead to any genuine solution, but only to the appearance of a solution, in which the individual deludes himself: he consoles himself, he makes believe; it is a simulated (*alsob*) compensation.

For instance, a man will try to compensate for his personal

failures or inferiority by overstressing the importance of his ancestors, his family, his university, or any other social allegiance. A typical example is Shakespeare's figure of Richard III. This form of self-defense is expressed in authoritarian and theatrical poses, in despotism, paternalism, maternalism, ambition, or blustering. Such an individual cannot tolerate being despised or weak, and develops an exaggerated desire for importance and power. It is an attitude which prompts him to serve a cause: family, political party, professional organization, the state, a scientific or religious idea. Everything becomes tactics in the service of this strategy, a means in view of the end. But because the motive force is a selfish thirst for prestige, any genuinely human contact becomes very hard, if not impossible. The individual concerned will aspire to make a name for himself as a sports champion, a movie star, a politician, a businessman, a professor, a speaker. The common denominator in all this is to be able to feel himself superior to the mass at his feet. In some very bad cases this tendency to overvalue oneself leads to actual megalomania.

A fairly common type of inferiority complex is that of the *domestic tyrant*. For instance, a young woman knows very little about housekeeping, but is much concerned with her husband's good opinion. She has a maid who is perfectly capable of handling the housework, leaving her free to attend to other things. But with unbelievable tenacity she will constantly throw wrenches into the works by criticizing and obstructing the maid's work. She always has something to find fault with and thus succeeds in poisoning the whole atmosphere of the home. The explanation is to be sought in her sense of inadequacy. She is building up defense systems to prove to herself and to her husband that she really is indispensable and that the help she receives is quite unsatisfactory. Here the compensation mechanism operates on a foundation of vanity and aggressiveness, combined, perhaps, with an undefined guilt sense.

Compensation as a defense system against guilt

The phenomenon is rendered more complex when the deficiencies relate not so much to what an individual *has* as to what he *is*; when the underlying problem is not some organic or intellectual inadequacy, but a moral and religious fault. In such a case, the individual's sense of dignity is particularly shaken, because his responsibility is implicated in this humiliating defect.

The only healthy reaction is contrition and confession of sin: asking pardon and a radical change of heart. But this solution appears very hard because the self must consent to an even more far-reaching disintegration by revising its existential purpose. And strength of mind, here, is not enough, for the will is affected and fixed in a structure which seeks compensation; this is the famous hardening of the heart.

The individual concerned will resort to diversionary tactics by substituting quantity for quality. Realizing that the vessel on which he is sailing is listing to one side, he tries to restore the balance by ballasting the other. The evil disposition or the misdeed which causes the feelings of shame and guilt is buried under a mass of good works. The haunting accusation is silenced by a chorus of witnesses for the defense; the censure is concealed behind a richly decorated façade of medals for heroic action. But the evil itself has not been uprooted. We simply try to equalize our virtues and defects; to establish a balance sheet.

Such compensatory reaction determines the development of a series of virtues and vices, and in that sense Nietzsche was quite justified in speaking about a *genealogy of morality*.

In children, this process is often palpably apparent. For instance, a small child will react against his feelings of jealousy and hostility to his little brothers and sisters by showing exaggerated concern for them. Or a boy will protect himself against his excessive feelings of tenderness and desire for affection by unruly and boorish behavior. Children mould the possibilities of living and action which are presented to them, and ultimately their personalities too, and thus integrate themselves in their environment to the general satisfaction.

In the same way, the adult will sometimes attempt to escape a painful conflict by strongly stressing the contrary element; by evincing an exaggerated interest in a question; or again by showering a person with attentions. Behind all this there is often some latent but persistent hostility. We have an unfortunately celebrated example of this in the person of the overprotective mother, who seeks, through excessive affection, to make up for her more or less unconscious refusal of her child, and thus to anesthetize her gnawing remorse.

Or again, take the case of a young woman, the eldest in her family, whose mother died prematurely and who had to look after her younger brothers and sisters. Now she is looking after her ailing father, and is exaggeratedly concerned about his diet, his sleep, his clothing. The slightest thing becomes a tragedy. It is not at all improbable that all this hides a repressed desire for her father's death. Experience shows that in such cases, once the dependent person has died, all kinds of confused guilt complexes arise, and the individual concerned will be overwhelmed with self-reproach: might not her unacknowledged and unexpressed desire for her father's death have really caused his death? The contrary phenomenon is also quite common: fanatics, with a crusading mentality, fight an idea, an organization, or a person, but are fundamentally in sympathy with the hated enemy. This is the case of the severe judge who regrets that he could not have shared in the crime.

The Gospels shows us certain types of men who make use of good works to lull their troubled consciences. Those, for example, who instead of reconciling themselves with their neighbors and thus giving themselves, believe that a sacrifice on the altar will suffice (Mt 5:23). Those who, instead of listening to the prophets and obeying God without reservations, prefer to adorn their tombs (Mt 23:29). Others, rather than enter into communion with God through love of their neighbor, prefer to sacrifice work to long prayers (Mt 6:7).

This compensatory action imperceptibly inclines toward magic, formalism, and ritualism. Its fundamental characteristic is that man does not give himself, does not give his heart, but looks for substitutes. He does not belong to God totally. His offering, his merits, and his visible efforts (Sunday Mass, abstinence, almsgiving, etc.) are intended to represent his own person by way of satisfaction and compensation.

The tendency to stifle guilt feelings by some good action, or by self-punishment, may perhaps be understood against the background of our childhood experiences. The small child notices that his parents or teachers become kind again after they have punished him. Sometimes, after a sound thrashing, they become more lenient than before and the child can then do all kinds of things to which they will close their eyes. This experience of a correction received conferring a right to subsequent transgressions may encourage the development of a venal superego, a mentality of balancing out, or a substitute morality.

The question arises, indeed, whether the compensatory personality structure is not really inherent in ethical man to the extent that he is not religiously oriented. Through good works and sacrifices, he seeks to achieve security. His efforts are confined to the observance of standards, to the observance and fulfillment of the law. In other words, he seeks to justify himself. But at the same time, he realizes more and more clearly that he always falls considerably short of his standards. He realizes that his *being* never reaches what it *ought to be*; that his gift is never adequate to the task he has set himself.

After showing how her mother's life had been prolonged for a few weeks thanks to modern medical science, Simone de Beauvoir concludes:

> We did derive undoubted good from this respite: it saved us, or almost saved us, from remorse. When someone you love dies, you pay for the sin of outliving her with a thousand piercing regrets. Her death brings to light her unique quality; she grows as vast as the world that her absence annihilates for her and whose whole existence was caused by her being there; you feel that she should have had more room in your life—all the room, if need be. You snatch yourself away from this wildness; she was only one among many. But since you never do all you might for anyone—not even within the arguable limits that you have set yourself—you have plenty of room left for self-reproach. With regard to Maman we were above all guilty, these last years, of carelessness, omission and abstention. We felt that we atoned for this by the days that we gave up to her, by the peace that our being there gave her, and by the victories gained over fear and pain. Without our obstinate watchfulness, she would have suffered far more.[2]

Daydreaming

We mention this phenomenon here because of its close connection with compensatory action.

When an individual finds no outlet for his inclinations in everyday reality, he may look for such an outlet in planning, in letting his imagination wander, and in daydreaming. Other tendencies may remain unfulfilled through circumstances beyond the individual's control, or because he has repressed them, having little clarity about his contradictory desires, or because he is unable to control an unreasonable desire and can find no real solution to the conflict. He will then begin to live an unreal existence, building castles in the air, borne up on the wings of his imagination. He seeks to escape the harsh reality which he cannot accept and to shake off his dissatisfaction or sense of limitation. He can do this consciously, by thorough and reasonable examination, or instinctively, under the pressure of his feelings. The compensatory tendency expresses itself mainly in the latter form; the sense of the ego tends to be enhanced, expanded, and enriched through wishful thinking.[3] The distressing past is blotted out. We have eyes only for pleasant situations or memories, which we constantly entertain and embellish. As in fairytale-land, Cinderella becomes a beautiful princess, and Aladdin's magic lamp eliminates time and space.

Daydreaming among children and young people appears to take place essentially along the lines of identification with certain figures (the ego-ideal):

> The successful hero, such as the movie star, the athlete, the pilot, the astronaut; the superman under the features of the explorer or adventurer;
> The misunderstood man, subjected to persecution;
> The fervently awaited savior who finally appears when there is a fire, a train accident, etc.;
> The adopted child who is finally taken into the family's heart.

Needless to say, such play with imaginary characters and events can stimulate the young and encourage them in their plans for the future (when I'm grown up . . .). But it becomes an unhealthy and neurotic form of compensation if it is in fact a flight from reality: daydreams which prevent us from doing what we could and should do. In consequence of some failure or weakness, for example, an individual experiences shame and guilt. He represents the situation to himself over again, but this time he acts cleverly, heroically, modestly, generously . . . In his imagination, he shows others his *real* worth and enjoys their admiration. Or he will turn his attention away from his real inferiority and devote it to a purely Utopian sphere; fiction will make up for reality. In fact, of course, he does nothing at all. Typical of this attitude is the vengeance planned by the very young, or the helpless, when they have been misunderstood or unfairly treated; or again, the devastating rejoinders and biting insults invented *post factum* by the timorous man who has remained speechless under rebuke. The film industry, that gigantic factory of dreams, offers our contemporaries the opportunity for escaping at will from the anxieties of their business and home life. Whence the success of stories with a happy ending, which provide endless material for daydreaming, especially during the monotonous hours of assembly-line work.

Compensation through self-punishment

In his *Genealogy of Morals*, Nietzsche defends the view that man's conscience is a pathological phenomenon. The blond beast has betrayed its real nature, which is that of a roving beast of prey given over to its instincts. It has let itself be captured and muzzled by society, which aims at peaceful coexistence, docility, and self-control. As a result of this unnatural kind of life, the instincts, which have been caged in like animals, decay from nostalgia for unbridled freedom. The guilt sense and remorse are the price we pay for a life unlived; aggressiveness cannot be directed against others, so it turns inward against the individual himself.

This theory seems in fact to be valid in certain cases, particularly in those where innate instincts are repressed or where guilt feelings cannot be constructively integrated in the personality through admission of guilt and pardon.

The need for self-punishment is an important element in unconscious guilt feelings. It is a masochistic aggressiveness directed against the individual himself as a result of a sort of identification with a hostile principle which has been incorporated in the personality. This introjection is at the basis of the *negative superego*—a punitive principle which causes the individual to live in a world of prohibitions, terrorizing him to the point where he is in a state of perpetual panic. It is characteristic of this superego that its reactions should be only black or white and automatic, without any reference to reason. It takes no account of the real

situation and knows nothing of pardon. According to the inexorable law of an eye for an eye and a tooth for a tooth, it demands
reprisals and is appeased only by self-punishment: expiation by
payment in kind.

When persons oppressed by this vindictive superego have been
guilty of some omission or transgression, they condemn themselves
to continual failures and disappointments. They concede themselves no joy or success. They become inextricably involved in
humiliating situations in which they cover themselves with ridicule
or do something deserving of punishment. They seek refuge in a
ruthless asceticism and melancholy, culminating in extreme cases
in suicide. All these forms of self-punishment are really an attempt
to eliminate the guilty self or a guilty part of the self.[4]

The defense mechanism through which the individual *identifies
himself with the aggressive oppressor* leads to the emergence of a
sadistic superego, a phenomenon clearly apparent in some children
brought up with excessive severity, but also in adults in certain
circumstances. In his haunting descriptions of the Warsaw ghetto
under the German occupation, Ringelblum examines the monstrous relations in a group where victims and executioners confronted one another.[5] Hunted persons would adopt the language,
gestures, and methods of their tormentors. Jews who had been
humiliated beyond bearing turned anti-Semitic. Prisoners who arrived later, or who were weaker, would be pitilessly persecuted by
their own companions in misfortune. This behavior rivaled the
brutality of their foes. The phenomenon of *change of front* took
place: the oppression directed against themselves gradually gripped
the victims (imitative aggression). The feeling of having been delivered without defense to the whim of the stronger aroused infantile reactions of self-defense (regression): it was a case of identification with and imitation of the aggressor.

Sociological research confirms the existence of this phenomenon; minorities easily adopt the stereotyped value-criteria of the
majority or of the elite. The identification mechanism, as described by Freud, explains this phenomenon. To identify oneself
with a person is to try to establish contact in order to enter into
communication with that person. In order to meet one of our
fellow men, we have in some way to go out of ourselves and
identify ourselves with him. The pathological alienation of the self

through which a man identifies himself with his oppressor generates a sadistic superego which oppresses in its turn. This is a form of self-protection against persecution; it also involves envy of the persecutor's superiority. The result is a partial or total destruction of the self, which is lost in the superego of the oppressor; the individual concerned adopts the oppressor's mentality and attitude. As a result, his personal autonomy is stifled and he acquires a most wretched "conscience." For he has been deprived of all sense of personal worth: *they* make me suffer; the powerful authorities punish me; therefore I am guilty . . .[6]

Although in most cases self-punishment is probably a defense mechanism functioning in the area of a still infantile conscience, in which man has not yet arrived at a personal value experience, an adult conscience as such is no guarantee against it. For the prospective and retrospective self-criticism of that conscience can also be repressed. The aggressiveness of the normative principle directed against the ego is only provisionally relegated to the background. The deeper existential guilt feeling is not eliminated thereby, and the need for self-condemnation remains as virulent as ever. And even if the judgment of conscience is not repressed and if sorrow and regret have access to the sinner's heart, all danger has not yet disappeared. As long as the confession of sin is not addressed to God with full confidence in His spirit of reconciliation, it remains as it were in the air and the mechanism of self-destruction retains its full force. We have a prototype of this phenomenon in the figure of Judas. Jesus' disloyal disciple condemns himself viciously. He does not justify his action. He confesses it and casts far from him the wages of his crime, as though the innocent blood which adhered to it were burning his fingers. He tries to wipe out his past and imprisons himself in his isolation. His destructive aggressiveness turns against him and, through suicide, he fixes and as it were eternalizes his sin, which he regards as irreparable. This is in direct contrast with Peter, who also betrayed Jesus, but emerges from his sterile isolation when he feels the Lord's glance turned toward him.

Contrition and the confession of our sins do not become truly constructive until we are prepared to ask pardon of God, to return to His love and grace and to revise our approach to life. Sincerely lucid and merciless self-criticism can be an extreme temptation to escape God's judgment. It can, in particular, signify utter despair and a refusal to abdicate one's former pride. The culprit will then flee to his final refuge: self-condemnation without hope of reprieve. The man who simply recognizes that he is reproved by God, while refusing the offer of God's pardon, is in fact persevering in his egocentricity and pride. For God does not simply condemn him; He also offers him an opportunity to start afresh. Actually, if we refuse God's proffered reconciliation, we are not really taking His condemnation seriously either; we indulge in a blustering that is both humble and arrogant about our perversion, and we wallow in our despair.[7]

Crime through a sense of guilt

Freud noted that many crimes were committed solely because they were prohibited. Their authors were suffering from a generalized, oppressive sense of guilt, of whose origin they were unaware. But hardly had they committed some transgression than their uneasiness was allayed: their sense of guilt was at least localized.[8]

An intense sense of neurotic guilt is capable of exasperating some people to the point where they perform actions which they know perfectly well are sinful: specific actions whose objective nature cannot be disputed. The knowledge of thus being in a state of sin for a definite reason appears to give them peace. They feel at least temporarily relieved of an intolerable (neurotic) anxiety and uncertainty. Remorse and punishment seem to them more bearable than the discomfort of unmotivated guilt. Masturbation in the young can sometimes come under this heading. They need something to confess. They want the absolute certainty that their immense need for pardon will be satisfied. They must have a well-localized sin in order to be able to enjoy absolution. They use it as an amulet to dissipate their generalized feelings of anxiety and guilt. Again, many offenders against the law deliberately let themselves be arrested because they have no heart left to struggle.

We might be able to explain the background of this strange personality structure along the following lines. Certain systems of education are based mainly on threat and punishment. The child does not feel secure in the affection of his parents and other adults unless he lives up to the demands made on him. But obedience is not always possible, whence the feeling of being rejected and excluded. Little by little there sets in a climate of isolation charged with remorse. To defend himself against a nameless sense of guilt, the individual will try to find specific faults—taints from which he may subsequently be able to purify himself. And when anxiety reaches its paroxysm, he will allow himself to be drawn into reprehensible actions: the only way to achieve props for himself.

Other elements, of course, will also enter into play, among others the need for autonomy and the desire to be rid of irksome bonds, and also jealousy, resentment, and rebellion against a sense of inferiority. To quote the principal character in Camus' *The Fall*: "I once knew a manufacturer who had a perfect wife, admired by all, and yet he deceived her. That man was literally furious to be in the wrong, to be blocked from receiving, or granting himself, a certificate of virtue. The more virtues his wife manifested, the more vexed he became. Eventually, living in the wrong became unbearable to him. What do you think he did then? He gave up deceiving her? Not at all. He killed her." [9]

In some cases we might even be justified in speaking of a *Samson complex*. For example, a man has for years been consumed with jealousy of his wife and lived at enmity with her. His sense of guilt becomes more and more deep-seated, particularly since he has kept his resentment to himself and never expressed his hatred. At all costs, the family reputation must be saved. But meanwhile he looks for secret ways of making life unbearable for his partner. And this aggressiveness creates new guilt feelings, and the stifling guilt noose gets even tighter. Until one day, when the tension becomes intolerable, he commits some act of violence against himself and his wife together—like Samson destroying his enemies and himself at the same time.

The tendency which we have just noted reaches pathological proportions in the *delirium of self-reproach*. There are people who protest, in season and out of season, that they are scoundrels, etc. They are innocent, of course, of the extraordinary crimes of which they accuse themselves. But what of all those other faults which they do not admit, which they refuse to admit even to themselves! Their guilt is latent and unconscious, because it has been repressed. Long accumulated, it seeks an issue at any cost, especially if some violent shock occurs to reactivate it. The offender needs material for accusation, and that is why he grasps at the first pretext, real or imaginary; what matters to him is relief and abreaction. The false and morbid guilt which often adheres to a genuine but repressed guilt triggers the self-punishment mechanism. Finding no other outlet, it turns against the individual concerned to satisfy his need to make amends.

Compensation in the form of obsessional acts

The exculpatory tendency is undoubtedly most clearly manifested in the form of manias and obsessional acts.

In many cases, such action, which is often but not always rightly described as scrupulosity, derives from a fundamentally sadomasochistic attitude. On the one hand, the person concerned seeks to satisfy his need for self-punishment. On the other, he terrorizes his entourage by an ostensibly altruistic dictatorship whose real object is to impose his own authority.

Some individuals suffer from a kind of compulsion to check everything. Is the gas turned off? Is the door locked? Is the light out? Was the letter mailed? If they do not follow up their urge, they are assailed by anxiety, accompanied by the idea that the nonexecution of the ritual of verification will bring misfortune upon those around them.

Others suffer from *arithmomania* and force themselves to count all sorts of objects and movements, either to themselves or aloud. Now it will be a matter of touching things in a certain order: doors, jambs, walls; now of reciting a particular prayer a certain number of times. Or again, an individual will go through elaborate ceremonies in walking: go upstairs starting with the left foot; on no account touch two flagstones at once. Only thus can he momentarily neutralize his anxiety. Or there is the *competitive* obsession: a job must not be begun before a certain date, nor completed later than that date; an objective must be attained before another attains it; a destination must be reached before another car reaches it. The aim seems to be to beat the other in order to overcome one's own sense of inferiority. Another very widespread obsession is concerned with washing: a person will constantly be trying to wash away imaginary stains, as though to symbolize an unconscious craving for inner purification.

The relation between the obsessional act and the mechanism of self-punishment may be understood in terms of the hypothesis—assuming that hypothesis to be well founded—that it is possible to repress a drive, a desire, a fault, or a deficiency. In that case it is certainly possible for an individual to banish his aggressiveness, his jealousy, his hatred, or his resentment, but not thereby either to eliminate it or to integrate it. He cannot shake off a vague feeling of anxiety and self-reproach. The attempt to get rid of this experiential guilt by making amends for the injustice committed or at least for the desire to hurt others, gives rise to various forms of self-punishment. This behavior takes obsessional forms and is crystallized in a sort of magic rite which is supposed to give the person relief and security. But it soon appears that obsessional self-punishment does nothing to extinguish the profound sense of guilt. There is no genuine reparation or reconciliation. Worry and anxiety persist and require ever new and more complex forms of expiation. That is why the individual will attempt to motivate his nameless uneasiness by scruples of conscience. He accuses himself of imaginary peccadillos or transgressions, while remaining unaware of his serious faults. It is a case of "straining out gnats and swallowing camels" (Mt 23:24).

Mounier says that the overly scrupulous probably began by genuinely seeking to conform to the moral law, albeit rather narrowly understood. Subsequently, however,

> their oscillations of conscience, more obsessive than anguished, become habitual to them. They settle down in them, between the abysses which they no longer see and the enthusiasms they no longer feel, in the tranquil satisfactions of the happy mean. Of their original scrupulousness there remains only a tendency to hesitate in their decisions and behavior, and the habit of enveloping insignificant actions in scrolls of subtle analysis. Whether fiery or niggling, scrupulosity is usually but a ruse of the lazy conscience designed to dissolve the great moral responsibilities which press upon it into small, inconsequent problems.[10]

In many cases—but not in all—it is not the fearful conscience which causes the anxiety and sense of guilt, as is still often believed. On the contrary, it is anxiety, and ultimately repression and existential guilt, which lead to scrupulosity.

Persons of such meticulous severity set off in quest of an alibi and try to rid themselves of their sense of guilt without changing their existential purpose and ego structure. Most of the time, scrupulous persons of this kind are convinced of the absurdity of the accusations they make against themselves. They know that *objectively* the transgressions are not serious; therefore they do not really believe that they are as responsible as they claim. But that is precisely what they want: accusations that really exculpate them. Thus a man ostensibly assumes responsibility for a host of sins which are not sins in order to evade the admission of a genuine but unacknowledged fault. This is really flight to an inviolable refuge in which one can curl up comfortably.

It is clear, moreover, that many people hope through obsessional acts not to have to concern themselves with their liberty and responsibility. The fact of being bound by their obsession frees them from the liberty which oppresses them. Various defense mechanisms come into play in this operation in a combination which it is sometimes hard to disentangle: repression, rationalization, compensation, projection, displacement, minimization, symbolization.

Compensation in the form of false humility

We may admit our guilt for a number of different reasons.

There is the sinner who repents, recognizes and confesses his fault and implores God's mercy. But there is also the self-analysis of the person who simply wants clarity about himself. Confession may be inspired by the desire to defend oneself, and also to torture others; for example, the principal character in Mauriac's *Vipers' Tangle,* who triumphs over the others at least posthumously. It is even possible to use an examination of conscience for purposes of delectation. Thus Don Juan in his old age likes to dwell on his memories in order to be able to enjoy them at his leisure. He renders his past innocuous, as it were, by placing it in the context of moral considerations. Thus there are phony confessions and admissions. Some people exaggerate their faults and condemn themselves too severely in the hope of disarming authority.

Under this heading of compensatory mechanisms we may look first of all at the phenomenon of *admission of guilt through vanity.*

From the very beginning, nearly all the great pastors and theologians have cautioned against the dangerous delusion of parading one's wretchedness not out of genuine humility but out of a desire to appear humble. They have pointed, in contrast, to the genuinely humble man, who sincerely desires to be regarded as unworthy without being admired for his humility. "There is also a pride of the humble, a possession of poverty and a pharisaism of antipharisaism," writes Jean Guitton.[11] We can make spectacular gestures of humility!

The parable of the Pharisee and the publican (Lk 18:9) is sometimes misinterpreted in this connection. All the emphasis is placed on God's mercy in dealing with the anxious conscience of the sinner. We then proceed to cultivate a *pride of the publican* by abasing ourselves and passing ourselves off as evil, as though by talking continually about our faults we could impress God or make Him disinclined to condemn us. For there are indeed exaggerated forms of abasement. Vanity is as apparent in such cynical confessions as was Diogenes' pride through his tattered coat.

Paraphrasing the Gospel text, we might describe such an attitude as follows: I thank you, Lord, that I am not as proud as that Pharisee over there. I am unjust, I lie, and I deceive others; I like my comforts, I am bad-tempered and resentful; I am sensual and do not stop short even at adultery; in a word, I am a selfish man. For that is the human condition, and mine too. But *I*, at least, am aware of it! And consequently I'm better, after all, than the common herd. Twice a week I indulge my sensuality, and not more than a tenth of my possessions has been acquired honestly. But don't you think, Lord, that I'm a fine person all the same, since I have no illusions about myself? Your angels should sound an alleluia in honor of this uniquely honest sinner! I display my wounds with disarming sincerity and do not hide my infamy beneath the folds of my garment, as does this humbug of a Pharisee . . .[12]

Such exhibitionist pride and such vain complacency in humiliation have reached epidemic proportions. Mounier writes: "To humiliate oneself in public when the offense is a common one is a way of making oneself interesting, of drawing pity upon oneself and of simulating virtue without changing one's life style. 'I, a sinner,' is a successful title if we are skillful enough to arouse complacency behind curiosity, and aggressiveness behind complacency, by maintaining as playthings sentiments which it would be dangerous to carry to their extreme." [13]

One of the most striking illustrations of this attitude in contemporary literature (the intention, of course, is to show it up), is undoubtedly that of the judge-penitent in Camus' *The Fall*, the man who regards himself as superior to others because of his ruthless self-criticism, and who feels strong because in this way he gives them no opportunity to humiliate him. [14]

Simeon of Mesopotamia, a fifth-century monk, noted that vanity and complacency could assume the character of compensation. "How can the man who does not allow his conscience to counsel him, or who refuses to listen to another, ever find any consolation? For he does not accept the remedies of justice with gratitude. He entertains only worldly ideas and pursues human glory and honor." [15]

Through long experience of spiritual direction, the early Christian monks learned that when a man represses the guilt he feels, he is taking a dangerous road. He falls into the trap set by Satan, who seeks to prevent sinners from seeing their own malice and wants them to see only their own virtues. Thus the devil leads them into darkness and into reliance on their own powers and subjects them to his power. For man is meant for truth, even in spite of himself. The man who refuses to submit to the judgment of truth never learns to know himself but is satisfied with illusions. He turns his eyes from what is painful to attend only to what is flattering. Simeon's worldly man looks at himself with the eyes of those around him, whose approval he desires. Men's esteem, which truth calls upon us to renounce, renders those who seek it dependent upon the judgment of others. The devout, too, are threatened with this danger, which often takes the form of a pseudo-humility. The man who honestly desires to amend his life must keep strictly to the truth and not accuse himself falsely on the pretext of humility. For here, too, Satan takes advantage of the situation. "He conceals the evil that really exists as though it did not exist, and evokes misdeeds that have not been committed." [16]

Notes

1. See R. Heiss, *Allgemeine Tiefenpsychologie*, Bern, Hans Huber, 1956.
2. Simone de Beauvoir, *A Very Easy Death*, New York, Putnam, 1966, p. 94.
3. Let us recall here the "daydreams" of the false prophets (Jr 14:13–14; 23:25–32). See above, chapter 3.
4. This is more or less what Jeanson calls the SATAN method: "Sanctification Assurée par Thérapeutique Auto-Négatrice" [Sanctification Assured by Self-Negating Therapy].
   "Suicidal folly . . . ; it enables a man to become less than nothing, the foremost in respect of helplessness . . . ; oppressed of all countries, oppress yourselves!" (F. Jeanson, *La foi d'un incroyant*, Paris, Editions du Seuil, 1963, p. 135). That, according to this existentialist atheist, is the essence of the Christian attitude to life!
5. E. Ringelblum, *Notes from the Warsaw Ghetto* (tr. Jacob Sloan), New York, McGraw-Hill, 1958.
6. See I. Caruso, *Soziale Aspekte der Psychoanalyse*, Stuttgart, E. Klett, 1962, p. 68.
7. See K. Barth, *Kirchliche Dogmatik*, IV, I, Zurich, Evangelischer Verlag, 1959, p. 662.
   In this connection, Greek mythology gives proof of astonishing psychological perspicacity. Perseus is to engage in combat with Medusa, a female character of fascinating beauty, but whose hair, consisting of snakes, paralyses the beholder with terror.
   Medusa's head symbolizes man's personal culpability, as well as his vanity. The man who is directly confronted with himself is in danger of remaining rooted in both horror and complacency. Looking at the beautiful monster that I am leads to panic, terror, and pride, by reason of my vulgarity. "The terror inspired by Medusa is but an equivalent for vanity: regret of seeing it fade away . . ." (P. Diel, *Le symbolisme dans la mythologie grecque*, Paris, Payot, 1952, p. 107).
   Perseus would be irretrievably lost if Pallas Athena, the militant goddess of truth and wisdom, did not come to his rescue. She gives him her shining shield, in which he can see Medusa's reflection without being petrified at the sight. For the mirror indirectly reveals man to himself. And thus he sees himself as he is in reality, and not as he imagines himself to be. Now Perseus is able to cut off the monster's head and triumph over his fault. Subsequently, Pallas Athena affixes Medusa's features on her shield, so that this mirrored image becomes her emblem. And she constantly shows men the truth which frees them and invites each one of us to recognize his

self-portrait of Medusa so that, like Perseus, we may through conversion triumph over our sin.

8. Freud, *Gesammelte Werke*, vol. X, p. 313.

9. A. Camus, *The Fall*, New York, Alfred A. Knopf, 1956, p. 19.

10. E. Mounier, *Traité du caractère*, Paris, Editions du Seuil, 1947, p. 716.

11. *Monde moderne et sens du péché*, Paris, P. Horay, 1956, p. 240. Cf. above, chapter 7.

12. H. Thielicke, *Das Bilderbuch Gottes*, Gütersloh, Gütersloher Verlaghaus, 1959, p. 179.

13. E. Mounier, *op. cit.*, p. 721.

14. See *The Fall*, pp. 139–143.

15. Fragment published by H. Doerris, *Die Beichte im alten Mönchtum*, in Festschrift Jeremias, Berlin, Tüpelmann, 1960.

16. *Ibid.*

10

Displacement and minimization

Underplaying faults

When the Soviets succeeded in orbiting a Sputnik, many Westerners found it hard to believe. "It's probably a lot of propaganda! And anyway, who can check on them?" For the Russians were reputed to be vastly lagging in the field of technology. It *could not* be true, therefore it was *impossible.*

Anxiety and jealousy lead to wishful thinking. We repress unpleasant perceptions and we interpret objective reality subjectively. And finally everything becomes ambivalent. Any dangerous object can have some less dangerous aspect. And that is the aspect which is stressed in cases of minimization, to the point where the rest will appear less important. We delude ourselves, concealing what is frightening, difficult, prohibited, or improper, and to that end we invent euphemisms.

Thus the initials "T.B." sound less frightening than the term "pulmonary tuberculosis." Again, as regards death, we speak of "falling asleep," of "closing our eyes," thereby attempting to repress or eliminate our fear. Modern man, like men of all times, avoids a head-on confrontation with death and does his best, at least in everyday life, to ignore it. Public opinion does not care to be reminded of death. It prefers a healthy *philosophy of living:*

227

thinking about death is too negative an attitude; it is evidence of cowardice and of flight from earthly duties . . . Recent studies on the funeral business in America reveal this tendency toward repression and minimization. For example, relatives wish the deceased to be spoken of as though he were still alive, and want his death to be presented as an accident which medical science, alas, has not yet been able to prevent. Freud's observation is confirmed to the letter: "We regularly emphasize the fortuitous occasion of death—accident, illness, infection, old age—and we thus betray our tendency to reduce death from a necessity to a fortuitous accident." [1]

Making a reality appear banal or unimportant amounts to playing with it to the point of emptying it of its content through a kind of semantic erosion. By confining it to a fugitive or artificial existence, we remove it from the sphere of its real existence.

Among the mechanisms operating in favor of exculpation is that of *minimizing displacement.* It may be described as a defense mechanism through which anxiety and remorse are attached to an insignificant action, so that the person concerned may turn his attention away from the real cause of his culpability. In contrast to projection, which transfers personal responsibility to another, minimization is flight into another culpability.

Given the ego structure, it is very hard for sinful man to recognize and admit his real guilt. When he refuses to lend ear to his conscience, which reproves a desire, a drive, a failing or an attitude, he represses that value judgment from his consciousness. But remorse and anxiety continue to inhabit his heart, with the difference that the guilt feeling has been detached from its object. It has become an anxiety void of content and unanchored. But at this point we are irresistibly impelled to motivate this vague sense of guilt through rationalization and concretization. And we shall be inclined to put forward a less unpleasant and humiliating cause than the real one; this is what is called screening action (*Deckhandlung*).

This false localization reduces the intense sense of guilt. An excellent illustration of the phenomenon is given by H. Haefner,[2] as follows. A woman of about thirty, who had had an abortion some years before, consulted a psychotherapist concerning her violent headaches. Questioned as to the possible origin of the malady, she answered: "It's my own fault; my husband always told me to be careful not to go outside without a hat in winter, because it's so easy to catch cold or 'flu.'" Thus the patient recognizes her responsibility for her pains. But instead of relating them to her abortion and her troubled conscience, she accuses herself of imprudence. Such imprudence, of course, is not culpable at all. By sleight of hand, then, she has displaced the guilt, making it insignificant and innocuous. A frank admission of guilt would have meant a profound restructuring of her existential purpose; she therefore prefers, through trivialization, to persist in that culpable purpose.[3]

This method is currently widely used to set aside guilt feelings on the pretext that these are consequences or symptoms of some organic disorder.

It is a fact that a forgotten or repressed fault is often activated and re-emerges from the unconscious when a crisis or an illness halts man in his progress and invites him to reflect. This circumstance is conducive to the operation of this defense mechanism. Since the conscience is not troubled in normal circumstances, that is, when the individual is in good health, it is easy to stigmatize guilt feelings as a pathological phenomenon, particularly since, when we are depressed, we often tend to reproach ourselves bitterly for minor infractions in the distant past; for example, for some carelessness on the road. Most of the time, therefore, both the patient and those around him are able to lull their uneasy consciences. For through minimizing displacement the deep-seated sense of guilt (I have lived selfishly; I've messed up my life) has been camouflaged.

It is nevertheless significant that the sick and the elderly often seek explanations for their uneasiness in emotionally highly charged areas of their lives. Memory or conscience recall failings in situations which were in some way important to the person concerned, although the point itself appears unimportant. Thus an individual will blame himself for not having acceded to some request of a spouse, a parent, or a child. This sometimes signifies: it is my fault that he died so early; I did not give him the necessary care. Another feels that it may have been his fault that one of his uncles, or a colleague, went bankrupt; I did not shoulder my responsibilities. A former officer cannot help recalling a dangerous patrol in enemy territory from which one of his soldiers did not return; did I fail to take all the necessary precautions? We are reminded of the old doctor in Bergman's film *Wild Strawberries*.

Obviously, in such cases maximum prudence is needed. Every fluctuation in the guilt sense should not be interpreted as a grave existential crisis, capable of stimulating a constructive self-confrontation. Nevertheless, there is too great a tendency in medical circles to deal with the phenomenon by means of sedatives and other medication. Frankl once suggested reflection on the following analogy. When the ocean tide recedes, the sandbanks and reefs appear at the surface. But these submarine realities did not originate with the low tide. They already existed, and the low tide merely makes them apparent. Similarly, a lowering of vitality in a man can lead to the emergence of deeper problems. It is unreasonable to reject all guilt feelings in such cases as though they were simply symptoms of depression.[4]

Its importance in pastoral action

If he is to be adequate to his task as a confessor and spiritual director, the pastor must never forget that specific sin is the product and symptom of a profound egotism. By concentrating on a particular fault (which in fact often appears quite trifling), we ignore the fundamental option of the sinful individual, which is also apparent in other areas of his life and of which he perhaps does not believe himself to be guilty.

A businessman, for example, will have only his own interests in view in his business dealings. He does not look upon his work as a service to his fellow men or to society—let alone God. He is ruthless and unscrupulous in his competition with other firms. And yet he is not in the least disturbed by all this. On the other hand, he experiences chronic remorse in connection with practices of onanism and masturbation. That, he believes, is his only weakness, his only problem. He is completely unaware that the fundamental attitude underlying these practices is absolutely the same one, and that its motto is: "everyone for himself and the devil take the hindmost." But it is so much easier to recognize and confess a specific transgression, particularly when all kinds of extenuating circumstances can be invoked.

The *prophet's role* is to help such persons to discover the dynamic background of their personality structure as a whole. He must bring the fundamental purpose which governs the man's whole conduct to the level of consciousness. He must get the man to ask himself: "Who am I? What am I doing? Where am I heading?" Only thus can the individual realize the real depth of his capital or radical sin, and come to realize that being Christian does not mean observing a law but entering into communion with God through service of his neighbor.

In this connection, an accusation often levelled at the Church by Marxists deserves our attention, while at the same time requiring elaboration. It is that for centuries the Church has shown itself very accommodating to the wealthy and has thus been associated in the shameless exploitation of the poor, while concentrating its main efforts on countering sexual sin. The ecclesiastical authorities, who have been responsible for the religious and moral training of humanity, have thus executed a more or less conscious diversionary maneuver on a large scale: they have failed to draw attention to situations based on patent injustice which favored their own interests. Ricoeur thus has good reason to assert that what we need most of all is a thoroughgoing, merciless "scouring" of the concept of sin. "Improperly accused, that is how man appears to us at the origin of his ethical experience . . . The real fault is a concealed fault . . . The morbid sense of guilt tends to place enormous affective stress on an unreal fault which masks the access to the more genuine levels of culpability." [5]

All too often, alas, the pastor is inclined to palliate, particularly if he has only just embarked upon his ministry. He believes he is doing a service to the person who confesses an offense or a sin by minimizing it and thus taking a load off the other's shoulders. He takes an attitude inspired by compassion and seeks to console and cheer the person up by variations on the theme: "It's all not as terrible as you think." A more critical consideration of the problem will show that basically the pastor takes seriously only man's instincts and drives, whereas he trivializes the more spiritual, specifically human experiences arising from conscience.

So often we hear the sad complaint of persons who for years have been leading intensely Christian and apostolic lives: "I'm not getting anywhere; I feel I'm still at the beginning of my ascent toward God . . ." But the priest who unreflectingly reassures them with an indulgent: "You're wrong; you're already far closer to God than you suspect; go on as you are doing now and your anxiety will eventually disappear," may be doing more harm than good. For, except in cases where the influence of a misdirected conscience or of a still-infantile superego remains the determining factor, we should not try at all costs to free a person from his sense of guilt, either by relieving him of responsibility or by minimizing that responsibility. The whole question is really this: how shall we render sinful man capable of recognizing his fault, accepting the judgment of his conscience, and imploring God's pardon? And to that end it may be better to keep a dressing in the wound to prevent it from healing too fast than to apply ointments which have only a superficial effect. Nondirective discussion is most useful in such cases, creating a climate in which the person concerned can best consider and explore his negative experiences.

If our considerations on the mechanism of displacement and minimization apply to the *normal sinner* who unconsciously uses them as a protection against the admission of his guilt, they apply to a far greater extent where there is a morbid sense of sin. For neurosis is very often only a means of placing a screen between the self and genuine culpability. Such persons will really be delivered from their guilt not by simply wiping out all obsessional remorse, but rather by gradually directing the experience of guilt to the real but still hidden defect.

A certain concept of sin, and the danger of theological banalities

Karl Barth [6] rightly cautions against attempts at exculpation based on various theological considerations—considerations which are correct and by that very fact dangerous. For instance, that man, however sinful, still remains God's creature, and therefore good and worthy of love. Or again, that the sinner is never radically and substantially evil, so that his sin, ultimately, is an accident.

We use these and similar principles, without even realizing it, as a pretext to keep our sin at arm's length, just as we distinguish a subject from its attribute and a being from its transitory action.

This clever distinction evokes the idea of a neutral self, clearly detached from its evil actions and barely affected by them. In that case we will of course deplore our sins, up to a point, but without becoming too greatly upset by them. We may even be prepared to confess our sins, but without feeling obliged to acknowledge that we ourselves are sinners: that is, the responsible authors of our sinful actions. From this it is but a short step to the notion of purely external sins, which take place more or less fortuitously and in a discontinuous manner in the form of thoughts, words, and actions. We tend to look upon sins as operational accidents, which we deplore as such, which we confess and make up for, but in which we are not really personally implicated. Instead of identifying ourselves with our sinful condition, we keep our distance from our blemishes. We remain calm and dignified, since our basic self is not really involved.

Another easy means of objectifying our sin is to distinguish between serious and less serious transgressions, between material and formal, unconscious and conscious sins. We do not claim, of course, to be wholly pure and spotless, but we isolate ourselves, as subjects, from the faults objectively committed by us. Gradually this attitude provides us with an increasingly thick screen behind which the sinners that we are can take shelter.

In the spontaneous reaction: "Through this transgression, have I committed a mortal sin?" there is often concealed a goodly dose of self-justification. We try to feel in good standing with God and to convince ourselves that we have not acted seriously against His will. It will then be impossible for Him to reprove us forever . . .

The Gospels, on the other hand, invite us not to seek security in certificates of good conduct which we complacently hand to ourselves, but rather to put our sole hope in the infinite clemency of God.

The Catholic Church teaches us, of course, that in the life of the faithful man there are sins which do not affect his relationship to God as that of a child to his father. But we are too quick to reassure ourselves that venial sin does not exclude us from the kingdom, that these are *only* weaknesses and insignificant blemishes in the life of grace—imperfections which do not jeopardize our communion with God.

To the extent that we are really talking about venial sins, we can subscribe to all this, although not without some clear reservations. The capital problem, however, is this: are we really sure that our so-called venial sins are only *venial?* It is of course possible to claim, and if need be to prove, that certain actions, measured by objective standards, constitute minor faults. An unkind word about another, or a minor omission, cannot in themselves signify a radical breach with God. But are we not too readily inclined to consider human actions as independent entities, that is, as parts which can be isolated at will from our over-all conduct? We thus carry out a sort of nuclear fission in our lives. And in this very widespread "atomic" context we tend to lose sight of the over-all structure of religious and moral attitudes. Fragmentation ignores the importance of man's fundamental disposition toward God and his neighbor. And we must remember that this fundamental orientation, which inspires and determines all our particular actions, is barely at the level of consciousness. That is why the Council of Trent defined that we can have only conjectural certainty as to whether we are in a state of sanctifying grace.

In this over-all perspective, our venial sins also take on real importance. It is not impossible, for example, that some lack of charity toward a neighbor, objectively only a minor offense, is really a symptom of a more deeply rooted egotism involving what is in effect indifference or a radical refusal in regard to God; in other words, the end product of a life in a state of mortal sin. And since we all constantly commit venial sins, we have constantly to ask ourselves, with a concerned conscience, whether we are not perhaps sinning in a much more fundamental way: whether we are persons who have not abandoned themselves to God whole-heartedly, although according to the objective moral code we live in a pious and irreproachable manner. That, ultimately, is why we may never believe, with arrogant assurance and a calm conscience, that all is perfectly well with us. And in that sense the Catholic Church also admits Luther's principle: "just and sinful at the same time." [7]

Generalization

As we saw earlier, displacement and minimization may be defined as the fact of turning our eyes away from that which is painful and troubling in order to disguise it.

But it is possible for a man to turn his gaze in two different directions. Either he will concentrate his attention on a detail, as in the case of trivialization, or he will not bother with specific facts but will turn his eyes outward and generalize.

When a person opens his heart and speaks to us of his difficulties, his illness, or his suffering, we are often inclinced to console him by referring to similar experiences in our own lives or those of others. We are afraid, as it were, and too vulnerable to envisage the situation in concert with the sufferer. We therefore try to mitigate the intensity of his suffering and to dull its edge by soothing and often inept generalizations.

Generalization is thus a kind of leveling. We eliminate the particular, individual, and unique character of a phenomenon, an event, a situation, or a person. We allow it to be blurred by reducing the unique given to a common denominator, to other analogous experiences. Individuality is thus stripped of the characteristics by which it is differentiated from all the rest.

The great merit of modern sociology is to have done something to open our eyes to this defense mechanism, which may rightly be called *idealizing generalization.*

Purely accidental external forms and standards peculiar to a particular time and place are easily regarded as the immutable expression of human nature, or indeed as the natural law.

From that point of view it is worth examining the image man formed of himself a century ago. The figure who in fact dominated the world and set the tone, as symbolized and personified in the ruling figures of public life, was a male, of mature years, belonging to the white race and the middle class. These four characteristics determined the figure of the human prototype, who was convinced of having all power in his hands by virtue of natural and divine right, both on the individual and on the collective levels. In the light of this view of man, all others were excluded on the grounds of inferiority and, in a number of cases, deprived of their most elementary rights: women, children, non-whites, the proletariat. If we compare that state of affairs with the situation today, and see how many key positions are in *other* hands too, we cannot avoid the impression that a profound and beneficial change has taken place.

Idealizing generalization consists in raising a situation which is related to the life of a group or a culture of a particular period to the level of a universal criterion. What is in fact only the expression of specific circumstances is regarded as the unshakable will of God, that will which is the foundation of the natural law and of the immutable structures of being.

This defense mechanism generally comes into play in an endeavor to maintain the *status quo* and to prevent the possible emancipation of "other" groups. It is a way of evading responsibility. The new situation is not seriously envisaged or given any real chance, because we feel disoriented and fearful before the unknown, which appears as a threat. For the man who suffers from myopia (scotoma) as regards the historical, sociological, or ethnological perspective, conservatism is the obvious refuge.

More than all others, teachers and educators, who are by nature the guardians of tradition and regard the rising generation with a critical eye, must not forget that what is old is not necessarily good. They are naturally inclined to be ever invoking the past, *when things were so much better*, and they easily give way to resentment because they are dethroned. The same warning applies to philosophy and theology, whose spokesmen are often too quick to appeal to eternal truth and natural law.

It is customary, incidentally, in clerical circles, to make a virtue of necessity. As a result, the clergy often lose sight of the fact that certain measures and institutions are only transitory and local in character, and sometimes cling even to an established disorder, which they respect and maintain as sacrosanct. We need only recall the "deep" reasons adduced for retaining so unhealthy a practice as the use of Latin in the liturgy: the superiority of that language, its immutability, which safeguards the liturgy against any heretical interpretation, its mysterious atmosphere, its value as a symbol of the universal oneness of the Church . . . A similar suspicion and a pious sentiment of reaction inspired—and still inspires—the attitude of certain Christians in the face of the progress of science and technology, democracy, the changed relations between social classes, the general welfare, family planning, etc. Instead of being the light of the world in these areas and taking the leadership, they are content to hobble along behind the rest.

We have to react, too, against the tendency toward generalization in connection with the exegesis of biblical texts and the directives of the Church. A fundamental principle of hermeneutics is that we must try to understand texts in the light of the circumstances in which they came into being. On the basis of this principle we shall try to grasp what the Scriptures and the Magisterium intended to propose, and what will require revision in the actual formulation of the text if we are to remain faithful to the message. For the point is not to stick stubbornly to formulas but to transmit the divine message of salvation to a humanity in constant process of development, and to transmit it in terms which humanity at any given stage can understand.[8]

Human language, and also God's through the Bible and the Church, is bound up with the possibilities of the language of a particular time and place and of a specific culture. This applies as much to the problems raised and the current assumptions as to the arsenal of ideas and images and the vocabulary. Thus St. Paul's remarks on the relations between master and slave, or between man and woman, are based on a sociological structure which is not necessarily the same for all cultures. We have thus to transpose his real meaning to other situations, and particularly to that of our own day.

In connection with the admission of guilt, we may note, finally, that the recognition of our sin in general is easily emptied of its substance to become a vague culpability, without content. The danger of a general and abstract admission of guilt is that, under the appearances of unconditional humility, we easily slur over our personal sin and faults. At once, conversion and the plea for pardon become unreal too. That is probably one of the reasons why the Council of Trent prescribed that we should state in confession the type and number of our mortal sins, and if necessary mention specific circumstances capable of modifying their character. We need hardly add that the Council was not advocating a fragmented morality or a sterile casuistry.

It is not so hard, wrote Kierkegaard, to admit our state of sin in general; but it is hard, by contrast, to recognize the implications of specific and definite sins, as the impartial Judge discovers them. That, he went on, is a difficult and arduous task, but one which is nonetheless salutary and useful.[9]

Notes

1. *Gesammelte Werke*, vol. X, p. 342.
2. See H. Haefner, *Schulderleben und Gewissen*, Stuttgart, Klett, 1956, p. 37.
3. See the analysis of scrupulosity in chapter 9 above.
4. Cf. chapter 1 and note 19 to chapter 6 above.
A distinction is frequently made between exogenous and endogenous depression. The first is caused by external factors; the second, by internal ones (e.g., the menopause, arteriosclerosis). But this alternative quickly leads to simplifications and dangerous conclusions, especially when endogenous is identified with organic, and when the psychosomatic unity of the human person is thus disregarded.
For a serious study of these concepts, see H. Tellenbach, *Melancholie. Zur Problemsgeschichte, Typologie, Pathogenese und Klinik*, Berlin, Springer Verlag, 1961.
5. "Morality Without Sin," *Cross Currents*, Fall 1955, p. 328.
6. *Kirchliche Dogmatik*, IV, 1, Zurich, Evangelischer Verlag, 1959, p. 447.
7. See K. Rahner, "Gerecht und Sünder zugleich," in *Geist und Leben*, Würzburg, Echter Verlag, 1963, p. 435, from which this presentation is borrowed.
8. See above, chapter 1, on the prophetic function.
9. *Religiöse Reden*, Munich, 1922, p. 159.

Postscript

The tragedy of sinful man—and we are all sinners (see Ps 143:2; Rm 3:20)—is that he neither knows nor confesses his sin. He suffers blindness. "Everybody who does wrong hates the light and avoids it, for fear his actions should be exposed" (Jn 3:20). The prophet Hosea, in a daring metaphor, indicates how impossible it is to extricate ourselves from sin: "The iniquity of Ephraim is carefully hoarded, his sin is safely stored away. Pangs as of child-birth overtake him, and a stupid child it is; its time is up but it does not leave the womb" (13:12–13).

Sinful man thus resembles a fetus which has arrived at term but which refuses to be born and to contemplate the light of life with God. It resists the efforts of the mother who bears it. For it is not like "the wise man [who] knows there will be a time of judgment" (Qo 8:5).

The purblind sinner with hardened heart cannot find the light because, being opaque, he prefers to remain in darkness. And thus the womb can become his tomb (cf. Ho 13:14). Nevertheless God wants to lead him to the life of salvation so that he may be born "from the everlasting word of the living and eternal God" (1 P 1:23), through the word of truth (Jm 1:18), by the breath of the Spirit (Jn 3:8; cf. Tt 3:5).

God therefore sends the prophet as a midwife to assist in this painful birth. Hosea, for example, calls: "Israel, come back to Yahweh your God; your iniquity was the cause of your downfall. Provide yourself with words and come back to Yahweh. Say to him, 'take all iniquity away!' " (Ho 14:2–3).

The duty of God's spokesman, the prophet, is not so much to speak of light to one as yet unborn, and who therefore cannot see, as to cure his eyes and help him to see. That means that he must go to find the blind man where the blind man happens to be, and

239

bring him imperceptibly to realize his fault and his need for pardon, so that he can go on to confess his sins and allow himself to be reconciled with God. That is why the prophet must act prudently. He must take into account sinful man's limited possibilities and offer him a mirror in which he can recognize the reflection of his face. He will speak in parables and expose the subterfuges of the exculpatory tendency. He will hope that the systematic disclosure of the defense mechanisms will enlighten man concerning himself and help him to avoid the eternal return of his aberrations.

You must want love more than anything else; but still hope for the spiritual gifts as well, especially prophecy . . . The man who prophesies [talks] to other people, to their improvement, their encouragement and their consolation . . . While I should like you all to have the gift of tongues, I would much rather you could prophesy . . . If you were all prophesying and an unbeliever or an uninitiated person came in, he would find himself analysed and judged by everyone speaking; he would find his secret thoughts laid bare, and then fall on his face and worship God, declaring that God is among you indeed (1 Cor 14:1–25).